How to Live a Good Life

How to Live a Good Life

A Guide to Choosing Your Personal Philosophy

EDITED AND WITH AN INTRODUCTION BY
Massimo Pigliucci, Skye C. Cleary,
and Daniel A. Kaufman

VINTAGE BOOKS
A Division of Penguin Random House LLC
New York

A VINTAGE BOOKS ORIGINAL, JANUARY 2020

Copyright © 2020 by Massimo Pigliucci,
Skye C. Cleary, and Daniel A. Kaufman

All rights reserved. Published in the United States by Vintage Books,
a division of Penguin Random House LLC, New York, and distributed
in Canada by Penguin Random House Canada Limited, Toronto.

Vintage and colophon are registered trademarks of
Penguin Random House LLC.

Pages 305–306 constitute an extension of this copyright page.

Library of Congress Cataloging-in-Publication Data
Names: Pigliucci, Massimo, 1964– editor. | Cleary, Skye, 1975–
editor. | Kaufman, Daniel, 1968– editor.
Title: How to live a good life : choosing the right philosophy
of life for you / edited and with an introduction by Massimo Pigliucci,
Skye C. Cleary, Daniel A. Kaufman.
Description: New York : Vintage Books/Penguin Random House LLC,
2020. | Includes bibliographical references.
Identifiers: LCCN 2019029484 (print) | LCCN 2019029485 (ebook)
Subjects: LCSH: Philosophy. | Religions. | Conduct of life.
Classification: LCC B21 .H69 2020 (print) | LCC B21 (ebook) | DDC DO—dc23
LC record available at https://lccn.loc.gov/2019029484

Vintage Books Trade Paperback ISBN: 978-0-525-56614-4
eBook ISBN: 978-0-525-56615-1

Book design by Christopher M. Zucker

www.vintagebooks.com

Printed in the United States of America
10 9 8 7

Contents

Introduction

Who needs a philosophy of life, anyway?

Do you have some idea, however vague, of how the world works? Do you have a sense of how to properly behave toward others? If you answered yes to both questions, congratulations, you have a philosophy of life! A philosophy of life is a framework that is made, at a minimum, of a metaphysics (i.e., an account of how the world works) and an ethics (i.e., a set of principles or guidelines to deploy when interacting with others). The real question, then, is not whether you have a philosophy of life, but rather if it stands up to scrutiny. That is, whether or not it's a *good* philosophy of life.

Most of us don't do what Socrates famously insists we should do: examine our life, since, as he put it, an unexamined life is not worth living. That's clearly an exaggeration. Plenty of unexamined lives turn out to be worth living, both by those who lived them and by the reckoning of those who examined them later on (e.g., by way of writing someone else's biography). But Socrates was onto something, we think: examining your life, at least from time to time, may help you make small corrections to your life's course, if need be, and occasionally may even prompt you to make some radical changes to your unfolding path. That has happened to two of us, and we think the experience was transformative and positive.

As she details in chapter 12, Skye began her adult life as what she describes as a good "capitalist worker bee," enrolling in an MBA program over the objections of her then-boyfriend, who thought she had too little time for him already, and at any rate, they would soon get married, so what was the point? Then she took a philosophy class, and her professor gave her a book by the existentialist philosopher and landmark feminist Simone de Beauvoir. The effect was extraordinary. As she recalls: "It was as though I had just been flashed by the world outside of Plato's cave. Philosophy waltzed into my life, seduced me by dancing around and gracefully shattering all the assumptions and expectations I had about life."

Massimo, for his part, was absolutely positive he would live his life as a scientist, and for more than a couple decades that's just what he did, his personal philosophy being a very no-nonsense version of secular humanism (chapter 15). But at the peak of his career, a midlife crisis struck. Rather than buying himself a red Ferrari (which he couldn't afford, anyway), he went back to graduate school, got a PhD in philosophy, and shifted fields. Moreover, he began to explore alternatives to his rather uncritical early acceptance of secular humanism at around age fifteen, after he left the Catholic Church (chapter 9), and serendipitously (via his Twitter feed!) hit on the Greco-Roman philosophy of Stoicism (chapter 5). It was love at first click, and his life hasn't been the same since (for the better, if you need to ask).

Some of the other contributors to this volume have had similar experiences; some have not. But they all were very happy, when we asked them, to reflect publicly on their choice of philosophy of life, explaining what is distinct in that choice and why it works for them. By the end of the book, you will have been exposed to a dizzying array of philosophical views on life: from ancient Eastern approaches such as Buddhism, Confucianism, Hinduism, and Daoism to Western ones such as Aristotelianism, Epicureanism, and Stoicism; from venerable religious traditions such as Judaism, Christianity, and Islam to modern ones such as Ethical Culture, existentialism, effective altruism, pragmatism, and secular humanism. There could have been many more, of course: from geographic areas such as Africa and North and South America; from philosophical realms such as utilitarianism; from religious traditions such as Jainism, Sikhism, and Rastafarianism; or from more politically oriented movements such as feminism, anarchism, liberalism, conservatism, and Marxism. And maybe there will be, in the next edition. After all, this is a sampler, not an encyclopedia. The point is: there are many ways of living one's life philosophically, and it is worth reflecting on the differences as much as on the commonalities (see Conclusion).

You will have noticed that we don't make a sharp distinction between philosophies of life and religions, and we think this is for good reason. It is true that some of the traditions we mention are more obviously philosophical (Aristotelianism, Epicureanism, existentialism, effective altruism, pragmatism, secular humanism) and some more obviously religious (Hinduism, Judaism, Christianity, Islam). Then again, some have clear elements of both (Buddhism, Confucianism, Daoism, Stoicism, Ethical Culture). The demarcation line exists, we think, but it is fuzzy, and its application debatable in any given instance. It is also rather pointless. So long as a system of thought has the two components we mentioned at the outset (a metaphysics and an ethics), it qualifies for this anthology. To the degree that the metaphysics includes a significant reference to a transcendental reality, and particularly to a god or gods, that tradition falls more on the side of religion than philosophy, but that distinction is not crucial.

This also means something that might surprise many readers: we all have a philosophy of life, because we were exposed to it when we were kids. More often than not that philosophy happens to be a religion, but of course secular humanists and existentialists also have children! Indeed, although we would love to see a systematic sociological study on this, it is likely comparatively rare that people consciously choose their philosophy of life, as Skye and Massimo have done, and even so, nobody ever really begins from scratch.

Why read the collection of essays you are holding in your hands? For at least three reasons. First, to appreciate the sheer variety of philosophical points of view on life and better understand other human beings who have chosen to live according to a philosophy different from your own. Understanding is the beginning of both wisdom and compassion. Second, because you may wish to know something more about your own—chosen or inherited—life philosophy; our authors are some of the best and brightest in the field, and their chapters make for enlightening reading. Last, it is possible that you, too, have been questioning your current take on life, the universe, and everything, and reading about other perspectives may reinforce your own beliefs, prompt you to experiment with another philosophy, or perhaps even cause you to arrive at a new eclectic mix of ideas.

The chapters of this book appear in rough chronological order of appearance of the different traditions in human history. The book is written to be read from cover to cover, but feel free to dip into the different traditions as they catch your attention. We also want to note that while many of the chapters are written by academics, this is not an academic book, and it does not engage in detached armchair theorizing and objective critical analysis. These authors are actively involved with their chosen philosophies of life, they're thinking through what these philosophies mean in an everyday sense, and their writings provide a glimpse of how the world looks through their respective lenses. Thus, we see this book as an opening of possibilities.

Philosophy, as you probably know, literally means "love of wisdom." Even though the modern academic version of it tends to be highly specialized and remote from everyday life (like pretty much any other academic discipline), philosophizing has been a life-changing activity for many people across cultures for more than two and a half millennia. Do yourself a favor and enter into conversation with at least some of these thinkers, using the present collection as a gateway to a world of ideas that has surprising, very practical consequences for how we live our lives.

—Massimo Pigliucci, Skye C. Cleary,
and Daniel A. Kaufman

Ancient Philosophies from the East

Buddhism, Confucianism, and Daoism

Eastern philosophies—particularly three of the most well known: Buddhism, Confucianism, and Daoism—tend to have a reputation in the West for being all about yoga and meditation. Although these are parts of what they are about, the essays by Owen Flanagan, Bryan Van Norden, and Robin R. Wang show that this conception is overly simplified, incomplete, and misleading. The risk of cherry-picking bits and pieces—such as meditation or yoga—without a fuller understanding of the underlying philosophy is that we end up with commercialized cults of the self, sacrificing credit cards and calories to the Yoga Fashion Gods Inc., which is a far cry from what the Buddha, Confucius, and Laozi teach. Buddhism, Confucianism, and Daoism are philosophies of life that present primarily practical guides for ethical behavior.

Buddhism is, by some estimates, currently the fourth largest "religion" in the world, after Christianity, Islam, and Hinduism, accounting for around 500 million people, or nearly 7 percent of the world's population.[1] It is hard to say how many people follow Confucianism and Daoism, because when polls are done in Korea and China, for example, only a small percentage say they officially belong to the "religion" of Confucianism, but most conform to and enact a Confucian way of life. Confucianism is more a cultural and philosophical affiliation than a religious one, and the ideas and texts of Confucians continue to exert deep cultural influences on billions of people.

The popular practices of Buddhism, Confucianism, and Daoism could have been included as religions in Group III, but we think they merit their own section, not only because they originated in Asia, but also because they do not worship deities in the same ways as more orthodox religious traditions (such as Hinduism). They often do make reference to deities or spiritual entities, and there are religious rites and temples associated with them, but intellectuals in each tradition typically regard them as "skillful means," that is, expedients for justifying or explaining the philosophical teachings to people. Moreover, their focus is on the individual, or the individual within society, rather than a god, and, as Flanagan argues, Buddhism in particular lends itself well to secularization for those looking for a spiritual and ethical, but not necessarily religious, philosophy.

Siddhartha Gautama, more commonly known as "the Buddha," was an Indian prince who lived around 500–400 BCE. At the age of twenty-nine, he traveled away from his palace to meet his subjects and was shocked by the sickness and suffering he witnessed. He became an ascetic and at thirty-five meditated under a bodhi tree for forty-nine days and, according to the legend, became enlightened. He set about spreading his wisdom on how to achieve enlightenment. Like Daoism and Stoicism (which we will come to soon), Buddhism aims to relieve pain and suffering. Key sources of our existential pain are emotions such as anger, resentment, and blame, which inflict suffering on ourselves as well as others. Buddhists check, or as Flanagan puts it, "deflate" their ego by exercising virtues including compassion, loving-kindness, sympathetic joy, and equanimity. "The ethical imperative," Flanagan says, "is always to love, to substitute compassion and love whenever and wherever there is suffering, violence, cruelty, and hate." This is part of the path to releasing ourselves from our attachments and freeing ourselves from the endless cycle of rebirth, so that we may find a state of serenity and, ultimately, nirvana. It is not always as simple as it sounds, though—and Flanagan talks us through the problem of whether a Buddhist would kill Hitler, a thought experiment that might for some end in a brain cramp.

About the same time that Buddhism was flourishing in India, China was having its own golden age of philosophy. Between 770 and 221 BCE there was intense interstate warfare in China, but also vibrant intellectual debate, as thinkers argued over the solutions to China's problems. This spurred a widespread enthusiasm for education and learning, leading to what was called the period of the "Hundred Schools of Thought," as new ideas flowed and flourished. This is when Confucianism and Daoism developed, along with Mohism (a form of impartial consequentialism); the School of Names (concerned with the philosophy of language and dialectics); Legalism (a philosophy of government based on clear laws that are strictly enforced); and the School of Yin-yang (which sought to understand and potentially control the course of history through the use of concepts such as *yin*, *yang*, and the Five Phases).

Kongzi, more commonly known in the West as Confucius, advocated compassion for others and personal integrity. Kongzi claimed that we have special obligations to those tied to us by personal relations such as kinship. This emphasis on filial piety is one of the best-known aspects of Confucianism. However, Confucians stress that we should have compassion not only for those close to us, but for "all under Heaven," since we are all interdependent. The Confucian way is to treat everyone as if they were our own siblings, parents, or children, because we exist within relationships, and good relationships make for a good life.

Compassion for others is a manifestation of benevolence, one of the four Confucian cardinal virtues, along with righteousness (integrity in the face of temptations), wisdom, and propriety (skillfulness in following social conventions such as etiquette and ritual). Confucianism is similar to Buddhism in advocating compassion. However, Buddhism sees attachments as the source of suffering, while Confucianism argues that a good life is one rich in healthy attachments, to family, friends, and humans in general. Confucians and Buddhists also disagree on the nature of the self. For the Buddhist, we are impermanent and without a fixed essence. A Confucian says that to deny the fact of individual existence, "is like closing one's eyes so that one does not see one's nose—but the nose is still there where it belongs," as Bryan Van Norden notes.

Another influential philosophy to emerge from the Hundred Schools of Thought was Daoism—sometimes spelled *Taoism* in English, but the Chinese characters are the same—or the "School of the Way," founded by the sages Laozi and Zhuangzi.[2] Whereas Confucianism is concerned with social harmony, Daoism is interested in the individual living in harmony with nature and the natural flow of the universe. As Robin Wang explains, we align ourselves with the Dao (the way) by putting our mind on a diet. We dig out the tangled weeds of anxiety and worry that clog up our mind, and clearing them out leaves some empty space for illumination and acuity. We prepare for and accept uncertainty, and go with the flow of the world, but focus on taking control of our body and nurturing it, like a garden. Happiness comes not from nirvana or relationships necessarily, but rather from trusting and following the flow and, as Mama Wang tells her daughters, when we "eat well, exercise daily, get plenty of sleep, and do well in school." Daoism's ultimate vision, however, is a spiritual transformation that brings the finite human life into an infinite cosmos.

Notes

1 Pew-Templeton Global Religious Futures, "The Future of World Religions: Population Growth Projections,

2010–2050," Pew Research Center (April 2, 2015): 102, https://assets.pewresearch.org/wp-content/uploads/sites/11/2015/03/PF_15.04.02_ProjectionsFullReport.pdf.

2 Laozi is also sometimes known as *Lao-Tzu*, *Lao-Tze*, or *Li Er* and means "Old Master." Zhuangzi, meaning "Master Zhuang," is also sometimes known as *Chuang-Tzu* or *Zhuang Zhou*.

CHAPTER ONE

Buddhism

Owen Flanagan

Let me tell you about the occasion on which I first vividly experienced Buddhism as both an utterly alien and extremely attractive form of life, simultaneously unimaginable given that I was already well socialized in another way of world-making, and yet worth emulating if I could change myself completely, becoming a different kind of person with an entirely different economy of heart and mind. Since then I have been trying to become more like that person, to absorb some Buddhist wisdom and Buddhist habits of the heart. I am still very much a hybrid being.

It was March 2000, and I was in Dharamsala, India, a hill station in the Himalayan foothills, for four days of meetings with the fourteenth Dalai Lama, Tenzin Gyatso; some of his fellow Buddhists; and a group of Western scientists, mostly psychologists and neuroscientists, to discuss the topic of destructive emotions and how to overcome them (see Goleman 2003 for a report on these meetings).

It became clear after a day or so of talks that Tibetan Buddhists believe that anger, resentment, and their suite of emotions are categorically bad, always unwarranted, wrong, and "unwholesome," as they are inclined to say. That was surprising by itself. We, denizens of the North Atlantic, don't categorically dismiss anger as inappropriate, but we do draw limits around its expression or magnitude, such as "Don't get too angry" or "Don't get so angry." Wrath, after all, is considered by Christians to be a deadly sin. Most of us do not think that we should never get angry (even if we could show such self-restraint) or that anger is always wrong. For us, justifiable anger demonstrates that one sees and cares about something genuinely valuable. Everyday anger and annoyance only show that one is human. Minimally, we expect and tolerate a certain amount of these emotions. Then there is the fact that most people I know were raised to think it okay, permissible, possibly sometimes required, to feel and express outrage. Righteous anger is something we ought sometimes to experience and express, something that certain people or states of affairs deserve.

I know that there are coping mechanisms and rules of decorum—"counting to ten," sublimation, or "tamping it down"—norms that keep us from expressing anger or that work to contain it, but not experiencing anger at all seems to me unnatural, weird, not human. Again, self-work to keep from getting pissy over small frustrations makes good sense and is certainly possible. But except for the rare bird of saintly even temperament, never experiencing anger—at the cosmos or the gods or especially evil people for their awfulness—seems close to a psychological impossibility. But then there was this kicker, even more mind-boggling: these Buddhists also believed that anger could be eliminated in mortals, that there are practices that actually work so that it is possible not to experience anger, practices that can extirpate anger, cleanse the soul of tendencies to anger.

I found myself posing this thought experiment to the Dalai Lama. Imagine that one were to find oneself in a public space—a park, a movie theater—where one realizes that one is seated next to Hitler—or Stalin or Pol Pot or Mao—early in the execution of the genocides they actually perpetrated. We, my people, think it would be appropriate first to feel moral anger, possibly outrage at Hitler et al., and second, that it would be okay, possibly required, to kill them, supposing one had the means. What about you Tibetan Buddhists?

The Dalai Lama turned to consult the high lamas who were seated behind him, as usual, like a lion's pride. After a few minutes of whispered conversation in Tibetan with his team, the Dalai Lama turned back to our group and explained that one should kill Hitler (actually with some martial fanfare, in the way—to mix cultural practices—a samurai warrior might). It is stopping a bad, a very bad, karmic causal chain. So, "Yes, kill him. But don't be angry."

What could this mean? How did it make sense to think of one human being killing another, being motivated to kill another human being, without feeling, without activating the suite of reactive attitudes such as anger, resentment, blame?

The thought is that Hitler is an unfortunate node in the way the world is unfolding. He did not choose to be the evil person he is. He deserves compassion, not anger. And he must die for reasons of compassion: compassion for him and all those who might suffer his awfulness.

Stoics, excellent warriors, thought something similar, that when effective action is required against an enemy, including his elimination, emotions like fear and anger get in the way, immobilize, cause one to under- or overreach, and undermine skillfully achieving one's aims. In *De Ira*, and in a direct challenge to Aristotle, Seneca writes: "It is easier to banish dangerous emotions than to rule them." The mature person is disciplined and thoughtful, whereas the angry person is undisciplined and sloppy; "anger is excited by empty matters hovering on the outskirts of the case."

Seneca, like other Stoics, thought that we confuse the occasional necessity of severe punishment and war with the necessity of anger. Aristotle, he says, claims that anger is useful for the soldier, although not for the general. But good soldiers, good Stoic warriors are never angry; otherwise they make a mess of what sometimes sadly needs to be done. Seneca's recommendation for anger: "Extirpate root and branch. . . . What can moderation have to do with an evil habit?"

I came to understand later that the requirement to extirpate anger in the Buddhist and Stoic cases has to do with the primacy of ethics in both philosophies. The aim of ethics is to do good, to reduce pain and suffering (*dukkha*), and, if possible, to bring happiness in its stead. Anger, at least in one standard mode, aims to hurt, to do harm, to inflict suffering. And one should never aim to do that. Anger is the handmaiden of the rapacious ego that demands satisfaction, and the grasping, rapacious ego that seeks to destroy what lies in its way is the problem, the main cause of suffering, not the solution.

In the Buddhist case, there is an additional reason to oppose anger that has to do with a uniquely Buddhist metaphysics of human agency. Hitler and his ilk are bad nodes in the way the universe is unfolding. He must be stopped. That is a practical imperative. But we who are positioned to stop him, and duty-bound to do so, must do so with love and compassion. Hitler, after all, could have been one's own self, one's child, or one's parent. The ethical imperative is always to love, to substitute compassion and love whenever and wherever there is suffering, violence, cruelty, and hate. This impulse to live compassionately, to try to relieve the suffering of all sentient beings is the key Buddhist idea. It is put forward as the only sensible response to the universal predicament of suffering. Where there is suffering, try to relieve it, and to bring happiness instead.

In the fertile spiritual ecology of northern India in the fifth century BCE, there was a plethora of spiritual practices promoting solutions to the problem of *samsara*, the cycle of birth and death. In the first instance, *samsara* refers to the simple fact that whatever arises or is born eventually dies, decays, and disperses. Each and every thing—plant, animal, and person—is born and dies. Each one of us will lose others whom we love and be lost to people who love us. Knowing even at the moment of birth that the precious and innocent child will suffer the slings and arrows of fortune, and will eventually grow old and die, shadows the happiness of welcoming a newborn into the world.

The concept of *samsara* poses a deeper problem in Indian philosophy than in the Abrahamic traditions, which conceive of life on Earth as a single cycle—ashes to ashes, dust to dust—with an afterlife (in heaven or hell) that occurs for each living thing only once. Indian philosophical traditions, including Buddhism and Jainism—with the exception of the materialist Charvaka philosophers—believe in reincarnation: an *eternal* cycle of birth, growth, decay, and death repeating across many lives.

Each of the competing philosophies offered ways to understand the repetitive cycle of *samsara* and offered differing prescriptions for liberation from it—an eventual release from the cycle of rebirths across multiple embodiments in animal and human forms, including possibly as devils and angels in inner and outer realms.

It is worth remarking, at this point, that there are around 500 million Buddhists in the world.[1] Half of those are in China, where they constitute a minority (a little more than 18 percent).

A large proportion of the rest are in several majority Buddhist countries, including Thailand, Myanmar, Bhutan, Cambodia, Sri Lanka, Laos, Vietnam, Japan, and South Korea. India, where Buddhism began, is less than 2 percent Buddhist. North America has close to 4 million Buddhists—about 1.4 percent. Most of these are from East and South Asia (Japanese Pure Land Buddhism is the largest single denomination), although there are, especially in "spiritual but not religious" precincts, growing numbers of well-off white people who identify as Buddhist.

According to the dominant Brahminic tradition in India ca. fifth century BCE, to which Buddhism was a response, liberation from *samsara* comes by excellence at ritual performance that is only open to the priestly caste—the Brahmins. Liberation (*moksha*) involves release from both body and mind, at which point *atman*, a permanent, immutable diamond in the rough that is one's essence is absorbed (really, reabsorbed) into the bosom of the universe, its source: *Brahman*. Release (*moksha*) typically takes numerous reincarnations during which one reveals by high-caste membership that one is deserving of a further and final ascent to the order of fully enlightened beings.

Buddha took aim at the twin pillars of *Brahman* and *atman*. Buddha did not deny that there might be a transcendental source behind creation, such as *Brahman*. Rather, he insisted that the supernatural prop of *Brahman* is not something humans can know about one way or another (notice he did not treat rebirth with the same skepticism). It is an esoteric matter that has no bearing on the practical problems of living and mitigating suffering. As for the permanent *atman*, Siddhartha was what we might call a radical empiricist. Experience teaches that everything is impermanent, and thus so am I. I have no *atman*. Sure, I am a person, a psychophysically connected and continuous being who exists for a time. I am conscious. Consciousness creates and keeps a story of who I am. But I don't have an *atman*.

The Buddhist concept of no-self (*annata, anatman*) is difficult and prone to misinterpretation. Note I just said that there are persons. I am one. And persons are conscious. I am; you are. We also have personalities and temperaments. We just don't have an immutable essence, *atman*.

We can avoid a certain amount of philosophical gymnastics and anachronistic attempts to assimilate what Buddhists mean by no-self to doctrines of Aristotle, Locke, Hume, William James, or Parfit by recognizing that Siddhartha's claim that each of us is *anatman*—not *atman*—is in the first instance a negative claim in a very specific historical context. It was a response to what he saw as the mysticism and puffery among the Brahmins who congratulated themselves by claiming that their essence (*atman*) was one and the same with the essence of the cosmos (*Brahman*). Both doctrines were esoteric and inconsistent with the Buddha's observation that everything is impermanent. Everything is in flux. There are no permanent essences, neither *Brahman* that stands behind the universe nor *atman* in you. The Buddha's last words were "Everything is impermanent. Strive on with awareness."

One could try to imagine what the Buddha would say about Abrahamic souls insofar as they are conceptualized as immortal. But it is important to realize that he was not directly talking to representatives of those faiths or to us modern, secular types. He was part of a different historical situation and a different conversation. In *How Buddhism Began*, Richard Gombrich writes:

> He was opposing the Upaniṣadic theory of the soul.
> In the Upaniṣads the soul, *ātman*, is opposed to both
> the body and the mind; for example, it cannot exercise

such mental functions as memory or volition. It is an essence, and by definition an essence does not change. Furthermore, the essence of the individual living being was claimed to be literally the same as the essence of the universe. . . .

Once we see what the Buddha was arguing against, we realise that it was something very few westerners have ever believed in and most have never even heard of.[2]

In any case, whereas Brahminic salvation (*moksha*) accrues from conscientious ritualistic performance, Buddhist salvation (*nirvana*) comes primarily from ethical excellence. If anything is rewarded, or is possibly its own reward, as we say, it is virtue not ritual. Ethical excellence is open to individuals of any social class. It does not depend on creedal religious beliefs of any sort. The universe somehow keeps track of the moral quality of one's actions (*karma*), and it rewards and punishes according to that moral quality. As Gombrich writes: "I do not see how one could exaggerate the importance of Buddha's ethicisation of the world, which I regard as a turning point in the history of civilisation."[3]

This "ethicisation of the world" suggests an interesting observation for how and why it is that Buddhism has, since the 1950s, become attractive to westerners. Among the Budd-curious, even among "practitioners" (more about them soon) in the West, most are attracted to Buddhism because they conceive it as congenial to secular sensibilities. Jack Kerouac and Allen Ginsberg were not religious, but they were very cool, and charmed by Buddhism. During the Vietnam War, Buddhist monks revealed themselves to be courageous self-immolating martyrs for peace, and hippies became interested in Buddhism as a source of their mantra "peace, love, and happiness." In the 1980s, Buddhist meditation was introduced as a mode of personal psychological hygiene for stressed-out "Masters of the Universe" and as a safe alternative to Valium. In the late 1990s and into the 2000s, the charismatic Dalai Lama claimed that Buddhism scored a trifecta: it was a friend of science, an ethics for the new millennium, and the way to happiness. This was all very good news for spiritual seekers in cultures where shared religious belief was no longer the means to bind together a moral community and where science was taken seriously.

Buddhism seemed uniquely suited to be an ethically serious form of life without requiring a belief in God. Indeed, the historical Buddha claimed indifference to the panoply of deities that eventually became the official gods of Hinduism. Across the many flavors of Buddhism, most are unimpressed by cosmological arguments for the existence of God, seeing no reason to posit a first cause, as opposed to an infinite beginningless regress of matter and energy.

Furthermore, although the Buddha's doctrine of no-self is not itself a naturalistic view of the self—he does not conceive of humans as 100 percent animal, a view favored by philosophers, psychologists, and neuroscientists—Buddhism has the potential to be read that way, since, like more biological conceptions, it emphasizes change and impermanence.

Although spirits abound in classical Buddhism, and consciousness can migrate from the dead to the living, Buddhists take a pass on worshiping an all-good, all-loving creator God. They are even skeptical of the idea that we need God to explain why there is something rather than nothing. It is perhaps no surprise, given this lack of any deep metaphysical foundation, the absence of any deep reason why we exist at all, that some have read Buddhism as being akin to existentialism in insisting on the urgency of making a decent life for oneself, given that there is no guidance from an überpower that makes sense of everything or sets out the single right path.

The development of Western Buddhism, what some call Buddhist modernism, is in many ways an unusual development. Although none of the Buddhist sects in the countries where Buddhism is a settled tradition conceive the self naturalistically—most are dualist and thus consider mental states to be nonphysical—and although hardly any sects deny rebirth, Buddhism is being adopted and changed by people who are naturalists, agnostics, and atheists. The great appeal of Buddhism to secular naturalists of the "spiritual but not religious" type comes from the original Buddhism lending itself so easily to being demythologized or naturalized and it remaining nonetheless ethically extremely serious. The world, recall, is ethicized.

I usually describe Buddhist modernism, the kind that at its best one finds nowadays in New York and San Francisco and their surround, as a threefold cord. It consists of three strands. The first strand consists of Buddhist wisdom, a minimal metaphysics, and a theory of human nature to the effect that:

- Everything is impermanent, and thus so are you, so am I, and so are all our cherished relations.
- The world is a fragile place, filled with suffering (*dukkha*).
- One major cause of suffering, and the only cause under human control, is the grasping ego.
- The ego is acquisitive and prone to anger and rage when it doesn't get what it wants (but doesn't in fact really need).
- Deflating ego makes me more attentive to what is outside of myself, the weal and woe of others.

- Everything that happens is part of a great unfolding.
- Opportunities to leverage and improve the world or oneself in the unfolding are few and far between.
- We must be attentive, ever mindful, if we are to catch the opportunities for diminishing suffering in ourselves or in others.

The second strand of the threefold cord is ethics. For the original Buddha, ethics (*sila*) consists of these four conventional virtues:

- *right resolve*: aiming to accomplish what is good without lust, avarice, or ill will
- *right livelihood*: doing work that does not harm sentient beings, directly or indirectly
- *right speech*: truth-telling and no gossiping
- *right action*: no killing, no sexual misconduct, and no intoxicants

Plus these four exceptional virtues:

- *compassion*: the disposition to alleviate suffering for all sentient beings
- *loving-kindness*: the disposition to want to bring happiness to all sentient beings
- *sympathetic joy*: the disposition to feel joy rather than envy at the excellences and accomplishments of others
- *equanimity*: the disposition to experience the well-being of all other sentient beings as of equal importance as one's own is accompanied by serenity in accepting that one is not the universe's main event

The third and final strand that makes the cord extremely powerful is mindfulness or meditation. Early Buddhists culled and put into practice a few gems from the thousands of techniques of the mental and physical discipline of yoga that originated in India.

Meditation on breath, bodily posture, and the stream of consciousness assists in understanding impermanence and no-self experientiality, as well as honing attentional skill and self-regulation. My breaths, my aches and pains, my worries, desires, obsessions, and anxieties come and go. None of them define me. Nothing in experience stays the same. I see no abiding self. But I do see that I—perhaps we should say "i"—go on without any of these desires, anxieties, obsessions defining me. This might help break the grip of the idea that I am the most important thing in the universe, and in the case of weird or unhealthy identifications, it might help me see that I am not defined by those identifications.

Meditation is also used as a skillful means for developing oneself ethically, akin to the way athletes visualize exactly what they want to do in a race before it begins. Loving-kindness (*metta*) meditation involves imagining oneself in a situation, for example, where a hungry person needs food, which you have and want to keep. Ideally, one experiences—or works to experience—one's better self yielding and sharing the food. There are also techniques to work on specific skills, on becoming more patient, or controlling anger, or becoming more courageous or sympathetic. The aim is to become a person who is more sensitive to suffering in others and attuned to respond to diminish it.

One thought is that to actually be a Buddhist—for Buddhism to be your philosophy of life—you should have some grasp of all three strands of the threefold cord. This seems like a fairly plausible requirement, but it has one interesting implication.

When Americans learn that I am interested in Buddhism, they ask if I practice. They almost always mean do I meditate, and more specifically, do I meditate a lot. They are not asking if I believe in impermanence and no-self, or whether I try to practice an ethics of compassion and loving-kindness.

This idea that Buddhism has mostly to do with meditation is a distinctively Northern Atlantic peculiarity. In 2011, I wrote a *HuffPost* column about what I called "bourgeois Buddhists" in which I pointed out that your average Buddhist layperson in East and Southeast Asia meditates very little, about the same amount that your average American Christian prays. Most meditation in North America and Europe, which advertises itself as Buddhist or Buddhist-inspired, is served up as a tool for becoming less frazzled and more serene. It is about the self, not about being less selfish.

This brings me to the question of whether being a Buddhist will make you happy. There is hype to this effect. What about that? It seems too good to be true. Buddhism warns of appeals to ego, and one could hardly think of a better advertising appeal to the ego than the promise of happiness. Remember, the original Buddhism focused on *dukkha*, the problem of alleviating suffering for all sentient beings, including oneself. But alleviating suffering is not the same as making one happy. Here is a cautionary tale about the rush to conflate the two.

I wrote an article for *New Scientist* in May 2003 called "The Colour of Happiness" in which I reported on two preliminary studies of the "positive effect" of Buddhism in (as revealed in the brain of) exactly one meditating monk. To my chagrin, news agencies such as Reuters, the BBC, and Canadian and Australian public radio were quick to sum up the message of my essay with hyperbole of this sort: "Buddhists Lead Scientists to 'Seat of Happiness.'" Matthieu Ricard, the French-born meditating monk, was declared to be the happiest person in the world. And I was one of the scientists who had discovered the happiness spot in his brain. (I wasn't even there!)

I did (too) many media interviews in a futile attempt to quell or at least rein in the premature enthusiasm for the idea that the brains of Buddhists were extremely frisky in the happiness department, and thus the owners of these brains were unusually happy people, perhaps the happiest of all, and that, in addition, meditation (whatever that is) was responsible for the very happy brains inside the very happy people. I was asked when I had discovered that Buddhists were the happiest people who ever lived and where exactly in the brain the happiness spot was. *Dharma Life* magazine, in an amusing headline of its own, called the scientists Richie Davidson and Paul Ekman, who performed the early studies on the meditating monk, "Joy Detectives."

I had joked for years about the way, for example, the *New York Times*'s Science News reported neuroscientific discoveries. Like most of my friends, I thought most of the hyperbolic hoopla foolish but harmless. But this Buddhism stuff was not funny. First, it was happening to me. Second, the situation felt Orwellian and thus vaguely dangerous. I sensed that many of the Buddhists I knew and respected were all too ready to buy into the hyperbole and sell their own Buddhist brand of snake oil, claiming for it certification by neuroscience as *the* way to happiness. Being allergic to magical, univocal spiritual solutions, I had to play skeptic. My Dutch Buddhist friend Rob Hogendoorn and I coined a word for what was going on: "Buddshit." Every spiritual tradition is prone to bullshit on its own behalf. "Buddshit" is simply distinctively Buddhist bullshit. The claim that Buddhism was the path to happiness was Buddshit.

It was puzzling, but not entirely surprising, that Buddhism would advertise itself as a way—the best way—to happiness. It was not surprising, because, well, modern Western people will say they want happiness more than anything else. The Dalai Lama, the leader of the Geluk sect and the most famous Buddhist on Earth, succumbed to this advertising tactic with his co-authored book *The Art of Happiness* (1998). Happiness is the coin of the realm. Pursuit of happiness is an inalienable right, after all.

But again, it was puzzling that the attraction of Buddhism had become the promise of happiness, because the original Buddhism did not promise happiness. The original Buddhism of 2,500 years ago offered practices that might mitigate suffering. And the original Buddha, no more than Confucius or Jesus, would not be someone we would call happy according to any modern conception. Siddhartha Gautama, as I have been saying, ethicized the universe. He did not personalize or hedonize or egoize the universe.

Still, there is something to this idea that Buddhism is a philosophy that might offer some of what modern Western people need or should want. What Buddhism offers is a metaphysical perspective, an ethics, and a set of practices that, taken together, deflate ego and might, if one is lucky, diminish a certain amount of magical thinking and produce a certain amount of serenity and equanimity.

Buddhism claims, first and foremost, to offer a solution, so far as one is possible, to the main existential problem faced by all humans: how to minimize suffering. It involves getting over one's self, deflating one's ego. Happiness, not being possible, is not much, or at least not the main thing, on offer in classical Buddhism—at least not until one has lived uncountable lives, at which point, if happiness is conceived as attaining *nirvana,* one becomes happy by becoming nothing, nothing at all, emptied of all desire.

If standard-brand happiness is not on offer from Buddhism,

what is on offer? What Buddhism might offer is a relatively stable sense of serenity and contentment, not the sort of feeling state that is widely sought and promoted in the West as the best kind of happiness. This serene and contented state comes, if it does, from the wisdom of impermanence and no-self, from mindfulness, and from enacting the virtues of compassion, lovingkindness, sympathetic joy, and equanimity. If one wraps oneself in this threefold cord, one aligns oneself with what is wise and good, and what can provide meaning, if anything can. Will one be happy? Maybe. But that is not the point.

Suggested Readings

Conze, Edward. *Buddhism: Its Essence and Development*. Mineola, NY: Dover, 1951/2003. A short philosophical primer on the essence of Buddhism.

Dalai Lama and Howard Cutler. *The Art of Happiness: A Guide for Living*. New York: Riverhead. 1998. A sales pitch for Buddhism as a way to be happy.

Flanagan, Owen. *The Bodhisattva's Brain: Buddhism Naturalized*. Cambridge, MA: MIT Press, 2011. My attempt to defend Buddhist metaphysics and ethics without the hocus-pocus.

Goleman, Daniel. *Destructive Emotions: How Can We Overcome Them*. New York: Basic Books, 2003. A report on the scientific-philosophical meetings with the Dalai Lama to discuss anger and other destructive emotions in 2000.

Gombrich, Richard F. *How Buddhism Began: The Conditioned Genesis of the Early Teachings*. New Delhi: Munshiramm Manoharlal, 1996/2002. A reliable classic on Buddhist philosophy.

Wright, Robert. *Why Buddhism Is True: The Science and Philosophy of Meditation and Enlightenment*. New York: Simon & Schuster,

2017. A defense of Buddhism as a way of life for contemporary Americans.

Notes

1 Pew Forum on Religion and Public Life, "The Global Religious Landscape," Pew Research Center (December 2012): 31–33, https://assets.pewresearch.org/wp-content/uploads/sites/11/2014/01/global-religion-full.pdf.
2 Richard F. Gombrich, *How Buddhism Began: The Conditioned Genesis of the Early Teachings* (London: Athlone Press, 1996).
3 Gombrich, *How Buddhism Began.*

CHAPTER TWO

Confucianism

Bryan W. Van Norden

Why do we like Einstein so much? Clearly we do. Think of all the dorm room posters and Internet memes with his likeness and quotations attributed to him (usually falsely). Einstein is also portrayed in countless films and television shows, and always favorably. Why does his very visage elicit an instinctive positive response from us?

The popularity of Einstein, believe it or not, is due to the influence of the ancient Greek philosopher Plato (died fourth century BCE). Plato argued that the best life for a human is one of theoretical contemplation. People who study things like pure mathematics, theoretical physics, and philosophy have transcended attachment to the mundane affairs of the everyday world. They are better than the rest of us: more pure, almost godlike.

In the novel *Cat's Cradle*, Kurt Vonnegut calls into question this ideal of the detached, superhuman scientist. The character Felix Hoenikker is intended as a caricature of the scientists who developed nuclear weapons without giving much thought to the ethical implications of what they were doing. (Hoenikker is referred to as "the father of the atomic bomb," a title given in real life to physicist J. Robert Oppenheimer, who led the Manhattan Project.) Hoenikker is portrayed as brilliant and intensely curious. However, he is also friendless, loveless, and utterly indifferent to other humans, including his own children. Hoenikker invents a substance, *"ice-nine,"* which will allow any individual who possesses even a drop to end all life on Earth. He is blithely unconcerned about who will gain control of *ice-nine*, and what consequences will follow from it.

I want to stress that I have absolutely no reason to believe that either Einstein or Oppenheimer was actually like Hoenikker. But certainly some great scientists are. Wernher von Braun was equally happy building rockets for the Nazis during World War II and building them for NASA during the Cold War. (As the comedian Tom Lehrer once quipped in a parody of von Braun: " 'Once the rockets are up, who cares where they come down? / That's not my department!' says Wernher von Braun.") I am hardly on an anti-science crusade. After all, philosophy gave birth to natural science, and we wish our progeny all the best! My only hope is that you will question the Platonic assumption that a life is admirable or worth living merely because it involves the exercise of purely theoretical reason.

But then what *does* make life worth living? Followers of Confucius (551–479 BCE) answer that a good life is one characterized by loving relationships with other humans. The paradigm of loving relationships is provided by the ideal family, in which parents guide and nurture children, and siblings care for one another. Analogously, political leaders and supervisors of every kind should work for the well-being of their subordinates, and we should have compassion for our friends, members of our communities, and all other people—just as we would for our own siblings. As one Confucian put it:

> The people are my siblings, and all living things are my companions. . . . All under Heaven who are tired, disabled, exhausted, sick, brotherless, childless, widows or widowers—all are my siblings who are helpless and have no one else to appeal to. To care for them at such times is the practice of a good son.[1]

This leads to a view of humans as largely defined by our relationships. Who am I, for example? I am Bryan Van Norden, but to say this is to identify myself as standing in a *relationship* with all other Van Nordens, including my parents and siblings, but also the Van Nordens who served in both the Union and the Confederate Armies in the Civil War, and those who fought on both the Revolutionary and Loyalist sides during the Revolutionary War. (I imagine that family reunions among my ancestors were somewhat awkward.) I am a professor, but this too is a relational property: I am a professor *of* a particular college and a teacher *of* particular students. I am an author, but this is a complex relational property involving me, the presses that publish my books and articles, my editors, and my readers. Even my most scientifically objective properties are relational: I am a member of the species *Homo sapiens*, but a species exists only because the members of the species exist. Had it not been for the survival of the first humans in Africa, I would not exist. Finally, insofar as I am a mere clump of matter, I am related to everything else *indirectly* through the Big Bang and *directly* through the force of gravity (which drops off with the square of distance but never disappears).

The fact that our qualities are relational has ethical implications. Since there is no "me" that is completely independent of my relationships, I live well to the extent that I do a good job at my relationships. Insofar as my identity is defined by being a teacher, I am living well when teaching well, and living badly when teaching badly. But isn't there more to life than one's job? Certainly! But insofar as my identity is defined by being a father, to be a good father is to be a good me, and to be a bad father is to be a bad me. As these examples illustrate, there is no fundamental tension between self-interest and concern for others, because a major component of living well is fulfilling the relationships that partially define us. Confucius expressed this very succinctly. When asked for insight into what a flourishing society would be like, he replied, "Let the ruler be a true ruler, the officials true officials, the fathers true fathers, and the sons true sons."[2]

One Confucian philosopher, Wang Yangming (1472–1529), argued that people are implicitly aware of the fact that they form "one body" with other things:

> This is why, when they see a child [about to] fall into a well, they cannot avoid having a feeling of alarm and compassion for the child. This is because their benevolence forms one body with the child. Someone might object that this response is because the child belongs to the same species. But when they hear the anguished cries or see the frightened appearance of birds or beasts, they cannot avoid a sense of being unable to bear it. This is because their benevolence forms one body with birds and beasts. Someone might object that this is because birds and beasts are sentient creatures. But when they see grass or trees uprooted and torn apart, they cannot avoid feeling a sense of sympathy and distress.[3]

Wang goes on to argue that we even "form one body with tiles and stones" because we feel regret at seeing beautiful old buildings or scenic cliffs "broken and destroyed."[4]

This Confucian view is in sharp contrast with what has been the dominant view in Western philosophy for more than two millennia: that humans are metaphysically distinct and politically independent. Philosophers who agree about little else—from essentialists like Aristotle (384–322 BCE) to existentialists like Simone de Beauvoir (1908–1986)—have taken it for granted that reality must somehow consist of independent individuals.[5] This fiction has had some positive consequences. The belief that humans are born as free individuals who innately owe nothing to one another led to social contract theory: the view that political power is justified by independent individuals reaching an agreement that respects the rights and interests of each. This helped provide a rationalization for respecting freedom of speech and religion.

Jean-Jacques Rousseau (1712–1778) gave pithy expression to the political myth of radical individualism by saying, "Man is born free; and everywhere he is in chains."[6] But we are not born free. We are born with obligations to the parents and other relatives who will raise us to adulthood, to teachers who shape us far beyond what is required to just earn a paycheck, and to the preexisting civilization that makes all our individual contributions possible. Daniel Defoe's *The Life and Strange Surprising Adventures of Robinson Crusoe* (1719) has become a literary paradigm of the independent individual who owns everything in his world because he creates everything himself. This is ironic, since those who have actually read the novel know that it is about the dependence of the individual upon the grace of God, and upon the accomplishments of earlier humans (as symbolized by the tools and resources that Crusoe recovers from his wrecked ship and requires for his survival).

However, the limitations of the myth that there are radically independent individuals are increasingly apparent. Only extremists really think that our rights are absolute and unlimited. Does the right to free speech license a high school teacher to host a white supremacist podcast?[7] Does my "right to keep and bear arms" entail that I can own a semiautomatic rifle that can fire sixty rounds a minute? Does someone's religious freedom allow him to refuse to bake a wedding cake for a gay couple?[8] And how do corporations—one of the most momentous and influential inventions of the twentieth century—fit into this scheme? They are currently treated as individuals for certain narrow legal purposes, but they are certainly not individuals in the way classic philosophers thought that persons are individuals.[9]

There are people who find the answers to the preceding questions less obvious than I do; however, the intractability of the debates on these topics suggests that we need a more accurate model of people and the universe in which we live: one that takes into account the fact that "no man is an island entire of itself; every man is a piece of the continent, a part of the main."[10] In judging what laws we should have and what rights we should protect, we need to acknowledge that we live in a universe of *inter*dependent people and things.

This does not mean that individuals do not matter: Confucians are always clear to distinguish their position from that of Buddhists, who defend the teaching of "no-self." When a king asked the Buddhist monk and philosopher Nāgasena (second century BCE) who he was, he replied, "Sire, I am known as Nāgasena. . . . [But] this 'Nāgasena' is only a designation, a label, a concept, an expression, a mere name because there is no person as such that is found."[11] An implication of this Buddhist doctrine is that affection for family, friends, and romantic partners is attachment by one illusory self to other equally illusory selves.

One Zen master explained the ethical consequences of the no-self doctrine: "If you meet a Buddha, kill the Buddha . . . ; if you meet your parents, kill your parents; if you meet your relatives, kill your relatives. Only then will you find emancipation, and by not clinging to anything, you will be free wherever you go."[12] This intentionally shocking kōan is a metaphor for the injunction to give up your attachments to particular individuals that occupy particular roles. This is why Buddhist monks and nuns in most cultures are celibate, shave off their hair, and wear identical clothes—to eliminate any attachments or individuality.[13]

Confucians argue that the Buddhist view fails to recognize that, while we are largely characterized by our relationships, there have to *be* individuals in order for there to be relationships *between* individuals. In order for there to be the relationship of motherhood, for example, there has to be at least one individual who is a mother and one individual who is her child. In order for there to be the relationship of friendship, there have to be at least two individuals to stand in that relationship. When a student bragged that he had transcended individuality, saying, "I no longer feel that my body is my own," his Confucian teacher teased him, "When others have eaten their fill are you no longer hungry?"[14] On another occasion, the same Confucian explained that accepting the teachings of Buddhism "is like closing one's eyes so that one does not see one's nose—but the nose is still where it belongs."[15] In other words, Buddhism simply ignores inescapable aspects of our experience as human beings.

The complementary aspects of Confucian metaphysics—the belief that everyone is interdependent combined with the belief that there really are individuals who stand in these interdependent relations—explain the complementary nature of the Confucian virtues. The two most important Confucian virtues are benevolence and righteousness. Benevolence is the virtue manifested in our compassion for others: it is expressed in the love you have for your parents, the feeling of alarm you have when you see a child about to fall into a well, your pity for a suffering animal, and even the visceral satisfaction you feel in contemplating plants, trees, and mountains in their natural state. Since we are all interdependent, our benevolence should extend to "all under Heaven."

However, we should not ignore the fact that we are also individuals with particular histories and distinctive relationships. Being the son of the particular individuals CVN and HVN is part of what makes me who I am, and their sacrifices and nurturing have given me opportunities they never had. The debt I owe to them creates an obligation to respect and care for them (filial piety) that I do not have to the same degree toward others. However, I should show some respect to all of my elders, in appreciation of the fact that earlier generations have helped create and maintain our society. Filial piety and respect for elders are two examples of differentiated care, which is a distinctive aspect of Confucian ethics. Differentiated care distinguishes Confucianism from ethical systems like utilitarianism, which enjoins us to produce the greatest happiness for the greatest number of people, and Kantianism, which claims that we ultimately owe nothing to anyone except for respect for their freedom and independence. In contrast, Confucians hold that we should show compassion to all human beings, but we have special obligations to certain individuals because of the specific relationships we have with them, relationships that make us who we are—family, community, and friendship. So part of the justification for differentiated care is the special debts we acquire through the relationships that help define us.

Another justification for differentiated care is that the family is the nursery of virtue. It is by loving and being loved by others in the family that we learn compassion for people in general; it is by respecting the boundaries of others and having our own boundaries respected in the family that we learn respect for people outside the family. Mengzi (fourth century BCE) is called the "Second Sage" of Confucianism, meaning the sage second in importance only to Confucius himself. He succinctly described the relationship between family affection and broader virtues:

> Among babes in arms there is none that does not know to love its parents. When they grow older, there is none that does not know to respect its elder brother. Treating one's parents as parents is benevolence. Respecting one's elders is righteousness. There is nothing else to do but extend these to the world.[16]

While benevolence is important, we should not completely dissolve into other people and things, because we are also individuals with our own distinct identity. The virtue of preserving one's personal integrity is righteousness,[17] which is manifested in our disdain for doing what is ethically shameful. It is expressed in our unwillingness to cheat at a game, our refusal to accept a gift given with contempt, and our disgust at the thought of selling out our principles for money. Usually, benevolence and righteousness motivate us in the same direction. For example, I would never make fun of someone for not being able to afford nice clothes: this is partly because it would make me feel bad to hurt another person's feelings (benevolence), but it is also because I would be ashamed to be the kind of person who thinks he is better than others for superficial reasons like wealth or clothes (righteousness). Sometimes, though, righteousness tempers benevolence. Mengzi refuses to accept an audience with rulers who fail to treat him with respect. One of his disciples pleads with him to bend his principles, because he might be able to benefit everyone if he could persuade a ruler to enact benevolent government policies. Mengzi replies that to allow himself to be humiliated would be to give up being a noble person, and "those who bend themselves have never been able to make others upright."[18] To put it in modern terms, you should show compassion for others, but don't be a doormat!

What if the disrespect you suffer is minor and the benefit to others of your sacrifice is huge? This is where wisdom, the third Confucian virtue, comes in. Confucian wisdom is not purely theoretical rationality. William Shockley (1910–1989) won the Nobel Prize as the co-inventor of the transistor, but he was also a vocal racist who died completely estranged from his own children.[19] Shockley had exceptional theoretical rationality (at least about electronics) but lacked the *practical* rationality that is wisdom in a Confucian sense. Wisdom is manifested in things like being a good judge of the character of others, having a prudent concern for one's own well-being, having the ability to work well with others (whether as a leader, follower, or colleague), and having a practical sense of how to get things done in the real world.

Wisdom is also the virtue that allows you to find solutions to dilemmas that result from conflicts between different values. Some of these are easy to resolve. Another philosopher asked Mengzi whether unmarried men and women should avoid physical contact. Mengzi replied that they should. (If this rule seems prissy, think about the extent to which it is prudent and appropriate for male and female coworkers to avoid physical contact today.) Obviously thinking that he had trapped Mengzi in an inescapable dilemma, the other philosopher crowed: "If your sister-in-law were drowning, would you pull her out with your hand?" Mengzi calmly answered: "To not pull your sister-in-law out when she is drowning is to be a beast. . . . To pull her out with your hand is discretion."[20]

Of course, wisdom can face more challenging dilemmas. Confucius met a duke who bragged that the people of his territory were so "upright" that a son turned in his own father for stealing a sheep. Confucius replied, "Among my people, those whom we consider 'upright' are different from this: fathers cover up for their sons, and sons cover up for their fathers. 'Uprightness' is to be found in this."[21] For those who insist on absolute impartiality in ethics, what Confucius recommends will seem like a terrible lapse in integrity. But ask yourself: As disappointed as you would be to discover that your father is a crook, would you actually turn in your own father to the police, or do you think that your obligation to him as your father trumps your normal obligation to report the guilty? What is your honest answer (not the answer you think you are supposed to give according to some abstract moral theory)? Confucianism is refreshingly realistic in its conception of our moral obligations.

The fourth cardinal virtue of the Confucian tradition is propriety. Propriety is manifested in our mastery of etiquette and ritual. These are merely social conventions, and propriety is the least important of the cardinal virtues. It is much better to be a kind person of integrity who is a bit of a social clod than a graceful villain. However, Confucians, always practical, recognize that we need to follow social conventions skillfully in order to interact with our fellow humans smoothly. Of course, part of propriety is recognizing when to ignore social conventions. There is a story that Queen Victoria hosted a state dinner for a visiting dignitary from another culture. When finger bowls were brought out for guests to clean their hands after the appetizers, everyone was aghast when the guest of honor drank the water in the finger bowl, mistaking it for soup. The lords and ladies in attendance turned toward the queen to see how she would react. Victoria promptly drank the water from her own finger bowl so that the guest would not be embarrassed. Although this story is too good to be true, it illustrates the fact that "the great person will not practice" what Mengzi aptly describes as "the propriety that is not propriety."[22]

One of the commitments of Confucians is that we all (or maybe all of us but the truly bestial) already have these virtues within us—but only incipiently. Human nature is fundamentally good, but we have to cultivate our innate virtues. Consequently, Confucianism (and every movement you are reading about in this volume) believes in the possibility of ethical cultivation. However, there are rationalizations and misconceptions that prevent us from seeing that we can become better people. Mengzi warns against becoming one of "those who are destroying themselves," by which he means those who "slander propriety and righteousness." You know this sort of person. They say, "All this talk of morality is crap! Everyone is just out for themselves!" This is true—of them. Or at least it has become true, because they believe it is true. Many other people are "throwing themselves away," because they "say 'I myself am unable to dwell in benevolence and follow righteousness.'"[23] This self-defeating denial of the possibility of moral improvement is common, but a moment's reflection reveals how implausible it is. We certainly think that people, through long and hard work, can get better at non-moral skills like playing tennis or poker, writing and painting, and appreciating fine wines or works of art. Wouldn't it be remarkably odd if being a good person were the only thing we could *not* get better at with practice, dedication, and education?

The practice of those who *do* believe in ethical cultivation is sometimes undermined by the misconception that it can occur only as the result of "sudden enlightenment." You might not know this phrase, which comes from Zen Buddhism, but you are familiar with the concept. We regularly see it in television sitcoms and dramas. A father has been emotionally cold toward his children for thirty years. Then, one day, one of his kids asks what Grandpa was like. The father explains that *his* father never expressed any approval of or affection for him. Close-up on the father's face: "Wait! I'm just like that! But now I see that is bad, so I won't be like that anymore!" Father hugs children; problem solved forever. Roll credits. (Older people like me remember the series *The Love Boat*, which had at least one plot line each episode featuring sudden enlightenment about some personal or relation-ship problem—one that occurred during a one-week vacation cruise to Puerto Vallarta, no less!) Sudden enlightenment is not merely unrealistic; it gives ethical cultivation a bad name, because when people realize that sudden enlightenment doesn't actually happen, they give up on *any* kind of self-cultivation. Real ethical development is hard work and takes a long time.

So how do we develop our ethical character? Through think-ing and learning. Confucius said, "If you learn without thinking about what you have learned, you will be lost. If you think with-out learning, however, you will fall into danger."[24] Learn from texts: read works with specific ethical advice, like the Confucian classics, but also biographies, historical works, novels, and poetry that explore the nuances and complexities of human motivations, virtues, and vices. But also learn from others. "When walking with two other people, I will always find a teacher among them," Confucius explained. "I focus on those who are good and seek to emulate them, and focus on those who are bad in order to be reminded of what needs to be changed in myself."[25] And always think about what you learn. What does it mean for *me, here, now*? Also think about your own actions and motivations. One of Con-fucius's disciples explained that every day he examines himself on three points: "In my dealings with others, have I in any way failed to be dutiful? In my interactions with friends and associates, have

I in any way failed to be trustworthy? Finally, have I in any way failed to put into practice what I teach?"[26]

The ultimate goal of ethical self-cultivation is to become a sage: an individual who has perfected at least some aspects of virtue. However, people have many misconceptions about what a Confucian sage is like. Contrary to the stereotype, Confucian sages do not sit quietly on mountaintops dispensing cryptic aphorisms. Sages are more than anything else *active* in the world. Over the course of his life, Confucius was an accountant (yes, really) and also a government official. He retired from public life and became a full-time teacher only because he could not find employment with a ruler who was not completely corrupt. Wang Yangming is another good example of a Confucian sage. During his long career, Wang was a general who led troops into battle against rebels, a provincial governor who promoted legal and economic reforms, and an official at court in charge of education. So if you want Western examples of sages, don't envision someone like St. Simeon Stylites (fifth century CE), who spent thirty-seven years sitting by himself on a high pillar contemplating God. Confucian sages are people who work to make the world a better place, like Abraham Lincoln, Martin Luther King Jr., Mahatma Gandhi, and Mother Teresa.

But isn't the idea that some people are sages dangerous? Can't it lead to the arrogance of assuming that you are perfect, or cult-like obedience to a guru? These are dangers only if you do not understand what a sage really is and does. If you *think* you are a sage, you definitely are not one, because you lack humility. As one influential later Confucian put it: "Sages do not know they are sages."[27] And even if you are fortunate enough to encounter a sage, the last thing you should do is follow him or her blindly. Wang Yangming told his disciples, "I have yet to attain any real insight into the Way, and my study of it remains crude and inept. You gentlemen have made a mistake in following me up to this point." He then complains that some people "say that you should not admonish your teacher, and this is wrong! . . . You gentlemen should begin your practice of encouraging goodness through reproof with me!"[28]

Given all of this, you might wonder what role sages play in our ethics. They are paradigms of what we can be like at our best. They give us examples of what we should aspire to, and because they are human, we have no excuse for not continually trying to be like them. One of Confucius's disciples tried to rationalize his failures by saying: "It is not that I do not delight in your Way, Master. It is that my strength is insufficient." But Confucius would have none of it: "Those whose strength is insufficient collapse in the middle of the Way. In this case, you draw a line."[29] In other words, the disciple's belief that he cannot aspire to become a sage is merely a rationalization that he talks himself into in order to justify his own inaction; it is a mistaken belief that becomes self-fulfilling.

So what concrete advice would Confucians give you about how to live? First, try to have a life filled with healthy personal relationships. Pick as friends and romantic partners people who make you feel good about what is good about yourself and who inspire you to become even better. You cannot choose your family, but you may have to remind yourself that you love them, because you do (whether you like it or not). This does not mean that your elders are always right. But you can love someone and respect what is genuinely admirable about them while being honest with yourself about their limitations.

Your choice of career is also important. Whatever profession you enter, ask whether the way you are pursuing that career is beneficial or harmful to others (benevolence), and whether it is shameful (righteousness). Confucius explained that, "Wealth and social eminence are things that all people desire, and yet unless they are acquired in the proper way I will not abide in them. Poverty and low status are things that all people hate, and yet unless they are avoided in the proper way I will not despise them."[30] (People who take positions in certain presidential administrations should keep this in mind.) So you can be a Confucian attorney, but be the kind of attorney who is honest and helps people use the law to achieve legitimate goals. Don't be the kind who files nuisance suits or prolongs a case just to line your own pockets. You can be a Confucian businessperson, but be the kind who makes quality products that people need, not the kind who buys a company, artificially inflates the stock price, and then sells it before the negative effects of your policies sink the company. Of course, you don't need a white-collar job to be a Confucian. Confucius once had a job as a sheep herder. If you are a Confucian general contractor, build a good house and charge a fair price. If you are a Confucian waiter or waitress, do your job well and cheerfully. But what if a customer is being a jerk to you? Don't forget that righteousness/integrity is a virtue, too. You should be able to look at yourself in the mirror each morning with self-respect.

I noted earlier that one of Confucius's disciples asked himself every day, "Have I in any way failed to put into practice what I teach?"[31] This is a question each of us should ask—including me. I am a deeply imperfect person, but I think I am a better human being to the degree that I have genuinely committed myself to Confucian principles and practices. Confucianism has helped me to recognize that the time I have spent helping to raise my children (who have become talented, flourishing adults) and the efforts I have made to be a good teacher to the majority of my students (who will never be professional philosophers) are not distractions from living well (as a Platonist might think). As a result,

I am able to do these things unreservedly and joyfully, rather than grudgingly. Confucianism has allowed me to appreciate that handling real-life ethical problems is not analogous to solving a mathematical equation (as many contemporary Western ethicists seem to think). As a result, I try to make ethical decisions with flexibility, imagination, and attentiveness to the messy details of each context. Confucianism has also taught me that, while I have an obligation to be informed about and to take a stand on issues of national and global importance, my most fundamental ethical tasks are to be kind and respectful to the people I encounter in everyday life. As Mengzi explained: "The Way lies in what is near, but people seek it in what is distant; one's task lies in what is easy, but people seek it in what is difficult. If everyone would treat their kin as kin, and their elders as elders, the world would be at peace."[32]

Confucius was once asked if there is "one teaching that can serve as a guide for one's entire life." He said that all you really need to know is the word *reciprocity*: "Do not impose upon others what you yourself do not desire."[33] Today, we know a lot more than Confucius did about how tastes can differ, and how experiences are affected by factors like race and gender. But in combination with learning and thinking about the experiences of others, reciprocity is still a good start to realizing your potential as a human being by living a life characterized by benevolence, righteousness, wisdom, and propriety.

Suggested Readings

Confucius. *The Essential Analects: Selected Passages with Traditional Commentary*. Translated by Edward Slingerland. Indianapolis: Hackett Publishing, 2006. A great translation of the sayings of Confucius that is actually faithful to the Chinese tradition.

Creel, H. G. *Confucius and the Chinese Way*. New York: Harper Torchbooks, 1960. Still the best general introduction to Confucius and his philosophy. Out of print, but check your local library or used bookstore.

Ivanhoe, Philip J. *Confucian Moral Self Cultivation*, 2nd ed. Indianapolis: Hackett Publishing, 2000. A readable introduction to the debates within Confucianism over how to become a better person.

The Four Books: The Basic Teachings of the Later Confucian Tradition. Translated by Daniel K. Gardner. Indianapolis: Hackett Publishing, 2007. This translation lets you understand the Confucian classics as Chinese students learned them for generations.

Van Norden, Bryan W. *Introduction to Classical Chinese Philosophy*. Indianapolis: Hackett Publishing, 2011. An overview of the intellectual context in which Confucius and his successors lived and taught.

Notes

1 Zhang Zai, "The Western Inscription," in *Readings in Later Chinese Philosophy*, trans. and ed. Bryan W. Van Norden and Justin Tiwald, (Indianapolis: Hackett Publishing, 2014), 135. Translation slightly modified.

2 "Kongzi (Confucius), 'The Analects,'" 12:11, trans. Edward Gilman Slingerland, in *Readings in Classical Chinese Philosophy*, 2nd ed., ed. Philip J. Ivanhoe and Bryan W. Van Norden (Indianapolis: Hackett Publishing, 2005), 36. Translation slightly modified.

3 Wang Yangming, "Questions of the *Great Learning*," trans. Philip J. Ivanhoe, in *Readings in Later Chinese Philosophy*, 241–42. Translation slightly modified.

4 Wang, "Questions of the *Great Learning*," in *Readings in Later Chinese Philosophy*, 242.

5 See chapter 4, "Aristotelianism" by Daniel A. Kaufman, and chapter 12, "Existentialism" by Skye C. Cleary.

6 Jean-Jacques Rousseau, *The Social Contract and Discourses*, trans. G. D. H. Cole (New York: E. P. Dutton & Co., 1913), 5.

7 Christopher Mathias, Jenna Amatulli, and Rebecca Klein, "Exclusive: Florida Public School Teacher Has a White Nationalist Podcast," *HuffPost*, March 3, 2018, https://www.huffpost.com/entry/florida-public-school-teacher-white-nationalist-podcast_us_5a99ae32e4b089ec353a1fba.

8 Tara Isabella Burton, "How religious groups are responding to the Masterpiece Bakeshop Supreme Court case," *Vox*, December 5, 2017, https://www.vox.com/policy-and-politics/2017/12/5/16719386/masterpiece-cakeshop-scotus-religious-arguments-amicus-briefs-gay-cake.

9 Adam Winkler, "Corporations keep claiming 'We the People' rights. And they're winning," *Los Angeles Times*, March 2, 2018, http://www.latimes.com/opinion/op-ed/la-oe-winkler-how-corporations-won-the-right-to-personhood-20180302-story.html.

10 John Donne, Meditation XVII: "No Man Is an Island," in *Devotions Upon Emergent Occasions* (London, 1624). Spelling modernized.

11 *The Questions of King Milinda*, ed. N. K. G. Mendis (Kandy, Sri Lanka: Buddhist Publication Society, 1993), 29.

12 "Selected Kōans," trans. Stephen Addiss and James Green, in *Readings in Later Chinese Philosophy*, 107–108.

13 For a more sympathetic portrayal of Buddhism, see chapter 1, "Buddhism" by Owen Flanagan.

14 "Cheng Hao, Selected Sayings," trans. Philip J. Ivanhoe, in *Readings in Later Chinese Philosophy*, 152.

15 "Cheng Hao, Selected Sayings," in *Readings in Later Chinese Philosophy*, 149.

16 "Mengzi (Mencius)," 7A15, trans. Bryan W. Van Norden, in *Readings in Classical Chinese Philosophy*, 152–53.

17 "Benevolence" is an adequate translation of the Chinese *ren*. "Righteousness" has become the standard translation of the Chinese *yi*, but I find that English speakers often immediately associate it with "self-righteousness," which is opposed to being *yi*. The English word closest to the meaning of *yi* is probably "integrity."

18 *"Mengzi*, Book 3B," 3B1, in *The Essential Mengzi*, trans. Bryan W. Van Norden (Indianapolis: Hackett Publishing, 2009), 36.

19 ScienCentral, Inc., and the American Institute of Physics, "William Shockley," PBS, 1999, https://www.pbs.org/transistor/album1/shockley/shockley3.html.

20 "Mengzi (Mencius)," 4A17, in *Readings in Classical Chinese Philosophy*, 138.

21 "Kongzi (Confucius), 'The Analects,'" 13:18, in *Readings in Classical Chinese Philosophy*, 39.

22 "Mengzi (Mencius)," 4B6, in *Readings in Classical Chinese Philosophy*, 139.

23 "Mengzi (Mencius)," 4A10, in *Readings in Classical Chinese Philosophy*, 137–38.

24 "Kongzi (Confucius), 'The Analects,'" 2:15, in *Readings in Classical Chinese Philosophy*, 6.

25 "Kongzi (Confucius), 'The Analects,'" 7:22, in *Readings in Classical Chinese Philosophy*, 22.

46 • *Bryan W. Van Norden*

26 "Kongzi (Confucius), 'The Analects,'" 1:4, in *Readings in Classical Chinese Philosophy*, 3. (This task of daily ethical self-monitoring has parallels in Stoicism. See chapter 5, "Stoicism" by Massimo Pigliucci.)

27 Zhu Xi, quoted in "Categorized Commentaries on the *Great Learning*," trans. Bryan W. Van Norden, in *Readings in Later Chinese Philosophy*, 184.

28 Wang Yangming, quoted in "Miscellaneous Writings," trans. Philip J. Ivanhoe, in *Readings in Later Chinese Philosophy*, 280.

29 Zhu Xi, quoted in "Collected Commentaries on the *Analects*," trans. Bryan W. Van Norden, in *Readings in Later Chinese Philosophy*, 200. For a profound meditation on this passage and how to apply it to your own life, see "Perspectives on Moral Failure in the *Analects*," in *Dao Companion to the Analects*, ed. Amy Olberding (New York: Springer, 2014), 199–221.

30 "Kongzi (Confucius), 'The Analects,'" 4:5, in *Readings in Classical Chinese Philosophy*, 11.

31 "Kongzi (Confucius), 'The Analects,'" 1:4, in *Readings in Classical Chinese Philosophy*, 3.

32 "Mengzi (Mencius)," 4A11, in *Readings in Classical Chinese Philosophy*, 138.

33 "Kongzi (Confucius), 'The Analects,'" 15:24, in *Readings in Classical Chinese Philosophy*, 45.

CHAPTER THREE

Daoism

Robin R. Wang

I want to talk about a time of uncertainty, in which people heatedly disagree about moral values, religious beliefs, and the right form of government. This is a time of conflict, in which inequality is rampant and people desperately compete for wealth, power, and prestige. This is a time of impending environmental disaster, in which human-made changes threaten populations. This is also a time in which people wish to live long, healthy, and sexually satisfied lives, but often find they are unable to do any of these things. This is a time in which everyone wishes for joy, but few achieve it.

I could be describing our lives today, but this account equally applies to life in China during the Warring States period, which took place over two thousand years ago. At that time, the philosophy of Daoism emerged, providing solutions to the existing problems of uncertainty, conflict, disaster, and joylessness. Although technology, social structures, and forms of government have changed significantly since the Warring States period, the basic problems of life have not, making Daoism as relevant as ever. Westerners, when thinking of Daoism, often envision a practicing Daoist as someone who lives a life of leisure, free of the demands of urban modernity; someone who "goes with nature." Laozi, a central Daoist figure and sage, is commonly represented as an old, wrinkled man with a long white beard who wears flowing robes, often depicted riding a buffalo or meditating in complete harmony within his remote mountain cave dwelling. These stereotypical portrayals uphold a superficial and simplistic view of Daoism. Daoism goes much deeper than the popularized idea of "being with nature."

One of the primary concerns of Daoism is how to handle uncertainty. Laozi offers remedies for our chaotic personal, social, and political predicaments. Like someone cultivating the trunk and roots (*ben* 本) of a flourishing tree, Laozi turns his attention to the vital foundation (*ben*) of life itself. Zhuangzi, another pivotal Daoist sage in the fourth century BCE, says, "Resign yourself to what cannot be avoided and nourish what is within you—this is the best." What is inside us is the path! We can discover it through *yangsheng* 養生, nourishing or cultivating our lives. This activation of our living root involves focusing on what is most important and what is within our control, such as our abilities, desires, plans, and daily routines. Through these teachings, we can learn the Daoist way to be comfortable with uncertainty and build a bridge between ancient Daoist wisdom and contemporary challenges.

The Illumination of the Obvious: A Phone for a Stone

The Daoist way encourages perspective-taking. In a course I taught with Paul Harris, "In Search of Slow Time," Paul asked us each to surrender our phone for the duration of the class, swapping out the device for a simple pebble.

In exchanging our phones for stones, we substituted a constantly engaging, moving, and interactive electronic screen for a still object to hold in hand. We changed our focus from an artificially constructed, attention-grabbing device to a natural, silent, contemplative—and seemingly empty—earthly element. The stone reflects time and a living energy. What's more, it represents one fragment in the myriad of natural things; one piece of the great Earth. In changing our focus, we participated in altering our perspective. We worked to disengage ourselves from our self-absorbed, single-minded electronic stare, refocusing ourselves on an authentic portion of the world.

The "phone for a stone" exercise illustrates the changing of viewpoints that Zhuangzi encourages. In one of the stories in the *Zhuangzi* (the collection of writings by Zhuangzi, or "Master Zhuang"), Huizi, Zhuangzi's friend, tells Zhuangzi that he was given a seed that grew into an enormous gourd, too flimsy to fill with liquid and transport, and too large to cut and use as a dipper. Unable to find a use for the gourd, Huizi destroyed it. Zhuangzi, surprised by Huizi's decision to crush the gourd, asks him why he didn't instead make it into a vessel that he could use to travel down a river. Zhuangzi criticizes Huizi's inability to see the use of the gourd from perspectives different from those to which he was accustomed, telling Huizi that he has "tangled weeds clogging up his mind."

We know the world from our various unique perspectives, which, like Huizi's, often become fixed and unbending. When we change our perspective, we see from Dao's perspective. Dao is the ultimate source of all things.

Zhuangzi outlines apprehending the Dao's perspective in a few stages. Within three days, Zhuangzi tells us, you are able to separate the world from yourself. After seven more, you can detach all things. After another nine, you can even part life itself. In this process, you are gradually letting go of your constructed self and the viewpoints into which you have settled during your life. In this, we see that a Dao-based vision of life relinquishes personal, one-sided perspectives and appreciates, even celebrates, different ways of looking at reality.

To see things from the perspective of Dao is to understand that the world is not an amorphous and undifferentiated flat plane but an unbounded plurality. This requires both the ability to appreciate diversified views and the capacity to see the bigger and more panoramic patterns of the world. It involves the reversal of ordinary thinking: overcoming attachments to personal viewpoints; loosening emotional reactions to events; releasing projected values and conditioned reflexes; and erasing oppositional extremism.

Our minds are easily fixed or locked into one perspective, making it difficult for us to see all dimensions. This single viewpoint, however, brings out unnecessary judgments and frustrations. Instead, we should work to take an unfixed perspective, something that I call the contemporary Realtor's mentality. Let me explain.

In the summer of 2017, I was shopping for a home, aided by a young Realtor named Garrison. He worked incredibly hard to select potential homes every week, drove me around despite heavy traffic, patiently listened to my every concern, and answered all of my questions, large or small. Months passed, and there was nothing I liked. Finally, I asked him, "How can you deal with the fact that your hard work might lead to nothing?" He responded that he did not let his mind fix on one client but rather constantly took the position "It is what it is." Garrison works with more than thirty clients simultaneously, knowing that only two or three may yield a sale.

This contemporary Realtor's mentality is what Zhuangzi calls "walking in two roads" or the axis of Dao. The "axis finds its place in the center" and "responds to all the endless things it confronts, thwarted by none." Consider the axis as the center of the circle, the point that remains unbothered by changes in the surroundings, like the Hula-Hoop, which moves in tandem with the movement of your waist without throwing off your balance.

This Daoist art of perspective-taking—recognizing the existence of various perspectives—is called the "Illumination of the Obvious" or the attainment of *ming* 明 (acuity, discernment). Interestingly, *ming* indicates both the light of the sun and the light of the moon, where the moon shines at night and the sun radiates during the day. With both the lights of the moon and the sun—both "sides" illuminated—we can see the world from all directions at all times. Thus, the "Illumination of the Obvious" serves as the illumination of the existence of other sides, of other perspectives from which we often are disconnected.

The way we reach *ming* is by emptying our minds and letting things go. It is by clearing the "tangled weeds" that Zhuangzi says clog the mind. Zhuangzi calls it *xinzhai* 心齋 (fasting of heart/mind), simply saying this: put your mind on a diet!

My daughter's New Year's resolution for 2019 is to get a tattoo on her left hand that reads "Let go." She wants to have a constant reminder to let go of anxieties, worries, and things holding her back; to encourage her to breathe, release, and let go, all which assist in mental fasting and reaching *ming*.

By releasing anxieties and worries, you empty yourself, which is what affords you the plasticity needed to gain acuity. This point is nicely illustrated by a special device for visualizing this natural pattern involving emptiness, known as the *qiqi* 攲器, which has been restored in the Forbidden City in Beijing. This container holds a certain amount of water. If it is filled with too much water, it will tip over; if it has too little water, it will also tilt. The perfect condition will contain just the right amount of water and leave a certain amount of empty space in the container. This right amount is measured by the amount of empty space. Like *qiqi*, our mind needs empty space to reflect and respond without storing. Only this emptiness provides the appropriate illumination.

The Daoist way cultivates the habit of embracing experience immediately, on its own terms, and without preconceptions. Zhuangzi suggests that our mind is like the mirror in stillness and the echo in responding. It focuses on removing judgments and obstacles caused by emotions while endorsing acuity.

Natural acuity—taking things on their own terms—is the key to living well. Having acuity is like getting the most out of the ingredients of life experience. Din Tai Fung, the most popular Chinese restaurant in Los Angeles these days, has a never-ending menu that optimizes a finite number of ingredients using infinite imagination. It finds ways to preserve and extend the ingredients it offers, combining them in different sequences, using different colors, textures, flavors, fragrances, and more. It focuses on getting the most out of ingredients and teasing them into productive relationships that allow their natural flavors to shine.

Open to the Sphere of Miao 妙 (Mystery, Subtleness, and Wonder) and Ziran 自然 (Self-so) for Attunement

Our world is full of complexity and paradox. Is there an effective way to deal with the fast-flowing uncertainties of the modern world?

One possible way appears in the *Daodejing* (*Tao Te Ching*), which describes *miao*. The *Daodejing* says Dao is *miao* that generates the realm of the unknown, yet is also operational within ourselves, the world, and the cosmos. The core of this mind-set is being open to mystery and the enigma of ourselves, others, and the world. We ensure this openness by remaining attentive and responding to our surroundings; by suspending our own subjective will and allowing things to unfold. Thus do we experience the magic and sheer chance that are so characteristic of life.

What's more, in remaining attentive and receptive to our surroundings and aware that time will unfold naturally—and often in pleasantly unexpected ways—we can better cope with our own difficulties. Consider this: Zhuangzi describes a man, Ziyu, who falls ill and becomes physically deformed. When Ziyu is asked if he dislikes his physically tangled state, he replies, "What is there to dislike? My left arm may become a rooster to announce the dawn and my right arm may become a crossbow pellet to aid me in hunting." Through Ziyu's openness to possibility and his acceptance of the mysteries of the future, he transforms his negative experience.

Miao also describes the Daoist idea of time. Time, in common usage, refers to a schedule or a series of unfolding events. We have all tried to arrange or organize time. But should we go along with the natural rhythm of things rather than the schedules we create? Have you ever wondered where that one hour goes or comes from when we reset our clocks twice a year as we "spring forward" or "fall back"? What about the ways in which we try to fix a sleeping routine? We set alarm clocks, but our internal circadian system lets us know if we are off the mark, as our alarm clock cannot really get us out of bed.

The Daoist time is a passing phase of *shi* 時 (time). *Shi* refers to three interrelated concepts: seasonal alteration, the current situation, and timeliness. Human perspectives or actions should allow time to do its work. That is, let time itself originate, emanate, spring, and radiate, like the plants in your backyard. No matter how much you want them *now*, they still grow in a timely fashion, not according to your subjective will.

Being open to cosmic time is not a failure to act or a decision not to act but is rather an attunement with your environment and the rhythm of all things. Timely action can be justified by the Daoist behavioral code: it acts in accordance with *ziran* 自然: self-so. The *Daodejing* tells us that Dao emulates what is spontaneously so. This self-so finds a point between aimlessness and the modern obsession with willpower.

Consider that in an anecdote in the *Zhuangzi*, Cook Ding, a special butcher, does not adhere to an abstract or other's principle imposed on him from the outside world, but instead readily follows the intrinsic natural patterns of the ox. In doing so, he is able to perfectly carve an ox without dulling his blade or destroying the meat. He follows the natural flow of things. Like Cook Ding, we must recognize that it is not conceptual principle but the inherent patterning of things that provides us with the necessary premise for effective action.

The Daoist way directs us to embrace, absorb, and embody the particular pattern in all things. To do so one needs to have a *de* (德), an internal power or circulation. After all, the greatness of Dao is its ability to transform and change. Zhuangzi explains that Dao is "responding by pairing or matching" and *de* is "responding by attuning." Both require a creative synergy. As Zhuangzi says, "Do not hurry [your mission] to completion. . . . Let yourself be carried along by things so that the mind wanders freely." In surrendering to cosmic time and allowing yourself to transform freely, responding to circumstances by adapting to them, it is possible to attune yourself to the natural movement of things; to experience *de*.

Being alive means precisely that a living thing has its own active and functioning systems of circulation *de*. We often think of systems of circulation (digestive, respiratory, limbic, and so forth) as internal, but some are also external, whether seasonal or ecological cycles. Each living thing or event maintains its existence because of the *de* circulation through energy flow. *De* is an internal circulatory force that "nurtures" (*yang* 養) all things, like a kind of rechargeable battery. Because of this, our obsession with "control" can be replaced by circulation. Things, events, and people all have their own active and functioning system of circulation. Control only blocks this rhythmic circulation and causes more problems. Pain—whether physical, mental, or spiritual—is caused by blocked or jammed circulation. Daoist physicians claim that sickness is a result of *butong* 不通 (not flowing), while *tong* 通 (flowing) is to be free of pain.

Nature has no option but to move with the rhythms of the universe. The belief that there are laws (*fa* 法), standards (*du* 度), patterns (*ze* 則), and coherence (*li* 理) underlying the world constitute the *ziran* (self-so, or "of self") vision. As exemplified by the movement of running water or the rustling of wind, we should act according to this self-so. The Daoist way follows these rules as "compliance" (*yin* 因), which means abandoning your own subjective likes or dislikes in order to see natural phenomena as law and to understand the truth of all things as they are or as they are unfolding. This "compliance" means "the *Dao* of unintentional action." "Compliance with time" (*yin yu shi* 因于时) means adapting activities to the changes of the four seasons, rather than in accordance with our own subjective desires. This reflects respect for the laws of nature and natural ecological wisdom.

Zhuangzi tells us a story of a man playing in water. There is a waterfall that is more than two hundred feet high, with a whirlpool that covers ninety miles; fish and turtles cannot swim there, and crocodiles cannot live there. However, a man goes in and out of the water with playful ease. He is asked what kind of skill he has. The man responds, "I enter by being loyal and trusting to the water and I come out following this loyalty and trust. This loyalty and trust lead me to throw my body in the current and I do not dare to act selfishly." You have to trust and follow the flow; this is the *Daoshu* 道術 (art of Dao).

This art of Dao celebrates the outcome of flowing naturally with situations and conditions. Consider that sunlight, water, and soil are the basic natural prerequisites for farming. Plentiful sunlight and timely rain secure a harvest that supports human life. Sun and water provide the basis for human actions, captured in the timing (or seasons) of heaven (*tianshi* 天時) and the advantages of earth (*dili* 地利). From the sun, you can learn to follow the rhythm of seasons; from the soil, you can investigate how to go along with the rhythm and circumstances of the earth, taking advantage of conditions without coercing things.

A great example is the century-old story of how legendary Dayu managed a flood. Instead of using force to combat the flood—putting up dikes to stop the water, for example—Dayu redirected (*shudao* 疏導) the water. He dredged new river channels to direct the water according to its natural flow, rather than resisting the tendencies of the water. These channels served both as outlets for the torrential waters and as irrigation conduits to distant farmlands. He thus successfully controlled the floods. His method serves as a metaphor of flowing along in attunement with the terrain to get things done with excellence, ease, and sustainability. This idea now serves as a popular expression of Dao: flowing like water!

Parenting illustrates the importance of this form of directing. For example, my daughter wanted to be a lawyer since the fifth grade. She enjoyed reading, arguing, and winning debates. However, during her last semester in college, her ambition flowed in a different direction. As she was writing her senior thesis, she discovered a natural, five-hundred-year-old Chinese silk-making process that depends on sun and water to dye the beautiful fabric. Deviating from her original desire, she declared, "I want to learn more about this amazing silk and be a fashion designer." Although I questioned her decision, wondering if the world needs another fashion designer, I still flowed with her creative energy. Rather than fighting against or offering an impediment, parental direction and support are much better.

A Way to Success: A Straight Line or a Zigzag Path?

We all want to be successful by planning and designing bright futures. Yet, there might be a gap between our plans and reality's plan for us. We cannot limit all of our complex existences into one single, linear arrow. As Zhuangzi tells us: "Drawing a straight line upon this earth then trying to walk along it— danger, peril. . . . My zigzag stride amid [brambles and thorns] keeps my feet unharmed."

What is the way to success? Is it by following a straight line or by taking a zigzag path? The popular view is that success comes from inspiration, determination, and willpower, which move us in a straight line. This seems easy as long as we have willpower and can keep everything under our control. Yet, reality is hard. It is not easy to pay our bills, stay healthy, and have fun. So many unexpected things can block the road to success. We need to avoid what might be called "gap characters," the space between our will and our success.

In college, I was a javelin thrower for the track and field team.

I was determined to do my best, getting up early each morning for strength training and practicing techniques every afternoon after my classes. For two years, I spent five or six hours each day with the long stick. If I understood the world from a linear cause-and-effect perspective, my efforts would have yielded the desired result. However, my progress was minimal and I came to realize the futility of my passion. I learned that the most important maneuver involved in making the javelin fly a good distance involves relaxing my arm when I draw it back, then suddenly concentrating all my power in the throw. Without this proper positioning, the zigzag maneuver, the javelin will not go far. However, this is not only a matter of knowing it, but, more important, of mastering it.

During this time, I also questioned my passion and ability in this sport. I wondered, am I using my best *shi* 勢 properly? *Shi* is a special Chinese term that can refer to power, force, influence, natural features, or the propensity of things. Everything has its own *shi*, and every individual contains his or her own *shi*. *Shi* is one's strength in all things and actualizes all things, goals, and destinations.

The world is in an endless flow with *shi*. We can take advantage of this flow in order to direct and create *shi* in our favor. However, if we try to control a chain of events, avoid chaos and uncertainty, and become blind to *shi* by relying on planning, modeling, and restricting, then the situation will not be managed. Frequently, chaos and uncertainty bring out a new *shi*, or new opportunities that can increase our own *shi*. My greatest *shi* actually resides in spending time at the library reading philosophy books, so I put down the javelin and moved to extensive philosophical training.

Success-making is usually something deliberate and rational—a planned activity. Clearly there is a tension between human calculation and the intervention of natural tendencies. *Shi* is not only about following particular trends, but is also about actively making use of every opportunity contained in the changing process—not being blocked into a predetermined disposition.

The Daoist way asks us to *shen shi* 審時 (to have an awareness of propensity or optimize possibilities). The difference between imposing your will and following *shi* is whether one sets up a goal for actions or allows oneself to be carried along by the propensity of things. Does one impose a plan on things or rely on the potential inherent factors in a changing process?

The Daoist text *The Art of War* by Sun Tzu illustrates this power of *shi*, which makes a stone float. *Shi* is visible in the onrush of water, which tumbles stones along. When water rushes rapidly, its impetus surges forward and this momentum can generate a dynamic force that makes a stone float. Two interesting points: one is that *shi* is vital in making important events unfold; the other is that the changing of *shi* results in surprise. It is clear that there is no preconceived view for a floating stone. Rather, things happen when *shi* emerges in unexpected ways. Importantly, water, like reality, is full of *shi* because it continuously reconstructs itself.

We become comfortable with uncertainty through a reliance on *shi*—the inherent potential of the changing situation. We rely on *shi* to maintain an equable attitude of adaptation and openness to situations as they evolve. Consider the experience of dealing with a bad boss or supervisor. In this difficult situation, no matter what you do, you are doomed to fail. Zhuangzi suggests that we should recognize two constraints in life: *ming* 命 (unavoidable limitations), such as the parents we have, despite what they are like, and *yi* 義 (responsibility, doing what fits one's position), such as being a student or an employee. Accepting these constraints is the first step to finding *an* 安 (peace or reconciliation) in them.

After finding *an*, we should try to create, direct, or build *shi* in going about our situation. We do so by keeping our own emotions at bay and accessing our own strength at different times and in different contexts.

Part of this *shi* is finding something to rely on. A Daoist text tells us, "The wise invariably rely on the right timing or opportunity. But there is no guarantee that the timing or opportunity will come, so one must also rely on ability, just like making use of a boat or a cart." What one relies on is the natural propensity of things, such as water's power or the tendencies of the human heart.

As a strategy, relying on our circumstances shifts the focus away from our own actions and powers, and instead orients us toward what is already available in a given situation. In different conditions, we need to figure out what kinds of things can be relied on. What are the resources available? Like a Chinese saying, "If you live by the mountain, then you will be fed by the mountain; if you live by the river, you will be fed by the river." This belief can also make clear why the concept of *guanxi* 關係 (connections), making all kinds of human and social connections at different levels, permeates all aspects of today's Chinese social life.

Good Days and Bad Days: Living Joyfully

Uncertainty is not something that is created by human failure. It is a continuous condition that is constituted and shaped by change. Change can bring out many unexpected things or surprises. The Daoist way teaches us to experience joy in good or bad days by engaging in bodily movement, maintaining an organic lifestyle, and pursuing a natural and organic affluence.

One might ask, what about really bad days in our life, the desperate conditions many people find themselves in? As we discussed above, Zhuangzi guides us to first accept, not resist our *ming* (unavoidable limitations or unexpected conditions), then wisely to focus on the solution while keeping our spirit intact. This Daoist spirit opens a new horizon and unique mode of human existence.

I have tried to bring up my daughters based on the Daoist teachings, starting with many small things in their daily lives. My daughters call them "Mama Wang's four principles: eat well, exercise daily, get plenty of sleep, and do well in school." They have often challenged me by asking, "What about my happiness?" I say, "Well, if you can do these four things well, you will be happy."

Our sensory organs desire sounds, scents, tastes, and so on. However, if one wants to find joy in these, it should originate in the heart/mind (*xin* 心), or derive from being with nature. Being with nature is the real source of joy. Zhuangzi calls it a heavenly joy (*tianle* 天樂): "One who in living moves according to the movements of heaven and who in dying follows the transformations of the myriad things knows heavenly joy." To have this joy, the heart/mind will need to be harmonized or balanced (*he* 和). To reach *he*, the heart/mind must be in sync with the natural order or pattern of things. Compliance with the ordering of things enables one to taste, smell, and see things with enjoyment.

The contemporary happiness industry manufactures our happiness. Bottled happiness tells us that a product can take away our anxiety or remove our depression—that it can eliminate our negative feelings and leave us living happily ever after. The Daoist way teaches us to leave the happiness industry and take control of our own lives, starting with the simplest and closest thing:

our own body, a unity of physical form, energy flow, and spirit. The body is a central space for Daoists to occupy. Often ignored, the body is the most basic, manageable, and beneficial resource we possess. Like a garden with various plants, the body needs cultivation and nourishment in order to thrive. The body is fundamentally connected to growth and change, yet brings a wider range of uncertainties to our expectations and the way of living.

The ideal body in *Daodejing* is not that of a gentleman, a king, or even any adult, but a newborn. The infant's body contains the fullness of power because "his bones are supple and his sinews are pliant" 骨弱筋柔 (*gu ruo jin rou*). This is to say that there are no blockages, either of a physical kind, like a clogged artery, or of a psychic kind, like tension or anxiety, and this allows circulation within the infant's body, which in turn endows the body with an almost superhuman strength. The body of the newborn manifests a potency of life.

Here is a simple bodily daily ritual rooted in Daoism. This practice is a way of resting the mind to attain healing, purification, and spiritual transcendence. It focuses on the guiding of *qi* to benefit the body and mind. It pursues the fourfold alignment of body, limbs, breath, and mind. The practice reaches a level of simplicity that allows us to let go of things, free from sensory overload, and embodies a joy, especially during bad days.

Throughout the day, whether it is a good day or a bad day, think of the term "Dao": a word, sound, and command. Four things happen when you think of Dao:

1. *Shouyi* 守一 (guarding the oneness): Focus on oneness and self-awareness at your core, your inner center. Hold the correct bodily posture and movement.

2. *Xu* 虛 (emptiness): Take a breath while fasting the mind. The breath is the bridge between body and mind, an expression of mental reality closely linked to emotions and nervous conditions. The more breath is deepened and calmed, the quieter the mind becomes, and the easier to suspend the critical factor and enter into serenity.

3. *Ming* 明 (clarity): Gaze at a horizon. Remain aware of the present.

4. *Ziran* 自然 (self-so): Find your own way to complete the task at hand with efficiency.

The *Daodejing* claims that the journey of a thousand steps starts with the first step. It also implies that there are a thousand more to go. Taking each small step at a time, the whole journey becomes easier. In not taking the first step, things become increasingly difficult. Each step involves a quantum leap of imagination and inspiration, yet also requires persistence and resilience. Like our daily physical exercise, this practice helps us to gain more resilience, an ability to bounce back from adversity and an emotional muscle that can be strengthened at any time.

Final Remarks

Life is fluid and creative. It is always pregnant with the vital energies of imminent transformation and incipient potentiality. Change is an intrinsic and everlasting condition of all configurations, regardless of human desire, will, or planning. Thus, uncertainty is a vital part of our lives. It is not something external or temporal. Uncertainty is not a problem that needs to be corrected but rather a condition to be prepared for and accepted. One can bear or react to uncertainty passively or embrace it and deal with it in an active and spontaneous way. Real strength entails flexibility; real wisdom entails uncertainty; real endurance entails resilience; real power entails humility.

The Daoist way is a process, a method, a narrative, and an accumulation of wisdom and practice. It teaches us to develop an ability to master our environments, autonomy, and self-acceptance. In fact, it requires a high level of self-regulation.

The Daoist way requires us to have the ability to challenge our own comfortable paradigm, opening ourselves to other paradigms, responding to unpredictable changes. The notions of order, stability, discreetness, control, sameness, certainty, and permanence should be accompanied by disorder, flux, interpenetration, dispersal, difference, and uncertainty. We don't invite uncertainty into our lives, yet we can never eliminate it. The world is not about rational control, but natural rhythm. Let's flow with Dao to live well!

Suggested Readings

Daodejing: The New, Highly Readable Translation of the Life-Changing Ancient Scripture formerly known as the Tao Te Ching. Translated by Hans-Georg Moeller. Chicago: Open Court, 2007. This is a complete and more accurate translation of the Daoist classic text *Daodejing.* It comes with basic interpretations in each chapter.

Moeller, Hans-Georg. *Daoism Explained: From the Dream of the Butterfly to the Fishnet Allegory.* Chicago: Open Court, 2004. A nice overview of early Daoism with some exciting and interesting text-based stories.

Slingerland, Edward. *Trying Not to Try: Ancient China, Modern Science, and the Power of Spontaneity*. New York: Broadway Books, 2015. This connects the Daoist idea of nonaction with modern science, especially cognitive science.

Wang, Robin R. *Yinyang: The Way of Heaven and Earth in Chinese Thought and Culture*. New York: Cambridge University Press, 2012. Provides a good comprehensive description of yinyang's function and influence in Chinese ontology, knowledge, logic, body cultivation, visual art, and way of life.

Zhuangzi: The Essential Writings, with Selections from Traditional Commentaries. Translated by Brook Ziporyn. Indianapolis: Hackett, 2009. This is an accessible translation of another Daoist classic.

Ancient Philosophies from the West

Aristotelianism, Stoicism, and Epicureanism

Around the same time the Hundred Schools of Thought were sparking philosophical debate in the East, the seeds of Western philosophy were beginning to germinate in Greece. In the late fifth century BCE, Socrates was wandering around Athens being a gadfly, challenging and questioning the beliefs of those whom he encountered. He annoyed the wrong people—or perhaps they were actually the right people—and was eventually sentenced to death by hemlock for impiety and corrupting the youth. However, Socrates influenced three philosophical titans who are discussed in this section: Aristotle (384–322 BCE), Zeno of Citium (334–ca. 262 BCE), and Epicurus (341–270 BCE). Zeno is not as famous as the other two, but he was a wealthy merchant from Cyprus who, after being shipwrecked, read about Socrates in an Athenian bookstore, went on to found Stoicism, and inspired the later Stoic icons Seneca, Epictetus, and Marcus Aurelius.

Aristotle, whose name means "the best purpose," was a student of Plato at his academy in Athens, and tutored Alexander the Great. The good life, for Aristotle, is one that is eudaimonic, meaning a life in which we flourish and strive for an all-around well-being. As Daniel A. Kaufman explains in the first chapter of this section, chapter 4, on Aristotelianism, "The eudaimonic life, for Aristotle, is one in which we have lived to the fullness of our potential; developed our distinctive capacities to their finest points; and accomplished in the world what we have set out to do." We should endeavor to do excellently in all aspects of our lives—morally, psychologically, and physiologically. If we succeed, we can be proud of that, and take pleasure in it. But perhaps not all of us actually will do excellently in life, even if we're really trying, because there are many things that are out of our control—such as the circumstances of time and place in which one is born.

For Aristotelians, virtue is necessary but not sufficient for a eudaimonic life, which they interpret as a life of human flourishing. For the Stoics, in contrast, virtue in itself is sufficient for a life worth living, even though one may not flourish. In this sense, the Stoics struck a middle ground between Aristotelians and Cynics by introducing the notion of "preferred indifferents." Preferred indifferents are external goods that are important and useful, but we ought never to become overly attached to them because they are neither necessary nor sufficient for eudaimonia.

Consider an example. Your life has been devoted to business and your partner steals all your money and leaves you bankrupt. An Aristotelian would likely say that this turn of bad fortune—in which your judgment as to the choice of business partners may also have come into play—has prevented you from flourishing. For the Stoics, however, so long as you acted virtuously, success in business is a preferred indifferent and does not affect your value as a person. Stoics do not say that we should not have nice things, but rather that nice things are not required in order for one's life to be a worthy one. As a Cynic, you would be as indifferent to failure as to success, neither preferring nor "dispreferring" them. (Diogenes, one of the founders of Cynicism and one of the most famous Cynics, lived in Athens from 412– or 404–323 BCE and was indifferent to wealth and others' opinions of him. He was famous for living on the streets in a ceramic pot, urinating on people he did not like, and defecating and masturbating in public.) As for the Epicureans, getting into an ambitious business is probably going to give you little pleasure and increase your chances of experiencing pain, so it should be avoided or minimized.

Stoics also think eudaimonia is the goal to aim for, and a fundamental part of this state of being is living ethically—which is why both Aristotelianism and Stoicism advocate for the virtues of temperance and practical wisdom, among others. The Stoics point out that there are lots of things that are "not up to us" and the challenge is to figure out what we can and cannot control. It is perhaps no surprise that these two schools have many important elements in common, since Socrates taught Plato, who taught Aristotle, and Zeno read Aristotle and was also influenced by Socrates.

The Stoics developed specific exercises to help deal with suffering from wanting what they did not have, worrying about losing what they did have, and becoming better people. (Not just twenty-first-century problems, apparently.) For example, philosophical diaries can help us to reflect on and learn from our experiences. Self-denial in the form of occasional cold showers or fasting, for example, can help us to be grateful for the small things in our lives that we often overlook. Stoics think that flourishing is great, but not at the expense of ataraxia, which Massimo Pigliucci describes as "tranquility of mind in the face of anything the universe throws at you."

Stoicism is often unfairly characterized as a quietist philosophy, but Pigliucci challenges this misconception by showing how Stoicism can help us to face adversity and challenges that inevitably affect our lives. It is not so far removed from the Buddhist practice of detachment on the path to *nirvana*. And this is not the only point that Western and Eastern philosophies have in common: Stoic cosmopolitanism is surprisingly similar to the Confucian idea that everyone ought to be considered part of our family; and both Stoicism and Aristotelianism have elements of living according to our nature, which is not so different from the notion of aligning ourselves with the Dao.

Both Aristotle and the Stoics influenced medieval and Renaissance Christian thinking. After falling out of general favor in the third century CE, they had a profound bearing on the philosophies of Thomas Aquinas, Descartes, and Spinoza, among others. Aristotle became particularly popular in the Islamic world after the Christian scholar Hunayn ibn Ishaq (809–873 CE) translated Aristotle, Plato, and other works into Arabic, and leading scholars such as the Persian polymath Avicenna (980–1037 CE) studied them. Stoicism has also faced a resurgence in popularity in the late twentieth and early twenty-first centuries, thanks not only to Massimo Pigliucci's own *How to Be a Stoic* (2017), but also Stoic-friendly celebrity author-entrepreneurs such as Tim Ferriss and Ryan Holiday—who are showing how Stoic philosophy can help with everyday problems such as perseverance and overcoming fear. Both Aristotelianism and Stoicism have influenced modern psychology—particularly cognitive behavioral therapy (CBT) and positive psychology. Alasdair MacIntyre, the Scottish moral and political philosopher, went through an Aristotelian phase and—along with other modern philosophers such as G. E. M. Anscombe, Iris Murdoch, Philippa Foot, Martha C. Nussbaum, and Michael Sandel—reinvigorated discussions about Aristotelian politics and virtue ethics.

Facing a different sort of revival is Epicureanism, a philosophy based on the teachings of a third-century BCE Athenian named Epicurus. Epicurus was much less impressed with Socrates's ideas than Aristotle and Zeno, and was both revered and vilified for it. Epicurus agreed with the Stoics that we should aim for ataraxia, and with Aristotle that flourishing and friendship are vitally important to our happiness. Nevertheless, Epicurus thought that Aristotle and the Stoics overvalued rationality and undervalued the role of feelings and instincts as guides to living. And while Aristotle proposed that we are political animals,

Epicurus disagreed and thought it obvious that we are pleasure-seeking animals. Consider babies: right from the moment they are born, they avoid pain and enjoy pleasure.

Hiram Crespo explains that while Epicureanism has become associated with being "a foodie and wine snob," Epicureans originally ate simple meals with friends while discussing philosophy in a school known as "the Garden," where women were welcomed as equals (which was highly unusual in ancient Greece). Also contrary to popular belief, Epicureans understand pleasure not as indulgence, but rather as the pleasant, grateful, or confident feeling that one experiences when pain, suffering, and fear are absent. To figure out what will bring the most pleasure, Epicureans do "hedonic calculus," which is a process of weighing the advantages and disadvantages of one's choices. For example, Crespo explains, the dehydration and lost productivity the morning after drinking three beers might not be worth the fleeting pleasure of the night before.

Epicurus was a prolific writer, but few of his works remain today. Epicureanism died out around the fifth century, partly because Stoicism became more popular, and partly because the Christian tradition scorned Epicureanism as immoral with its focus on pleasure and the body and lack of fear of God. Later writers such as John Locke, John Dryden, Thomas Jefferson, Karl Marx, Lord Alfred Tennyson, José Mujica, and utilitarian philosophers revived Epicureanism, and in the twenty-first century, people still advocate for the philosophy of happiness and friendship that Epicurus envisaged. One of the most prominent philosophers today, Michel Onfray, has even established a university in France based on Epicurean principles.

CHAPTER FOUR

Aristotelianism

Daniel A. Kaufman

Ralph Waldo Emerson wrote that "a foolish consistency is the hobgoblin of little minds, adored by little statesmen and philosophers and divines," and one only has to consider those whose lives seem overly deliberated, planned, routinized, controlled, and enamored with intellectual virtues to see the truth of it. And yet, a life lived without thoughtful reflection and due consideration—without at least sometimes taking the long view and effecting some integration of oneself, one's relationships, one's activities, and one's values—is hard to imagine as being a fully developed or fully realized one.

So, one must have a philosophy of life, but not *just* a philosophy of life. An ethnic or religious heritage; a spouse and children; an extended family; a circle of friends with whom one enjoys long-standing and close relationships—these are the elements that make up a good and flourishing life, for they are what engage us at the deepest levels of our being and provide the particular relationships and experiences that give a life its substance. It is not enough, then, that one admire a philosophy for its intellectual qualities. It must be well suited to the type of person one is and the type of life one leads, an ill-fitting philosophy being even more obvious and awkward and ultimately useless than an ill-fitting suit.

In my own case, my preferred philosophy of life—I will call it Aristotelianism—interacts with my ethno-religious heritage (a cultural Ashkenazi Judaism), my relationships with my wife and daughter and our circle of friends and their children, and my being part of and strongly devoted to a particular family, with a particular history. It is a philosophy that I not only admire intellectually, but which suits the kind of person that I am, the kinds of people with whom I associate, and the kind of life I lead.

The text at the heart of my Aristotelianism is Aristotle's *Nicomachean Ethics*, and it will feature heavily in what follows. Early in that work, Aristotle articulates the wisdom just expressed, namely that philosophical theorizing can only provide us with a general, largely abstract, and ultimately incomplete guide to something as complex and steeped in particularity as a good human life. We should be suspicious, then, of philosophies that instruct us too much and in too great detail. If a philosophy purports to tell us specific things we should or shouldn't do in particular situations, then it is likely one that misunderstands the extent to which philosophical theory can inform practice. As Aristotle put it:

> Our discussion will be adequate if it has as much clearness as the subject-matter admits of, for precision is not to be sought for alike in all discussions. . . . We must be content, then, in speaking of such subjects and with such premises to indicate the truth roughly and in outline,

> and in speaking about things which are only for the most
> part true, and with premises of the same kind, to reach
> conclusions that are no better . . . for it is the mark of
> an educated man to look for precision in each class of
> things just so far as the nature of the subject admits; it
> is evidently equally foolish to accept probable reasoning
> from a mathematician and to demand from a rhetorician
> demonstrative proofs.[1]

Aristotelianism is a form of *eudaimonism*, from the Greek *eudaimonia*, which means human "excellence" or "flourishing." Sometimes translated as "happiness," it should not be confused with the modern, hedonic sense of the term, in which it means "pleasure" or "good feeling," though this will be a *part* of what it means to achieve it. The eudaimonic life, for Aristotle, is one in which we have lived to the fullness of our potential; developed our distinctive capacities to their finest points; and accomplished in the world what we have set out to do. It is a life that we should take pleasure in—Aristotle treats the pleasure one takes in one's own flourishing as evidence that it is genuine—but one which, more important, is admirable, in the sense described in my opening remarks; a life of which a person can be *rightly* proud.

It is also a life that one can fail to realize despite one's best efforts. One of the things that is most controversial about Aristotle's eudaimonism is that flourishing depends to a significant degree on so-called external goods, as well as luck. By the former is meant some measure of material well-being and positive native endowment, and the point is that you can do everything the right way and still fail to flourish in your life, either because of a lack of crucial material goods, inadequate personality or bodily traits, or vicissitudes of fortune, which may include everything from natural disaster to war, to being born to a lousy family, to prodigal children and crooked business partners. This is why Aristotle maintains that we can develop a truly accurate picture of the quality of a life only well after the person who lived it is dead. Just as we can get the full measure of a movement or a period only once sufficient time has passed for it to have a legacy that we can examine and evaluate, we can get the full measure of a person only from a position at which it is possible to see how the relationships he formed and the things he did have played out.

The idea is alleged by many to be elitist, which, in itself, of course, is no reason for thinking it untrue, but regardless, the charge is baseless. Nothing about Aristotle's view entails that in order to flourish one must be a millionaire or look like a super-model or have everything always go right. Rather, it suggests that there is a floor beneath which flourishing becomes increasingly difficult to nigh impossible; a level of poverty or material deprivation or compromised intelligence or physical ugliness or suffering of whatever kind below which a good life in the eudaimonic sense simply cannot be achieved.

That eudaimonia is entirely self-sufficient certainly is a comforting thought and one that appeals to modern sensibilities by satisfying the modern preoccupation with individual autonomy—how *dare* anyone suggest that *my* flourishing is something that *I* don't control?—but in my view, the idea either represents a misunderstanding about the nature of eudaimonia or is part of an (often unconscious) exercise in self-deception. Flourishing, after all, occurs (or not) *in the world, by way of our relationships and activity*, which means that it is dependent on people and events and things that we do not control. This becomes obvious when we consider the excellence or flourishing of things simpler than human beings. Whether a flower or an animal flourishes, for example, is due in part to facts about its environment: the flower cannot flourish in a catastrophic drought, and the animal cannot flourish if it is consumed by a predator before it has had the chance to be what it is and do what it does. And this is clearly the case with people, too, if we focus on the individual parts of our lives. Someone might be a technically proficient and mentally tough tennis player, for example, but if he is unfortunate enough to have spent his best years in a period in which there was no strong competition, though he may have been ranked number one for years, the comparative evaluation of his excellence as a tennis player will always be less than that of others who dominated the game in more competitive times.

Far from its dependence on external goods being a defect of Aristotle's eudaimonism, then, it is one of its greatest strengths, as it reflects a realistic, honest, and mature outlook on life. That effort alone is not enough; that in a fundamental sense I exist among and depend upon others; that social, political, economic, and natural forces are capable of overwhelming and destroying me and the things I have created; that it matters whether or not I *actually* have succeeded, as opposed to simply having tried to, and that I refuse to deceive myself about this—these are hard truths about our lives and our flourishing, the acceptance of which is part of what characterizes a mature outlook on life. Indeed, I would go further and say that to the extent to which in the modern era we have rejected these hard truths—in good measure, under the influence of Immanuel Kant's philosophy and its radical conception of autonomy—in favor of more comforting illusions regarding our self-sufficiency, is the extent to which our civilization as a whole exhibits less maturity than that of Aristotle's day, his views regarding the central role played by material circumstances and good fortune having been shared, notably, by the great Greek tragedians. Fortunately, in recent years, the significance of what I am calling "hard truths" about our flourishing has been reaffirmed by contemporary thinkers like Martha C. Nussbaum in *The Fragility of*

Goodness[2] and Thomas Nagel in "Moral Luck,"[3] which have forced contemporary philosophers to contend with them once again.

Eudaimonia, for Aristotle, is complex and encompasses more than moral virtue, another element of his philosophy that not only appeals to me, but represents a realism about human life that recommends it beyond personal taste. As human beings, we are defined by the capacity to *reason*, which, for Aristotle, means much more than the ability to comprehend and apply logic. Divided into two broad categories, practical/deliberative and intellectual, reason makes possible a number of distinctively human activities and thus provides the ground for a multifaceted kind of flourishing, of which moral virtue is only one—and for Aristotle, not necessarily the most important—kind.

Beyond moral virtue—by which Aristotle means excellence in the conduct of our personal and social lives—practical reason is the crucial mode of thinking involved in all manner of arts, crafts, and, more generally, *making* of any and every kind. It is reasoning about activity, about *what should I do?* and is employed whether we are interacting with a neighbor, voting in an election, carving a sculpture, or building a bridge. Thus, just as one can flourish as a social and political being, one can also flourish as an artist, a craftsman, and an engineer.

And then there is the purely intellectual side of reason—the side that is involved not in action, but in the pursuit of knowledge and understanding. It is the faculty we employ when engaged in all manner of scholarship—whether in philosophy, mathematics, or science—and though its fruits may be brought to bear upon one's practical reasoning and, thus, one's activity, it is a distinct kind of thinking in its own right. One can flourish in the pursuit of knowledge, then, and for Aristotle, this life, the "life of contemplation," is in fact the most admirable of all the kinds of life that we might lead, for it is not just a distinctively human life, but rather, as he puts it, "the life of a god," to which some very able and very well-situated people (there's that crucial role of natural endowment and luck again) can aspire.

My interest here, however, is not in Aristotle's hierarchical conception of the different ways in which human beings can flourish, but rather in the idea that we should flourish in *some number of them*, rather than just one or two; that the fewer the ways in which we flourish, the less admirable our lives are overall. Certainly, we admire the brilliant painter, who has mastered his craft and produces works of extraordinary beauty, but if we discover that he is terrible to his wife and children, crooked in his business, and involved in ugly politics, our estimation of his life, generally, will be poor. That is, while we may continue to admire him *as a painter*, we will not admire him *as a man*. And the same obviously would be true if we swapped our painter for a Nobel Prize–winning theoretical physicist, the rest of whose life is shameful and a shambles.

None of this is particularly controversial, but strangely, it becomes so when one shifts the focus to moral virtue, where we find that many esteemed philosophers, as well as ordinary people, suddenly find single-mindedness an admirable trait. But I reject the idea that the person who is morally virtuous and fails to flourish in any other respect has led an admirable life, any more than has our painter or theoretical physicist, and Aristotle, more than any other philosopher, gives us the tools with which to explain why. For it is he who has become famous for preaching a message of moderation, one that applies not just to moral virtue (which we will discuss in a moment) but to human life as a whole:

> Let us consider this, that it is the nature of such things to
> be destroyed by defect and excess, as we see in the case of
> strength and of health . . . ; exercise either excessive and

defective destroys the strength, and similarly drink or food which is above or below a certain amount destroys the health, while that which is proportionate both produces and increases and preserves it.[4]

For Aristotle, then, the idea of the flourishing life cannot be disentangled from that of the balanced one, and the person who pursues moral virtue at the expense of all else—who views moral considerations as always overriding of all others—is by definition one whose life is unbalanced. To flourish as a human being is to fully develop and exercise one's distinctive capacities, and, as we have seen, these capacities support any number of forms of life, aside from the moral. To pursue the moral above and beyond all else, then, is to fail to fully and healthily develop as a person, and the life that follows cannot be one in which one can be said to have flourished. As the philosopher Susan Wolf explains it in her paper "Moral Saints":

> The ideal of a life of moral sainthood disturbs not simply because it is an ideal of a life in which morality unduly dominates. The normal person's direct and specific desires for objects, activities, and events that conflict with the attainment of moral perfection are not simply sacrificed but removed, suppressed, or subsumed. The way in which morality . . . is apt to dominate is particularly disturbing, for it seems to require either the lack or the denial of the existence of an identifiable, personal self.[5]

Of course, moral virtue is an important part of the eudaimonic life, and here, again, Aristotle shines, for not only is his message of moderation sorely needed in the moral sphere—a very common, though pernicious idea is that being moral involves *always* or *never* doing certain things—so too is his conception of the relationship of theory to practice. Ours is a picture of morality obsessed with principles and rules, and Aristotle is going to show us why there cannot—and should not—be any.

I've said that one cannot disentangle Aristotle's conception of flourishing from that of a balanced life, and this is because eudaimonia is properly understood as a kind of well-being, one that encompasses physiological, psychological, and moral "health." As our physical and mental well-being is sustained by moderation in temperament and conduct and undermined by extremes of personality and action, the moral dimension of our well-being is, too. Hence, Aristotle's famous "doctrine of the mean," according to which a particular moral virtue will always represent the average in terms of temperament and conduct, relative to the relevant vices, which will always exemplify extremes, either of excess or deficiency.

Consider, for example, a moral virtue like honesty. The person who fails to tell the truth often enough suffers the relevant vice of deficiency and is labeled a "liar," while the person who tells the truth too much suffers from the relevant vice of excess and is called "indiscreet." The person who tells the truth in the "right amount" has the relevant virtue and is the one whom we identify as "honest." Or think of the virtue of temperance. The person who fails to control himself enough when it comes to food, drink, and other sensual pleasures suffers the relevant vice of deficiency and is deemed "gluttonous," in one way or another, while the person who exercises too much self-control and refuses ever to indulge himself suffers the relevant vice of excess and is identified as "insensible." It is the person who controls himself to the proper extent that has the relevant virtue and whom we say is "temperate."

Notice something about this doctrine of the mean. All it really tells us is the *relative position* of virtue and vice. It does *not* tell us—or even help us to discover—what *counts* as moderate, excessive, or deficient, and thus what is virtuous or vicious, in any given situation. Moreover, the very same thing may count as moderate on one occasion, excessive on another, and deficient on yet a third. This past September, I threw a big party at a local restaurant to celebrate my fiftieth birthday, with dozens of family and friends attending. The affair cost in the thousands of dollars, and the drinking and other festivities carried on well into the late hours. To do such a thing on such an occasion seemed not only like an appropriately good time, but an expression of love and generosity toward those who are dearest to me. To do it every week, however, would not represent munificence and a fun-loving attitude, but rather a pathological lack of thrift, not to mention a drinking problem. And to never do it or anything like it at all, under any circumstances, would not represent healthy caution and restraint, but would suggest, rather, that one is a cheap bore.

It is telling that in our society, "temperance" is a word that often is used to describe a movement of teetotalers—i.e., people who will not drink at all—as it indicates that we are commonly inclined to identify moral virtue with extremes of personality and behavior. In good part this is a legacy of Christianity and its celebration of asceticism, something that I think is misguided, not just because it reflects the sort of unbalanced personality that we already have discussed, but because it closes a person off to any number of experiences that may contribute to their flourishing. This is why it is so important that Aristotle makes it clear that the person who enjoys himself too little is just as bad as the one who enjoys himself too much, for it reflects the deep and essential idea that our flourishing requires us to be open to experience, something with which a morality based around extreme forms of prohibition interferes.

In Aristotle's view, no action, conceived neutrally, is intrinsically virtuous or vicious, but depends on the circumstances for its moral valence. Consequently, there can be no general moral rules—"Don't kill people," "Don't take others' property against their will," "Give money to the poor"—that apply unconditionally, irrespective of context. (One can easily imagine contexts in which it would be right to kill, take others' property, and the like.) We need to *figure out* what the right thing to do is, in any given situation. If that wasn't the case—if one could simply memorize a list of dos and don'ts—there would be no need for practical reason, which, if we think about the actual experience of ethical life, there clearly is. But practical reason alone also is not sufficient, if we are to determine what duty requires of us in any particular set of circumstances, for all reasoning concerns things characterized at some level of generality. One cannot reason with regard to the particular. To be able to identify the moderate and thus the right thing to do in a specific situation depends on one's being able to *see* it. Aristotle observes:

> The end cannot be a subject of deliberation, but only the means; nor indeed can the particular facts be a subject of it, e.g. whether this is bread or has been baked as it should; for these are matters of perception.[6]

The baker may know that his bagels should not be baked too much or too little, but rather, the right amount, and consequently, practical reason may lead him to bake at a certain temperature, for a certain duration, but knowing, at any particular point, whether a particular bagel has been baked enough is something that can only be seen, not reasoned to. Analogously, while I may know that pleasures should not be indulged in excessively or deficiently, and reason may lead me, as a general matter, to situate myself and behave in certain ways, what constitutes the right amount of drinking or eating on a particular occasion is only something that can be "seen," not deduced. This is why, for Aristotle, moral excellence is not just a matter of excellence in practical reason, but in a kind of perception, and what is called "practical wisdom" is a combination of both. It is also why, for Aristotle, moral virtue is not something that can be developed solely as a result of instruction, but requires substantial experience, as is the case with excellence in baking or bridge building or any other practical endeavor. One can teach a person how to reason, by way of explicit lessons, but the ability to *see* rightly, in various situations and circumstances, is something that can be developed only by *doing* whatever it is that is under consideration.

I fear that some of my readers may be disappointed. I have provided no inspirational aphorisms; no mantras; no meditation regimens; no exercises to do every morning; no steps to follow of any kind. Of course, this is entirely on purpose. A philosophy just is not the sort of thing that can guide us that specifically. At best, it can provide a general orientation, a basic set of ideas that comprise the barest of frameworks within which to consider what sort of life one should lead. One thing that I like so much about Aristotle is that he understands this and, even more important, *admits* it. He neither overstates nor oversells, as so many philosophies of life seem to do. Much of what he tells us requires no formal apparatus to grasp, as it belongs within the realm of common sense. And yet the combination yields a definite orientation—an attitude that makes Aristotle's a distinctive and, in my view, useful philosophy of life. Remain as open as possible to experience;

don't deceive yourself about what constitutes success or failure; develop as many of your capacities as fully as you possibly can; understand and appreciate the necessity of experience, beyond formal education; and recognize and accept the role played by luck. This is about as much as a philosophy legitimately can tell a person with regard to how one lives a good life. The rest must be discovered on one's own.

Suggested Readings

Aristotle. *Nicomachean Ethics*. Translated by David Ross. Oxford: Oxford University Press, 2009. The most accessible, readable, and well-known translation of Aristotle's *Ethics*.

Lear, Jonathan. *Aristotle: The Desire to Understand*. Cambridge: Cambridge University Press, 1988. One of the best and most accessible secondary sources on Aristotle's philosophy, with a particularly excellent analysis of the most important ideas in the *Nicomachean Ethics*.

Williams, Bernard. *Ethics and the Limits of Philosophy*. New York: Routledge, 2006.

———. *Philosophy as a Humanistic Discipline*. Princeton: Princeton University Press, 2006. All of Williams's work is grounded in the idea that philosophy is a human activity and an expression of the core elements of our nature. Of the philosophers of the last century, he was one of the most resistant to the idea that philosophy and especially ethics provide any kind of transcendent or extrahuman perspective from which to guide (or prescribe) our actions. Among his corpus, these two books resonate the strongest with this idea, which strikes me as quintessentially Aristotelian.

Notes

1 Aristotle, *Nicomachean Ethics*, trans. David Ross (Oxford: Oxford University Press, 2009), 4.

2 Martha C. Nussbaum, *The Fragility of Goodness: Luck and Ethics in Greek Tragedy and Philosophy* (Cambridge: Cambridge University Press, 1986).

3 Thomas Nagel, "Moral Luck," in *Mortal Questions* (Cambridge: Cambridge University Press, 1979).

4 Aristotle, *Nicomachean Ethics*, 25.

5 Susan Wolf, "Moral Saints," *Journal of Philosophy* 79, no. 8 (August 1982): 424, doi: 10.2307/2026228.

6 Aristotle, *Nicomachean Ethics*, 44.

CHAPTER FIVE

Stoicism

Massimo Pigliucci

A few years ago I was leisurely checking my Twitter feed when I saw something that read "Help us celebrate Stoic Week" followed by a URL that mentioned "Modern Stoicism." I thought: *What on Earth is Stoic Week? And why would anyone want to celebrate Stoicism, of all things?* Little did I know that that tweet was going to be the serendipitous beginning of a radical transformation of my life. For the better, I shall add.

I followed the proffered link with some curiosity, and it brought me to a site called Modern Stoicism.[1] I dutifully downloaded their handbook, and "lived like a Stoic" for a week. Which meant reading about Stoic philosophy, studying some of the ancient texts, and especially engaging in a number of practices, from visualization exercises to the writing of a personal philosophical diary to mild forms of self-denial (e.g., refraining from buying things, or fasting, or going out underdressed in cold weather). By the end of the week I was sufficiently intrigued as to commit to "live like a Stoic," so to speak, for the rest of the year (a few more weeks, at that point). After that, I committed to practice for one more year. Several years later, I'm still at it, and I have seen a number of improvements as a result. I think I'm at least a slightly better person, I don't get as anxious or angry as before, and I've developed an attitude of equanimity toward whatever the universe throws at me: if good, I enjoy it without becoming too attached to it; if bad, well, you can't always win, and there will possibly be better days ahead.

But what, exactly, is Stoicism? Isn't it about suppressing emotions and going through life with a stiff upper lip? Why would anyone want to do that?

Stoicism is an ancient Greco-Roman philosophy, which originated during the Hellenistic period, that is between the death of Alexander the Great and the rise of the Roman Empire. It was founded around 300 BCE by Zeno of Citium, a Phoenician merchant who had lost much of what he had in a shipwreck, made it to Athens, and walked into a bookshop, looking for solace. He read Xenophon's *Memorabilia*, a book about Socrates, and got intrigued by the possibility of studying philosophy. He asked the bookseller where he could find a philosopher, and the fellow pointed to someone who was walking by and said, "Follow *him*."[2] That man happened to be Crates of Thebes, a Cynic (that word did not then mean what it does today), and Zeno became his student.

Eventually, Zeno studied with several other philosophers belonging to a variety of schools, and ended up founding his own sect, which soon became known as the Stoics, because of their unusual habit (for philosophers) of meeting and lecturing in public, by the Stoa Poikile, or Painted Porch, in central Athens. The basic idea of the new philosophy was that in order to figure out how to live a life worth living, a eudaimonic life, as both modern philosophers and psychologists still refer to it, we have to master two things: we need to develop a decent understanding of how the world works, so not to engage in wishful thinking and waste a lot of time and resources; and we need to reason as well as we can about things, or we risk arriving at the wrong conclusions as to what to do and how. The Stoic recipe, then, looks something like this:

> "Physics" (study of how the world works, what we today call natural science and metaphysics) + "Logic" (study of reasoning, including cognitive science) => Ethics (study of how to live) => Eudaimonia (flourishing life)

This approach spread throughout the ancient world, and eventually the center of Stoicism moved to Rome, then the political, financial, and cultural capital of the Western world. It is from Rome that we get the three most famous Stoic writers of antiquity: Seneca, who was tutor and then adviser to the emperor Nero; Epictetus, the slave who became one of the most revered teachers of ancient Rome; and Marcus Aurelius, the emperor-philosopher. Stoicism gradually died out as a formal school after the second century CE, together with all the other Hellenistic philosophies. But its ideas survived by virtue of being incorporated into Christian thought, influencing major philosophers throughout the ages, from Augustine of Hippo to Thomas Aquinas, from René Descartes to Baruch Spinoza.

Stoic ideas then resurfaced during the twentieth century, possibly because of the turmoil that gripped society (two world wars and the civil rights struggles, to mention a few), just like in Hellenistic times. Stoicism provided the inspiration for cognitive branches of modern psychotherapy, including rational emotive behavior therapy and cognitive behavioral therapy. Since 2010, an organized movement of modern Stoicism has developed, with a strong online presence,[3] an increasing number of local groups, and international events like Stoicon held during "Stoic Week," which got it all started for me.

But what, exactly, does Stoic philosophy consist of? And why is it relevant to people living two millennia after Zeno, Seneca, Epictetus, and Marcus Aurelius?

There are two crucial ideas underlying Stoicism, and they each correspond to one major promise the philosophy holds for its practitioners. The first crucial idea is that life is fundamentally about being a morally good person, which is achieved through the continuous practice of four cardinal virtues. The second idea is the so-called dichotomy of control, the notion that some things are "up to us," as the Stoics say, and other things are not. The first idea promises, if followed, to lead to a eudaimonic life, the sort of life you can look back on at the end and think that it was worth living. The second idea promises something called ataraxia, or tranquility of mind in the face of anything the universe throws at you. And who wouldn't want to live a good and serene life?

A life of virtue, or a moral life, is—for the Stoics—a life lived "according to nature," because human nature is that of a social animal capable of reason. So applying reason to the task of making this a better world for everyone, including ourselves, is the natural and right thing to do. As Marcus Aurelius puts it: "Do you have reason? I have. Why then do you not use it?"[4] Or, more explicitly: "If the intellectual is common to all men, so is reason, in respect of which we are rational beings: if this is so, common also is the reason that commands us what to do, and what not to do; if this is so, there is a common law also; if this is so, we are fellow-citizens; if this is so, we are members of some political community."[5]

This is the central Stoic notion of cosmopolitanism: we are all on the same boat (planet Earth) together, and we are dependent on each other to make it so that the boat stays afloat and its occupants thrive. In this sense, there is no sharp distinction between my interests and those of the rest of humanity, something that is particularly relevant and urgent in these days of global environmental catastrophe and constant threat of war.

The way the Stoics put all of this into practice is by means of the four cardinal virtues: practical wisdom, the ability to navigate complex situations, especially morally salient ones, in the best way possible; courage, of the moral kind, as in the courage to stand up and do the right thing; justice, meaning treating others as worthy of the respect and dignity that comes with being fellow humans; and temperance, responding to situations in just measure, without excess or defect.

These four cardinal virtues were later incorporated into Christian doctrine by Thomas Aquinas, who added the three virtues that are peculiar to his interpretation of Christianity: hope, faith, and charity. Modern comparative social psychology has found that these same virtues (and two others, which the Stoics recognized but did not call virtues: humanity and transcendence) are valued by nearly every literate culture in the world.[6] You may object that living this way is very demanding, and you would be right. Then again, the reward is the sort of life that you will think on your deathbed was in fact worth living. Moreover, any other philosophy of life or religion is demanding as well, if actually practiced. It's not easy to be a good Christian, or Buddhist, or whatever else. If that parallel still doesn't do it for you, think of an analogy, which was, in fact, often used by the ancient Stoics themselves: taking care of your body. Sure, it's not easy to eat well, exercise regularly, and so forth. But the reward is a longer and healthier life, something well worth overcoming your habits as a couch potato, no?

How, exactly, does one go about "practicing virtue," though? The Stoics were nothing if not pragmatically oriented, so they had a number of exercises and tricks they used in their quest to become better persons. One of the most important of these is the evening philosophical diary, a tool of self-reflection to aid us in learning from our experiences, to forgive ourselves for our mistakes, and to prepare for a better day tomorrow. Seneca explains in detail how and why to do it:

> The spirit ought to be brought up for examination daily. It was the custom of Sextius when the day was over, and he had betaken himself to rest, to inquire of his spirit: "What bad habit of yours have you cured to-day? What vice have you checked? In what respect are you better?" Anger will cease, and become more gentle, if it knows that every day it will have to appear before the judgment seat. What can be more admirable than this fashion of discussing the whole of the day's events? How sweet is the sleep which follows this self-examination? How calm, how sound, and careless is it when our spirit has either received praise or reprimand, and when our secret inquisitor and censor has made his report about our morals? I make use of this privilege, and daily plead my cause before myself: when the lamp is taken out of my sight, and my wife, who knows my habit, has ceased to talk, I pass the whole day in review before myself, and repeat all that I have said and done: I conceal nothing from myself, and omit nothing: for why should I be afraid of any of my shortcomings, when it is in my power

> to say, "I pardon you this time: see that you never do that anymore"? . . . A good man delights in receiving advice: all the worst men are the most impatient of guidance.[7]

Another powerful tool in the Stoic toolbox is always to have ready a series of pithy phrases to remind yourself of what to do, or how to react, in any situation. Stoics memorize these and silently or vocally bring them up when they are in difficulty, reminding themselves of what they have learned and what follows from it in terms of how to actually live their lives. Here are some of my favorites:

- **Why won't you do the job of a human being?** Having trouble getting up in the morning and facing your day? You are in good company: the emperor Marcus Aurelius himself. And yet, as he says, we were not born to just comfortably huddle below warm blankets: "At dawn, when you have trouble getting out of bed, tell yourself: 'I have to go to work—as a human being. What do I have to complain of, if I'm going to do what I was born for—the things I was brought into the world to do? Or is this what I was created for? To huddle under the blankets and stay warm?'"[8]

- **The obstacle is the way.** Running into a brick wall? Charging it may not be the best strategy available to you. Try climbing on it, or going around it: "Our actions may be impeded by [other people], but there can be no impeding our intentions or our dispositions. Because we can accommodate and adapt. The mind adapts and converts to its own purposes the obstacle to our acting. The impediment to action advances action. What stands in the way becomes the way."[9]

- **It seems so to him.** Often people do things that we think are obviously wrong. If an injustice has been done, by all means oppose it. But Stoicism teaches us not to judge others (or ourselves), and this phrase is a reminder that other people also think they are doing the right thing: "A good guide, when he sees someone wandering astray, doesn't abandon him with a dose of mockery or abuse, but leads him back to the proper path. So you too should show him the truth and you'll see how he follows. As long as you fail to make it clear to him, though, you shouldn't make fun of him, but should recognize your own incapacity instead."[10]

- **Everything has two handles.** There is always more than one way to look at a situation, especially in terms of our relations with other people. See that you adopt the more positive stance, not the confrontational one: "Everything has two handles, and it may be carried by one of these handles, but not by the other. If your brother acts wrongly toward you, don't try to grasp the matter by this handle, that he is wronging you (because that is the handle by which it can't be carried), but rather by the other, that he is your brother, he was brought up with you, and then you'll be grasping the matter by the handle by which it can be carried."[11]

- **There goes my cup.** This is to remind myself that everything is impermanent. From the least important material things (the cup in the quote) to the most meaningful relationships in my life (my daughter, my wife, my siblings), everything is subject to the laws of the universe, and everything will end: "This is what you should practice from morning to evening. Begin with the smallest and most fragile things, a pot, or a cup, and then pass on to a tunic, a dog, a horse, a scrap of land; and from there, pass on to yourself, to your body, and the parts of your body, and to your children, your wife, your brothers. Look around you in every direction, and cast these things far away from you. Purify your judgments so that nothing that is not your own may remain attached to you, or become part of yourself, or give you pain when it comes to be torn away from you. And say while you're training yourself day after day, as you are here, not that you're acting as a philosopher (for you must concede that it would be pretentious to lay claim to that title), but that you're a slave on the way to emancipation. For that is true freedom."[12]

Lest you think that Epictetus is advising us not to care about ourselves or our loved ones, that is not his point. He is reminding us that—as he puts it elsewhere—everything we have is actually "on loan" from the universe, and the right attitude is to enjoy it while we have it and relinquish it when it is gone. Indeed, precisely because it will one day be gone, it is all the more precious while we have it.

There are several other very useful phrases, and many additional exercises,[13] which the *proficiens* (the one who makes progress) learns along the way, by reading both the ancient and the modern texts, or by practicing with like-minded students of the philosophy.

The second important Stoic idea—after the notion that it is crucial to live a moral life—is that of the dichotomy of control.

As Epictetus puts it: "Some things are within our power, while others are not. Within our power are opinion, motivation, desire, aversion, and, in a word, whatever is of our own doing; not within our power are our body, our property, reputation, office, and, in a word, whatever is not of our own doing."[14] The idea should be familiar, since it is found in a number of different traditions. Perhaps most famously, for modern Christians it takes the form of the Serenity Prayer, adopted by a number of twelve-step organizations, and originated by the American theologian Reinhold Niebuhr around 1934: "God, grant me the serenity to accept the things I cannot change, courage to change the things I can, and wisdom to know the difference."

But the same concept is present in Judaism, as exemplified by a saying attributed to the eleventh-century philosopher Solomon ibn Gabirol: "And they said: At the head of all understanding—is realizing what is and what cannot be, and the consoling of what is not in our power to change." Similarly, Shantideva, an eighth-century Buddhist scholar, wrote:

> *If there's a remedy when trouble strikes*
> *What reason is there for dejection?*
> *And if there is no help for it*
> *What use is there in being glum?*

This isn't counsel for laying back and passively accepting life. Stoicism is no quietist philosophy, as we are reminded by its practitioners, ancient as well as modern, who are people of action. Cato the Younger gave his life in the fight against the tyranny of Julius Caesar. James Stockdale survived seven years as a prisoner of war in Vietnam thanks in part to what he learned from Epictetus.

The idea, rather, is more subtle and wise. We need to approach everything in life keeping in mind the dividing line between our efforts, judgments, and decisions (which are under our control) and the outcomes of those efforts, judgments, and decisions (which are not under our—complete—control). Cicero explained this by way of a powerful metaphor. Imagine you are an archer, attempting to hit a difficult target, perhaps a moving enemy soldier. You have control of your shooting practice, of the choice of bow and arrows, of the amount of tension to apply to the bow, and of the exact moment when you let go of the arrow. But once the arrow itself has left your hands, everything else is no longer up to you. A gust of wind could ruin the best shot. Or the enemy might see you at the last second and duck the fatal blow.

Similarly in life. You may do your best to get a promotion at your job, but whether you get it or not depends on a number of factors you don't control, from the possible competition of your colleagues to the mood of your boss. Or you may wish for the love of another person, but this is up to her or him, while for your part what you can and should do is be the best, most genuinely lovable person you can be to them. In other words, the Stoics counsel to shift our goals from external outcomes to internal efforts: so long as we have done all we could, we should be at peace with whatever happens. If the results are good, we rejoice, always keeping in mind that it could have easily gone otherwise. If the results are not good, we accept that as a natural part of life, and we prepare for the next challenge.

If we manage to really understand and practice the dichotomy of control, Epictetus tells us, the reward is well worth the effort: "no one will ever compel you, no one will restrict you; you will find fault with no one, you will accuse no one, you will do nothing against your will; no one will hurt you, you will not have an enemy, nor will you suffer any harm."[15] That's because you will have approached the state of ataraxia, a tranquility of mind—similar to the Buddhist enlightenment—that comes from truly understanding the world and your limitations, doing your best while at the same time being at peace with yourself if things do not work out. It's a truly powerful insight, which makes Stoicism a truly powerful philosophy.

This is all nice and fine, you might say, but life isn't made just of virtue and a serene mind. We have to make a living, we want to fall in love, we wish to achieve things. What do the Stoics have to say about all that? According to Stoic philosophy, everything that is not under our control—which means everything other than our efforts, judgments, and decisions—falls into two broad categories, labeled with the delightfully oxymoronic phrases of preferred and dispreferred indifferents.

Consider, for instance, wealth and its opposite, poverty. Obviously, not even Epictetus could reasonably argue that it isn't better to be wealthy than to be poor. (Or, similarly, healthy rather than sick, or educated rather than ignorant.) In that sense, wealth is "preferred" and poverty is "dispreferred." But—and here is, I think, the philosophical stroke of genius of the ancient Stoics—wealth or poverty make no difference to our ability to be good people, to live a life of moral integrity, to practice the four virtues. In this sense, wealth and poverty are "indifferent." This is further demonstrated by the fact that one can be wealthy and yet use his wealth for evil (or perhaps have acquired it in unvirtuous ways). Conversely, one can be poor and yet be honest and good. Of course, there are also many good wealthy people and many bad poor ones. Which is precisely the Stoic point: wealth and poverty are irrelevant to being or not being a good person. And it is the latter, remember, that is the conduit to a eudaimonic life.

There is yet another way to grasp the issue of preferred and dispreferred indifferents and how they relate to a life of virtue. Modern behavioral economists have developed the concept of lexicographic preferences. They realized, contrary to the common assumption in classical economics, that not everything can be traded by way of a single currency. Rather, people put things into different categories, some of which are qualitatively more important than others. My A category, for instance, may include the welfare of my daughter, while my B category could include (if I had sufficient funds) a Lamborghini—orange, to be specific. Now, while I would trade a significant amount of money (also in the B category) for a Lamborghini, I would never trade my daughter for the car! She is simply in a different category, one from which no trade can be considered against objects belonging to a lower-ranked category.

In Stoicism, virtue is in the A category, because acting morally toward other people, being a good person, is the thing of utmost importance, from which everything else follows, and which is necessary to live a flourishing life. Wealth, health, education, and the like, by contrast, are in the B category. They can be traded with each other and we can pursue them accordingly, but never at the cost of selling our moral integrity. That would be like trading my daughter for a Lamborghini. It may result in some fun rides, but it is precisely the sort of thing I would deeply regret on my deathbed.

What about our emotive life, the fact that we get angry, fall in love, or experience fear or joy? Contra popular misconception, Stoics do not seek to walk around like emotional zombies, nor to live with a stiff upper lip permanently set on their faces, like Mr. Spock from *Star Trek* (who, as it turned out, later in life discovered that "logic is the beginning of wisdom, not the end").[16] If you don't believe me, just listen to Seneca:

> Cato used to refresh his mind with wine after he had
> wearied it with application to affairs of state, and Scipio

would move his triumphal and soldierly limbs to the sound of music. . . . It does good also to take walks out of doors, that our spirits may be raised and refreshed by the open air and fresh breeze: sometimes we gain strength by driving in a carriage, by travel, by change of air, or by social meals and a more generous allowance of wine: at times we ought to drink even to intoxication, not so as to drown, but merely to dip ourselves in wine: for wine washes away troubles and dislodges them from the depths of the mind, and acts as a remedy to sorrow as it does to some diseases.[17]

We do distinguish between emotions that are healthy and unhealthy, and we seek to reduce or eliminate the latter, while at the same time cultivate and nurture the former. Think of it as a constant exercise in shifting our emotional spectrum: away from fear, anger, and hatred, and toward joy, love, and friendship. Unhealthy emotions are paralyzing and destructive. Even if we become angry for the "right" reasons, say in response to an injustice we have witnessed, we still allow ourselves to be controlled by a pernicious emotion, one that will likely result in an unreasonable response, possibly making a bad situation worse. Stoics seek to deny assent, as we say, to negative emotions, by reminding ourselves that they are the result not of objective facts about the world, but rather of our own judgments—judgments that we have the power to change: "So make a practice at once of saying to every strong impression: 'An impression is all you are, not the source of the impression.' Then test and assess it with your criteria, but one primarily: ask, 'Is this something that is, or is not, in my control?'"[18]

Consider a common example: someone insults you, possibly with the intent to hurt you. There are several things you should contemplate on such occasions. First off, was the "insult" actually a valid criticism? In that case, you should accept it gratefully and attempt to do better. Was the criticism false? Then the joke's on the other guy, since he is uttering something that is demonstrably wrong.

Second, are you positive that the intent was to hurt you? Maybe the other person said what he said in good faith, or without thinking carefully, or based on the premise that he had a right to say it. Unless you are sure about his motives, giving him the benefit of the doubt is going to go a long way toward defusing the situation.

Finally, what if the fellow really wanted to hurt you? It follows from the dichotomy of control that the attempt is up to him, but the outcome is actually up to you. Only if you react in a way to show that you are, indeed, offended, will the barb have achieved its goal, the arrow hit its target. But as Epictetus tells his students: "Remember that it is we who torment, we who make difficulties for ourselves—that is, our opinions do. What, for instance, does it mean to be insulted? Stand by a rock and insult it, and what have you accomplished? If someone responds to insult like a rock, what has the abuser gained with his invective?"[19]

In the end, Stoicism is one of several positive philosophies of life, and it will or will not speak to you, depending on your cultural background, upbringing, natural predispositions, and the specific time of your life and what is happening during it. But Stoicism is potentially helpful for everyone, rich or poor, healthy or sick, educated or ignorant. The power of the philosophy relies on a set of profound insights into human nature and psychology, as well as a set of practical exercises to actually live the best life you can.

In a nutshell, then: the most important things in life are to maintain moral integrity and be helpful to others, which can be achieved by a constant, mindful practice of the four cardinal virtues. A crucial thing to understand and use on every occasion is the dichotomy of control: some things are up to us, and others are not, which translates into the idea that we should internalize our goals. Everything else, such as the pursuit of careers, wealth, and other externals, is fine, so long as it doesn't get in the way of virtue. And our emotional lives are going to be better off the more we move away from destructive and unhealthy emotions and nurture constructive and healthy ones. Now, that's what I think of as a life worth living!

Suggested Readings

Aurelius, Marcus. *Meditations*. Translated by Robin Hard. Oxford: Oxford University Press, 2011. In my opinion the best modern translation of this classic, the private diary of the philosopher-king Marcus Aurelius, in which we can see one of the five "good emperors" struggling with his personal shortcomings and striving to be a better person.

Becker, Lawrence C. *A New Stoicism*, revised edition. Princeton, NJ: Princeton University Press, 2017. The most comprehensive attempt to update ancient Stoicism to modern times. Recommended to readers with at least some background in philosophy and logic. Otherwise, read this multipart summary of its main arguments: https://howtobeastoic.wordpress.com/tag/a-new-stoicism/.

The Cambridge Companion to the Stoics. Edited by Brian Inwood. Cambridge: Cambridge University Press, 2003. A scholarly, comprehensive, yet accessible overview of ancient Stoicism, including chapters on its history, physics, metaphysics, theology, logic, ethics, and so forth. Best approached by readers with some background in philosophy, though this is not strictly required.

Epictetus. *Discourses, Fragments, Handbook*. Translated by Robin Hard. Oxford: Oxford University Press, 2014. One of the quintessential texts of ancient Stoicism. Begin with the *Discourses*, which are more in-depth and yet accessible, and use the *Handbook* as an advanced student would: a *vade mecum* full of useful practical reminders.

Irvine, William B. *A Guide to the Good Life: The Ancient Art of Stoic Joy*. Oxford: Oxford University Press, 2008. An eclectic guide to modern Stoicism, with more than a flavor of Epicureanism. Beware of the author's treatment of the dichotomy of control and his attempt to turn it into a trichotomy. Most modern Stoics think this was misguided.

Pigliucci, Massimo. *How to Be a Stoic: Using Ancient Philosophy to Live a Modern Life*. New York: Basic Books, 2017. My own introduction to Stoicism, by way of a series of imaginary conversations with Epictetus, while walking down the Roman Forum, through the Colosseum and the Domus Aurea (Nero's villa in Rome). Each chapter tackles a practical issue, from love and friendship to disability and death. The last chapter includes a guided set of Stoic exercises.

Robertson, Donald. *Stoicism and the Art of Happiness*. London: Teach Yourself, 2013. A very practical approach to modern Stoicism, written by a cognitive behavioral therapist. Engaging and immediately useful.

Seneca, Lucius Annaeus. *Anger, Mercy, Revenge*. Translated by Robert A. Kaster and Martha C. Nussbaum. Chicago: University of Chicago Press, 2010. Three essays, including *On Clemency* (dedicated to Nero, and containing an interesting balance of advice and veiled threats to the new emperor) and *The Pump-*

kinification of Claudius the God (a satirical essay written after the death and deification of the emperor Claudius). But by far the most important entry is *On Anger*, a must-read text not just for people interested in Stoicism but, well, for everyone.

———. *Hardship and Happiness*. Translated by Elaine Fantham, Harry M. Hine, James Kerr, and Gareth D. Williams. Chicago: University of Chicago Press, 2014. This collection contains some of Seneca's best and most insightful writings about Stoicism: the three letters of consolation, *On the Shortness of Life*, *On the Constancy of the Wise Person*, *On Tranquility of Mind*, *On Leisure*, *On the Happy Life*, and *On Providence*. A must-read for the curious student of Stoicism and for anyone appreciating beautiful prose.

———. *Letters on Ethics: To Lucilius*. Translated by Margaret Graver and A. Long. Chicago: University of Chicago Press, 2015. A beautiful collection of letters written by Seneca to his friend Lucilius at the end of his life. But, more importantly, a very articulate and compassionate introduction to Stoic philosophy, as well as Seneca's de facto philosophical testament.

———. *On Benefits*. Translated by Miriam Griffin and Brad Inwood. Chicago: University of Chicago Press, 2011. This completes the explicitly Stoic writings of Seneca, with an in-depth analysis of how to give and receive benefits, and how and why to express gratitude. He wrote that philosophy teaches, above all else, to owe and repay benefits well.

Notes

1 Modern Stoicism, last accessed July 13, 2019, https://modernstoicism.com/.

2 Diogenes Laertius, *Lives of the Eminent Philosophers*, trans. Pamela Mensch (Oxford: Oxford University Press, 2018), VII.3.

3 The largest online Stoic community I know of is the Stoicism Group on Facebook, facilitated by the author Donald Robertson (Stoicism Group [Stoic Philosophy], Facebook, https://facebook.com/groups/466338856752556). As of August 14, 2019, it has almost 52,000 members.

4 Marcus Aurelius, *Meditations*, trans. Robin Hard (Oxford: Oxford University Press, 2011), IV.13.

5 Aurelius, *Meditations*, IV.4.

6 Katherine Dahlsgaard, Christopher Peterson, and Martin E. P. Seligman, "Shared Virtue: The Convergence of Valued Human Strengths across Culture and History," *Review of General Psychology* 9, no. 3 (2005): 203–213, doi: 10.1037/1089-2680.9.3.203.

7 Seneca, "On Anger," III.36, in *Anger, Mercy, Revenge*, trans. Robert A. Kaster and Martha C. Nussbaum (Chicago: University of Chicago Press, 2010).

8 Aurelius, *Meditations*, V.1.

9 Aurelius, *Meditations*, V.20.

10 Epictetus, *Discourses*, II.12:3–4, in *Discourses, Fragments, Handbook*, trans. Robin Hard (Oxford: Oxford University Press, 2014).

11 Epictetus, *Enchiridion*, 43.

12 Epictetus, *Discourses*, IV.1:111–113, in *Discourses, Fragments, Handbook*.

13 Massimo Pigliucci and Gregory Lopez, *A Handbook for New Stoics: How to Thrive in a World Out of Your Control* (New York: The Experiment, 2019).

14 Epictetus, *Enchiridion*, 1:1.

15 Epictetus, *Enchiridion*, 1:3.

16 Spock, logic, and wisdom: John Kolencik, "Logic is the beginning of wisdom not the end," YouTube video, 0:46, posted May 2013, https://youtu.be/A4XPTmmvVow/.

17 Seneca, *On Tranquility of Mind*, XVII, trans. Elaine Fantham, in *Hardship and Happiness* (Chicago: University of Chicago Press, 2014).

18 Epictetus, *Enchiridion*, 1:5.

19 Epictetus, *Discourses*, I.25:28–29, in *Discourses, Fragments, Handbook*.

CHAPTER SIX

Epicureanism

Hiram Crespo

Reconciling the Soul with the Body

I began adopting the label Epicurean in 2012, after realizing that Epicurean philosophy was the most satisfying for me. I had been raised Catholic, rejected that faith, and studied various religions. Buddhism had intrigued me at one point, and even helped me to accept the impermanence of jobs and people I loved and lost. The International Society for Krishna Consciousness had taught me to cultivate the higher pleasures—vegetarian food, sweet music, wholesome association—but ultimately made bizarre supernatural claims and required full submission at the feet of a guru. I realized that my deeply ingrained Western values impeded me from delving deeper into these Eastern traditions. I had been reading books by the new atheists when I came across Epicurean teachings.

As you say of yourself, I too am an Epicurean. I consider the genuine (not the imputed) doctrines of Epicurus as containing every thing rational in moral philosophy which Greece & Rome have left us.

—Thomas Jefferson,
in a letter to William Short

Most people, when they read Jefferson's "life, liberty, and the pursuit of happiness" passage in the Declaration of Independence, do not stop to consider America's Epicurean roots. Jefferson's letter to his friend the diplomat William Short, and his mentorship at Monticello of Frances Wright—the author of *A Few Days in Athens* (1821), the great Epicurean masterpiece of the English language—reveal a deep familiarity with, and an intense, focused engagement in Epicurean ethics. Even his edition of the Bible, in which he removed all supernatural claims, can be seen as an active, Epicurean reinterpretation of the Gospels. Modern Greek Epicureans cite Jefferson's example when they engage in happiness activism by lobbying the European parliament for the adoption of the Declaration of Pallini, which calls for the formal recognition and enshrinement of "the right to happiness" for all citizens of the European Union.

A quick online search for the word *Epicurean*, in addition to "disciple of Epicurus," yields the following definition: "a person devoted to sensual enjoyment, especially that derived from fine food and drink."[1] A search for "epicure" yields: "one devoted to sensual pleasure; one with sensitive and discriminating tastes especially in food or wine."[2]

As for being devoted to food and drink, I'm to a small extent guilty as charged! I could be described as a foodie, but not to excess. I do not drink alcohol or consume drugs, generally eat moderate portions, and am usually in bed by ten. So how did "epicure" come to mean foodie and wine snob? And, for that matter, why were Epicureans called "pigs" by their enemies in ancient Greece? And why is "apikores" (derived from "Epicurus") a hated designation in Judaism for a heretic or pagan?

It's possible that no school of philosophy has suffered as much slander as Epicureanism. This may be attributed to any number of reasons: the religious animus against the body, nature, and sensuality; Platonic-Aristotelian hegemony in academia; common insecurities concerning pleasure;[3] and the cult of reason—which often sacrifices the irrational part of human nature at the altar of the rational . . . but leaves people only half-fulfilled.

Let me revisit my story from the beginning, to contextualize how in Epicurean philosophy I have been able to find not just clear ethical guidance that is in line with science and that does not produce cognitive dissonance, but crucially that also suggests a way to reconcile my soul with my flesh. The Catholic faith I was raised in had convinced me that suffering was good—a source of virtue, even—and that pleasure, particularly the types of pleasure that my body was capable of experiencing, was evil. This is persistently reinforced via disturbing imagery of a corpse hanging on a cross, of weeping virgins, of saints who carry agony on their faces. We were told we had to "carry our cross" while alive, and then upon death we would have bliss—after having endured the one nonrenewable life we were allowed. I wanted to live, on the other hand, a happy life and avoid misery. With the soul at war with one's body and instincts, it is impossible to live a healthy and happy life.

I was also taught to be credulous, to believe without questioning, and that no evidence was needed for my belief—whereas the entire system of Epicurean philosophy is based on the evidence that nature presents to our faculties.

Upon reaching puberty I discovered that I was gay. I spent years hating my own body and myself. Unlike less fortunate souls—who grow up terrified of hell—I did not believe I would go to hell, nor did I find that I was irreparably evil. I grew up, however, confused by the lies that were perpetrated against me as a child. Self-respect required that I leave behind the beliefs of my ancestors. Years later, after evaluating many other ways of seeing the world, I learned that in Epicurean philosophy it was possible for one's conscience to be fully reconciled with the flesh; that it was possible to apply philosophy to one's body and instincts and with integrity, using one's natural faculties rather than fighting against them—and that it was possible to be both authentic and happy.

The Canon, the Physics, and the Ethics

Epicurean doctrine consists of the canon, the physics, and the ethics—all of which are coherently interwoven. The canon explains how to think about nature—how it reveals itself and how we perceive it—or, in other words, epistemology. The physics explains the nature of things as being fundamentally made up of particles and void. The ethics explicates the art of living.

Canon, meaning "measuring stick," is the set of faculties that nature gave us to apprehend reality: the five senses, the pleasure and aversion faculty (feeling, or hedonic tone), and the anticipations (a faculty that helps to recognize abstract patterns). The three sets of faculties are known together as a tripod: it is said that the canon stands on these three legs. These faculties report evidence from nature with no judgment. Each set of faculties has unique jurisdiction over an aspect of nature: only the ears can report noises, only the nose can report smells, only the hedonic tone can report what is choice-worthy, etc. If a shape is distorted by being underwater, for instance, we will have a final verdict on its shape only once our eyes have confirmed the shape of the object outside of water, so that ultimately only the eyes have jurisdiction over sight, etc.

Notice that reason is absent from the canon. Reason is considered an auxiliary faculty to the canon. It does not itself have a direct connection with nature, but is used to interpret the data that our canonic faculties furnish, and it is in the interpretation process where mistakes can take place. I will later have more to say about this dethronement of Divine Reason (Athena) by Divine Feeling (Aphrodite). I wish to note, for now, that this is not merely a fanciful or self-serving choice by the first Epicureans: it is understood that, rather than people setting up arbitrary ideals, we believe that it is nature itself that provided us with these specific faculties and set the standards of truth.

> There is an infinite number of worlds, some like this world, others unlike it. For the atoms being infinite in number, as has just been proved, are borne ever further in their course. For the atoms out of which a world might arise, or by which a world might be formed, have not all been expended on one world or a finite number of worlds, whether like or unlike this one. Hence there will be nothing to hinder an infinity of worlds.
>
> —Epicurus, in a letter to Herodotus

As for the physics, our tradition establishes that bodies are made of particles. This was first proposed by the Atomists, whose conversations are gathered in Epicurus's *Epistle to Herodotus*. These ancient Atomists (who shared an awe for nature very similar to Carl Sagan's in our own time) developed a full cosmology based on the theory that all things are made of elementary particles and void.[4] They rejected all supernatural opinions, posited an early theory of relativity, developed a "doctrine of innumerable worlds," and 2,300 years ago were speculating about extraterrestrial life based on their initial observations about the nature of things. Recent research on exoplanets—thousands of which have been found in recent decades[5]—confirm the insights found in Epicurus's *Letter to Herodotus*, which established a doctrine of innumerable worlds based on the infinity of particles and space in all directions, coupled with limited possibilities of combinations of them. Modern Epicureans take great pleasure in the study of science.

The Ethics: Choices and Avoidances

In the ethics—the art of living—is where we find the ripest and sweetest fruits of Epicurean doctrine. The ancient Epicureans observed that, since we are all made of particles and we observe no sentience after death, fear-based religion is unnecessary and people should focus on living well. After we die, the particles in our bodies return to nature and are recycled into other bodies. There are important ethical repercussions once we accept that we get only one life.

> We are born only once and cannot be born twice, and must forever live no more. You don't control tomor-

row, yet you postpone joy. Life is ruined by putting
things off, and each of us dies without truly living.
—Epicurus, *Principal Doctrines*

The acceptance of feeling as a guide is one of the things that
sets Epicureans apart. We see the human as a complete being, not
merely a "rational" one. We accept the irrational, the instinctive,
the sensual self. We fully accept ourselves as natural beings. Epicurus saw that Platonism and idealism had replaced nature with
ideas, had alienated people from their immediate experience, and
had the effect of denaturalizing and decontextualizing morality
and philosophy. He taught us that we should philosophize with
our feet on the ground, with our eyes open, using our faculties.
Our direct, immediate experience tells us that pleasure is choice-
worthy for its own sake and that pain is avoidance-worthy for
its own sake. Epicurus refused to subject these insights to syllo-
gisms, logic, or word-juggling. We see newborn babies, and how
they shun pain and seek pleasure, and from this observation we
conclude that it is in our nature to seek pleasure and avoid pain.
We believe that any compassionate, useful system of ethics has
to accept the insights of the pleasure-aversion faculty, which to
us is the most important component of the moral compass that
nature gave us.

Wherefore we call pleasure the alpha and omega of a
blessed life. Pleasure is our first and kindred good. It
is the starting-point of every choice and of every aversion, and to it we come back, inasmuch as we make
feeling the rule by which to judge of every good thing.
—Epicurus, *Epistle to Menoeceus*

The pleasure-aversion faculty is also unmediated, pragmatic and universally useful for everyone, regardless of their background or education. Women can use their faculties as well as men, children as well as the elderly. No priests, prophets, logicians, or mediators are needed to carry out our choices and avoidances, and so the Epicurean canon empowers us and emancipates us from traditional authorities.

> And since pleasure is our first and native good, for that reason we do not choose every pleasure whatsoever, but will often pass over many pleasures when a greater annoyance ensues from them. And often we consider pains superior to pleasures when submission to the pains for a long time brings us as a consequence a greater pleasure. While therefore all pleasure because it is naturally akin to us is good, not all pleasure should be chosen, just as all pain is an evil and yet not all pain is to be shunned. It is, however, by measuring one against another, and by looking at the conveniences and inconveniences, that all these matters must be judged. Sometimes we treat the good as an evil, and the evil, on the contrary, as a good.
> —Epicurus, *Epistle to Menoeceus*

Epicureans, from the beginning, rejected idealisms and absolutes that divorced people from context and from nature, and chose to engage reality instead. Our morality is contextual. Rather than hand down absolute dos and don'ts, the first Epicureans elaborated methods by which we can most effectively use our faculties.

All choices and avoidances are relative to concrete circumstances. The answer to moral questions is always: carry out hedonic calculus. Measure the advantages versus the disadvantages. Since a pleasant life is the goal, we must avoid or defer instant gratification if it carries disadvantages greater than the pleasure it brings. We therefore sometimes choose disadvantages in the hopes of a greater, longer-term pleasure.

So here is where I choose Epicurean moderation: here is where I reject the stereotype that led to the slander that led to the redefining of the epicure as a slave of the senses. Maybe one beer boosts our mood, but we should know our limits, and—as for myself—by the time I'm having the third beer, I begin to lose lucidity. The following morning, I'm dehydrated and can't be as productive. So the annoyance is bigger than the pleasure. Notice that a true epicure would never say "beer equals pleasure." Using his faculty of pleasure-aversion, he would experience the first beer as pleasant and the third one as unpleasant. The same sense-object can be pleasant or unpleasant at different times, but our faculties guide us at all times.

Another example of hedonic calculus in my life deals with academic achievement. I worked very hard to complete my university education while being underemployed and very poor. But the great sense of satisfaction after this ordeal, as well as the expectation that it may bring me a higher income in the future, allowed it to pass my hedonic calculus.

Sacred Friendship

Another area where I have frequently found myself calculating advantage versus disadvantage is friendship. Epicurean sources say that friendship is one of the most important components of the pleasant life. Friends bring enjoyment, security, and stability. Sometimes the pain of not having a friend or loved one is so great that we are willing to make huge sacrifices for them. We make excuses to see our friends often. But then—as per *Principal Doctrine* 39[6]—our wisdom tradition teaches that we can't be friends to everyone. There can be false friends who like only to praise us rather than provide honest assessments that we expect when we trust someone. With some people the disadvantages are too many, and it's best to avoid them. There must be concentric circles around us and boundaries. French hedonist philosopher Michel Onfray coined the word *eumetry* (the "good measure"): the right measure of safe distance that must be kept with "relational delinquents" in order to secure a life of pleasure.

In America, there's a crisis of isolation and depression. A study from Nicholas Christakis of Harvard Medical School and James Fowler of the University of California, San Diego, shows that happiness is contagious (and so is depression).[7] Another study by Christakis, along with researchers from the University of Chicago and the University of California, San Diego, shows that isolation is a health risk factor on par with obesity and smoking.[8] These studies place friendship in the category of natural and necessary desires.

We did not evolve to live in large cities surrounded by strangers to whom we never talk, whom we pass by while paying attention only to our phones. Many people today have become used to loneliness and see it as normal, or, in a show of false pride, have even set the arbitrary goal of being a "lone wolf" as an ideal in order to normalize their isolation. "Tribalism," we are told, is one of the great "problems" of our society. It keeps us divided, we are told. We evolved to live in social units, and communities, tribes, clans, and families help us feel properly human and healthy.

I gently awaken their sleeping faculties.
—a fictional Epicurus in
A Few Days in Athens by Frances Wright

In Vatican Saying 21, Epicurus says: "We must not force Nature, but gently persuade her." This is a key passage to understand if we want to pragmatically apply Epicurean teachings to our lives. Human beings are a tribal species, and it is pointless and unhealthy to repress our tribal instinct. Instead, we should learn to channel the tribal instinct in the healthiest manner possible. Epicurus's advice is that we should surround ourselves with intimate friends frequently. I believe this is the healthiest outlet for our tribal instinct and to neglect it is extremely dangerous. Today, in the absence of fathers or proper mentors, gang culture hijacks tribal instinct by using bonding rites through initiation, song, symbols, and violence to provide a community young boys and men might otherwise lack.

Norman DeWitt, in his book *Epicurus and His Philosophy*, writes that the ethics of Epicureanism are based on friendship. An Epicurean must build a tribe, a circle of friends, as an outlet for his tribal instinct. Ancient Epicureans were known as "the twentiers" because they had "feasts of reason" on the twentieth of every month to study philosophy among friends. Any excuse, however, was used to get together. Birthdays were particularly festive. Other healthy outlets for the tribal instinct today are sports teams, groups related to hobbies, volunteer associations, professional organizations, youth groups, and other extracurricular social clubs.

Conversely, we do not need innumerable friends: according to the anthropologist Robin Dunbar, the human brain can only process approximately 150 interpersonal relations. This is known as Dunbar's number, and it's about the size of a small tribe.

The Hierarchy of Desires

Epicureanism has more to say in helping us in our hedonic calculus. Unlike Buddhism, Hinduism, and other ascetic traditions that categorize all desire as dissatisfaction and therefore inherently a cause of suffering, in our tradition there is a hierarchy of desires. With some, nature does not give you a choice: you must attend to them. With others, you can live without them but use them to add variety to your hedonic regimen.

> Of desires some are natural, others are groundless; and that of the natural some are necessary as well as natural, and some natural only. And of the necessary desires some are necessary if we are to be happy, some if the body is to be rid of uneasiness, some if we are even to live.
>
> —Epicurus, *Epistle to Menoeceus*

All desires that do not lead to pain when they remain unsatisfied are unnecessary, but the desire is easily got rid of, when the thing desired is difficult to obtain or the desires seem likely to produce harm. Those natural desires which entail no pain when unsatisfied, though pursued with an intense effort, are also due to groundless opinion; and it is not because of their own nature they are not got rid of but because of man's groundless opinions.

—Epicurus, *Principal Doctrines* 26 and 30

Natural and necessary desires were known as the "chief goods" by Philodemus of Gadara—who taught Epicurean philosophy in the first century. These include safety, a home, warm relations, food, water, health, and happiness. This does not mean that we limit our pleasures to these goods. On the contrary, *Principal Doctrine* 20 says that it is not in our nature to shun pleasure. The natural, unnecessary pleasures serve to add variety and spice to life. We do not shun them, but we also know that we do not need them, that as long as we have the natural and necessary goods, we can "compete with Zeus" in happiness and self-sufficiency. If we understand these things clearly, and if we are grateful to nature for having made the needful things easy to procure, our choices and avoidances will lead to a life of true pleasure and satisfaction.

The Laughing Philosophers

Another aspect of the Epicurean art of living has to do with our willingness not to take ourselves too seriously. There seems to have always existed a culture of comedy among the Epicureans, as seen in the works of Lucian, Horace, and even at times Lucretius. The ancient, obese Epicurean poet Horace once called himself a "pig of Epicurus's sty," cheerfully owning the insult that was frequently hurled against our school. While mocking conventional superstitions, Lucretius in *De rerum natura* (*On the Nature of Things*) joked about how Jove would have needed to descend from heaven and get closer to the ground to more accurately strike mortals with lightning.

Lucian of Samosata, in his brilliant comedy *A True Story*, treated Epicureanism as a parody religion and imagined a paradise—the Isle of the Blessed—where the souls of all the Cyrenaics[9] and Epicureans would go to experience eternal bliss. He comically explained how the Stoics, Aristotelians, and other schools failed to get to the island—a lesson in each of these adventures.

Lucian also wrote *Alexander the Oracle Monger*, an exposé of a religious fraud who, as a result of this mockery, attempted to have Lucian killed. The Roman Senate would not prosecute Alexander, out of fear of violence from the false prophet's followers. Reading Lucian from the perspective of the twenty-first century, it's impossible not to be reminded of the *Charlie Hebdo* attack and the threats against satirists, writers such as Salman Rushdie, and other public figures who have criticized or mocked religion in recent times.

Epicureans belong to the lineage of the laughing philosophers, which begins with the first atomist, Democritus, who was known for frequently making fun of human nature. This makes sense: when one studies the nature of things and then looks at the beliefs of the majority, it's hard to escape the absurdity. Humans are capable of great intelligence, but also very good at allowing themselves to be easily duped by superstition. Epicurus was known for his attribution of funny epithets to his philosophical rivals. The historian Diogenes Laertius reports that he called Plato "the Golden One," and Nausiphanes "the Jellyfish." He also had epithets for some of his intimate associates. He was adored by his companions—who named the school after him rather than Metrodorus, Hermarchus, or Polyaenus, all of whom were equally influential—so this must have been done in a spirit of cheerfulness and trust.

Laughter is a healthy way to deal with tribulations and difficult, shameful, or uncomfortable situations. It's also a way to soften parrhesia—frank criticism, which is one of the societal roles of the philosopher. Philodemus of Gadara said that there are two forms of parrhesia: public criticism, which helps society's moral development, and private criticism for individuals. (Another way to soften criticism is through a virtue that ancient Epicureans were also known for: suavity, or the art of sweet speech.) Comedy as parrhesia serves a didactic purpose, but it also helps to encourage authenticity, to shun superstition and other undesirable traits, to deflate empty pretensions, and to clear the air. It's an important source of pleasure and a social lubricant—and this does not take away from its great utility.

Epicurean Economics

At one and the same time we must philosophize, laugh, and manage our household and economics, while never ceasing to proclaim the words of true philosophy.

—Epicurus, *Vatican Saying* 41

The doctrine concerning how the natural and necessary pleasures (for life, health, and happiness) have unique priority certainly has economic and political ramifications. Autarchy (self-sufficiency, self-government) is both an economic and a philosophical principle. The philosopher is expected to be self-sufficient in terms of not caring too much about public opinion, and in terms of being able to secure natural and necessary goods with ease. He should not toil, or engage in hard labor. Instead, Philodemus of

Gadara—in his scroll *On the Art of Property Management*—proposes that the philosopher should have fruitful possessions (that is, he should own means of production), have multiple streams of income (teaching philosophy, rental property income, and business ownership that employs others have special priority over other sources of income), and that his revenue must more than meet his immediate needs: it must facilitate a dignified life of leisure. We should ask ourselves today what might be the best ways to encourage ownership of assets and means of production in our communities in order to diminish wage slavery as much as possible and ultimately allow citizens to live pleasantly. Philodemus also argued that association is important in labor, and that we must choose our employees, employers, and business associates prudently. Ideally, they should be one's—or our—friends as well.

Epicurean contractarianism—the theory that there is no absolute justice, but that instead justice is based on contracts of mutual benefit—also informs how we think about business and autarchy. Self-reliance does not mean that we cease to be embedded in networks of mutual advantage. On the contrary, the same symbiosis we see in nature is replicated in the economy. By finding what is of mutual advantage between us and all our relations, we can more easily secure safety and prosperity for all. This is true in business-to-business relations, and in the case of conventional employment: the employee capitalizes her time via salary, pension, and health-care coverage, while the employer gets value from the labor and skills provided.

Philodemus of Gadara believed that there is a natural measure of wealth needed to secure the natural and necessary goods. A 2010 study by researchers at Princeton University demonstrates that, in American society, happiness correlates to income only up to $75,000—beyond that, happiness is more affected by health, relations, and other factors.[10] Understanding the limits set by nature for our desires is extremely important if we are to avoid the unnecessary anxiety that comes with consumerism and limitless desires. It's also crucial to see that we draw more happiness from experiences and relations than from possessions. As with the natural measure of community, per Dunbar's number, Philodemus's concept applies to food, shelter, and money.

Epicurean doctrine could be interpreted as saying that it is appropriate to tax only wealth and income beyond what is needed for an individual or family to secure housing, safety, food, health, and happiness. A growing number of intellectuals and influencers, and some cities, have been proposing and experimenting with Universal Basic Income (UBI), where all citizens are guaranteed an untaxed amount of funds to cover their basic needs. Critics say UBI is expensive. Defenders claim it's inevitable. It's possible that societies may have to experiment with a diversity of models of basic income before they settle on the UBI models that are most pragmatic.

The trends related to automation of labor are increasingly being seen as an opportunity to reinvent the workweek. Intuitively, it makes sense that the more people become the owners of the machines that replace them, the more they can profit from robot labor, but we are far from a comprehensive solution to automation. Eventually, as populations grow and jobs disappear, governments will have to advance a new labor paradigm involving shorter workweeks and/or early individual *semi*retirement accounts that would have greater liquidity than conventional retirement accounts. Here in the United States, when one draws from an IRA, there is a 10 percent fee. Could this be waived to allow for cyclical or partial retirement models? The question for an Epicurean is: How do I live most pleasantly while also being productive?

Epicureans Today

Many small but vocal groups and individuals are awakening to Epicurus's call to philosophize with our feet on the ground and to create lives filled with the pleasures that nature makes easily available to us.

In France, one of the most prominent public intellectuals is Michel Onfray, who has argued that Platonic and Abrahamic conventions have for too long enjoyed hegemony in the academic world, and proposes that a counterhistory of philosophy "from the perspective of the friends of Epicurus and the enemies of Plato" is needed to rectify the wrongs that Epicurean philosophy has suffered throughout history. He calls Platonism "the great neurosis at the heart of Western civilization." He has written more than a hundred books and founded the Université de Caen in order to rectify the problems he criticizes.

In the Americas, several of us are employing the pen (or the keyboard, in any case) to "strike a blow for Epicurus"—to quote from Lucian of Samosata. For example, the former president of Uruguay José Mujica has in recent years cited Epicurean teachings as a salvation from our modern Western existential crisis now that, he says, "Christianity has failed us" and people are dissatisfied with insatiable consumerism.

Back in Epicurus's homeland, several communities in various Greek cities have requested that the European Parliament recognize European citizens' right to happiness, and they celebrate annual symposia in February in memory of Epicurus's birthday.

Epicurus's message resonates today as ever: the prevalence of consumerism and the traditional religions' gradual erosion in credibility have many people questioning their inherited values; globalization and the automation of labor produces economic insecurity; the fiscal crisis in Greece (where most Epicureans live) has people asking questions about the natural limits of our desires; rates of suicide in the United States have risen in recent years as people are increasingly isolated and confused about their values; and global policies set by governments concerning many issues—most urgently, on the environment—suffer from lack of empirical evidence. If we base our solutions to all these problems on the study of nature, as Epicurean philosophy advises, we'll be able to efficiently and confidently tackle these and many other symptoms of societal dysfunction.

> Enjoy, and be happy! Do you doubt the way? Let Epicurus be your guide. The source of every enjoyment is within yourselves. Good and evil lie before you. The good is all which can yield you pleasure; the evil, what must bring you pain. Here is no paradox, no dark saying, no moral hid in fables.
>
> —Frances Wright, *A Few Days in Athens*

Suggested Readings

DeWitt, Norman Wentworth. *Epicurus and His Philosophy*. Minneapolis: University of Minnesota Press, 1954. DeWitt is somewhat neglected by academia, but is widely regarded as essential for anyone who wants to understand Epicurean philosophy on its own terms. The author has a good grasp on the canon, and here—as well as in his other writings—he exhibits a clear appreciation for the way ancient Epicurean communities organized themselves.

Onfray, Michel. *A Hedonist Manifesto: The Power to Exist*. Translated by Joseph McClellan. New York: Columbia University Press, 2015. The most complete English-language introduction to Onfray's thought. Rather than provide new insights, Onfray focuses on teaching historiography and on weaving together multiple threads into a coherent and forward-looking tapestry.

Philodemus. *On Death*. Translated by W. Benjamin Henry. Atlanta: Society of Biblical Literature, 2009. Perhaps the wisest and most worthy of study of all the scrolls from the villa at Herculaneum. It catalogues all the ethical repercussions of the Epicurean doctrine concerning death.

———. *On Property Management*. Translated by Voula Tsouna. Atlanta: Society of Biblical Literature, 2012. Most of the writings of Epicurus of Samos and Lucian of Samosata can easily be found online; however, the scrolls that survived the eruption of Mount Vesuvius in the year 79 CE are not widely available. This book contains a commentary on estate management by Philodemus.

Stenger, Victor J. *God and the Atom*. New York: Prometheus Books, 2013. A defense of classical atomism that focuses on how modern science and cosmology are still fundamentally aligned with Epicurean and Lucretian ideas.

Notes

1 "Epicurean," *Oxford Living Dictionaries*, s.v., accessed March 12, 2019, https://en.oxforddictionaries.com/definition/epicurean/.

2 "Epicure," *Merriam-Webster Dictionary*, accessed June 6, 2019, https://www.merriam-webster.com/dictionary/epicure.

3 Michel Onfray in *A Hedonist Manifesto* writes: "Pleasure
   scares people. They are scared of the word and the actions,
   reality, and discourses around it. It either scares people or
   makes them hysterical. There are too many private and
   personal issues, too many alienating, intimate, painful,
   wretched, and miserable details. There are secret and hidden
   deficiencies. There are too many things in the way of just
   being, living, and enjoying. Hence, people reject the word.
   They produce spiteful critique that is aggressive and in
   bad faith or that is simply evasive. Disrespect, discredit,
   contempt, and disdain are all means for avoiding the subject
   of pleasure" (Michael Onfray, *A Hedonist Manifesto: The Power
   to Exist* [New York: Columbia University Press, 2015], 26).

4 The first Epicureans argued that all bodies exist as
   elemental particles and void (this is what is meant by
   "conventional bodies": atoms and void), but that does not
   mean that things like time, or the attraction of a magnet,
   or pleasure and aversion, or other chemical reactions *between*
   bodies do not exist. They do not exist as conventional
   bodies, but they exist as interactions and reactions between
   bodies. In Epicurus's *Letter to Herodotus*, these are known as
   "emergent" or "relational" properties.

5 As of June 2019, exoplanets.org listed a total of 5,747
   confirmed (3,262) and candidate (2,485) exoplanets;
   however, this number is constantly increasing.

6 Epicurus's *Principal Doctrines* and *Vatican Sayings* are
   summarized conclusions on the most fundamental aspects
   of Epicurean philosophy. They are cited and elaborated on
   frequently by students.

7 James H. Fowler and Nicholas A. Christakis, "Dynamic
   Spread of Happiness in a Large Social Network," *British
   Medical Journal* 337 (2008): 1–9. doi: 10.1136/bmj.a2338.

8 John T. Cacioppo, James H. Fowler, and Nicholas A. Christakis, "Alone in the Crowd: The Structure and Spread of Loneliness in a Large Social Network," *Journal of Personality and Social Psychology* 97, no. 6 (December 2009): 977–91. doi: 10.1037/a0016076.

9 The Cyrenaics were the first philosophical school to propose an ethics based on pleasure. They were founded by Aristippus of Cyrene and were so named because they were most active among the Greeks of the North African city of Cyrene. Neo-Epicurean historian of philosophy Michel Onfray considers them so important—yet neglected—that in his book *L'invention du plaisir: Fragments cyrênaïques (The Invention of Pleasure: Cyrenaic Fragments*, 2002), he calls them "a philosophical Atlantis."

10 Belinda Luscombe, "Do We Need $75,000 a Year to Be Happy?," *Time*, September 6, 2010, http://content.time.com/time/magazine/article/0,9171,2019628,00.html.

Religious Traditions

Hinduism, Judaism, Christianity,
Progressive Islam, and Ethical Culture

Philosophy and religion have not exactly been on good terms throughout history. Rejecting or questioning religion, as philosophers such as Socrates did, was sometimes considered heresy—and was one of the reasons Socrates was sentenced to death. Nevertheless, as we noted in the introduction, the boundary between the two realms is indistinct. Alister McGrath remarks that early Christian writers thought of Christianity as a philosophy rather than a religion, and in early Christian artwork, Christ sometimes wears a philosopher's cloak. Jews and Muslims have been engaging in philosophy for hundreds of years, while the relatively recent Ethical Culture is based on a philosophy derived explicitly from ethics—a branch of general philosophy.

The Christian philosopher Søren Kierkegaard once jibed (pseudonymously), "for why do we have our philosophers, if not to make supernatural things trivial and commonplace?"[1] Religious traditions do make more space for the supernatural, the mystical, and the spiritual, which is why faith is a core element of religion and rarely so in philosophy. It is also why religions can be at peace without definite answers and give answers to some questions that are unanswerable for philosophers (because they often defy logic or rationality). Religions have rituals to be followed, prophets to be listened to, and often deities to be worshiped. While Ethical Culture is nontheistic, it does have rituals and a spiritual element. Hindus have many gods, and Judaism, Christianity, and Islam have one God (though some would argue that Christianity's Trinity of the Father, the Son, and the Holy Spirit makes it cryptically polytheistic). Religions often propose an afterlife or, as in Eastern religions like Hinduism, reincarnation, which rewards or punishes behavior in this life. Despite these differences, one key common thread shared by philosophies and religions is that they all grapple with the meaning of life and the question of how to live within ethical frameworks.

Because religions are so incredibly diverse and there are countless denominations and variations, it is difficult to generalize about them. Given their histories, geographic spread, and sheer number of followers it is no wonder that around 84 percent of the world's population is affiliated with a religion.[2] Thus it is important to point out that the authors of the chapters in this section are also diverse in their approaches to practicing their religions. At times, ritual clashes with modern living—a dilemma that Deepak Sarma faced and discusses in the first chapter of this section, chapter 7, on Hinduism. At other times, religious practices evolve in new directions and dimensions, as Adis Duderija shows in his chapter on Progressive Islam, chapter 10. Rabbi Barbara Block notes that, in Judaism, multiple voices and truths are not only allowed, but encouraged, since there might be multiple paths to the same goal; hence the quip, "Two Jews, three opinions." And Alister McGrath says, "generalizing about Christianity is notoriously difficult, and tends to be undertaken primarily by those with scores to settle and axes to grind."

We are not grinding axes here; rather, we are presenting five individual perspectives of religious philosophers who are navigating the complicated nexus of the philosophical and the religious. We have intentionally included a mix of interpretations and approaches to religion—some classic (such as Rabbi Block's Judaism) and some more unusual (such as Adis Duderija's Progressive Islam)—with the aim of opening up the reader's views about religion by featuring a selection of the diverse ways that people engage with them. It is an invitation to discover new aspects of the more spiritual philosophies of life, in a way that can be learned only through insights into the authors' subjective experiences.

Hinduism is an Indian religion with around 1.1 billion followers,[3] making it the third-largest religion in the world. By some accounts, Hinduism is the oldest religion in the world, partly because it is based on several other ancient religions that consolidated right around the time Aristotle, Zeno of Citium, and Epicurus were expounding their philosophies (ca. 500–300 BCE). Hinduism is unique because, unlike the philosophies we have encountered so far, it cannot be traced back to a particular person. As Deepak Sarma points out, Hinduism is a *beginningless* philosophy, which is intimately tied to the notion that we have an enduring self that is caught in a beginningless and endless cycle of birth and rebirth. Our current predicaments are a result of the meritorious or demeritorious *karma* that we've accumulated in an infinite number of past lives. And generally the idea is that we should be good in this life, so as to build up "good" *karma* for our future lives. Some Hindus use this notion to explain and justify the class system, which, as Sarma notes, creates deep tensions with the ideals of equality and social justice.

Like Hinduism, it is hard to know how old Judaism is. However, some pinpoint its beginning to Abraham, who was probably born around 2000 BCE in the city of Ur (now in Iraq) and emigrated to Canaan (now Israel). He was a shepherd credited as the first person to make an enduring covenant (a pact with God). In Genesis, God gives Canaan to Abraham and his descendants. In return, God requires Abraham and his male descendants to be circumcised.

Though there are around fourteen million Jews in the world, making Judaism smaller than the other religions in this section, it is the oldest of the monotheistic religions and the source of what we call Abrahamic traditions, in memory of their patriarch—

including Christianity, Islam, Bahá'í Faith, Rastafarianism, and many others.[4] Rabbi Block, the daughter of Holocaust refugees, discusses how it is possible for her to believe (when her father could not) in a God who would allow six million Jews to be murdered. Her approach to Judaism finds that God is not omnipotent, but rather needs our help to repair the world. Partnering with God in a covenant, with a focus on community over individual achievement, is among the central themes and challenges of Judaism.

Christianity began as a sect of Judaism, developing from the teachings of Jesus during the first century, which were later collated into the New Testament. Christianity has grown to be the most popular religion in the world, with around 2.3 billion devotees (or 31 percent of the global population).[5] Alister McGrath settled on Christianity after exploring a number of other traditions, including atheism. Channeling C. S. Lewis, he argues that part of Christianity's appeal is that it transcends the "surly bonds" of empirical facts to look at our lives as part of a greater scheme and provides a kind of mental map for living in a coherent and orderly world (even if we have not yet come to know the full "big picture"). It aligns the story of followers' lives to that of Christ. By helping followers to search for authenticity and fulfillment, Christianity gives them a sense of self-worth (because God loves them) in a universe in which it is all too easy to be overwhelmed by our insignificance, and also provides a narrative (betrayal, torture, crucifixion, and resurrection) for coping with trauma. As McGrath explains, "the central Christian narrative of the crucifixion and resurrection of Christ provides what is, in effect, an exemplary narrative of posttraumatic growth, with the potential to illuminate and transform the human situation."

Islam, the second most popular religion in the world with around 1.8 billion followers, emerged during the seventh century in Saudi Arabia.[6] Whereas Judaism's most important figure is Moses (he is credited as the author of the Torah) and Christianity's is Jesus Christ, Muslims (believers of Islam) consider Muhammad ibn 'Abdullāh (ca. 570–June 8, 632 CE) to be the last and most important prophet. The Qur'an is the sacred Islamic text, based on the messages that Muhammad received from Allah via the angel Gabriel, and was codified about thirty years after Muhammad died.

Adis Duderija writes about his engagement with a progressive form of Islam, which he discovered in the wake of the 9/11 terrorist attacks. Perhaps contrary to some popular beliefs about Islam, Duderija's progressive form of the religion can be, at a conceptual level, reconciled with the Universal Declaration of Human Rights (UDHR). It also promotes moral equality for all people regardless of beliefs or backgrounds, religious pluralism, laws guided by reason-based ethics that should evolve with humanity, environmental sustainability, and gender justice—including women's reproductive rights and leadership. Like Stoicism, Progressive Islam places a heavy emphasis on cosmopolitanism and, like philosophies such as Aristotelianism, it deeply values human flourishing.

There is some debate within Ethical Humanism (also called "Religious Humanism" and, as Anne Klaeysen refers to it, "Ethical Culture") as to whether it is a religion, since there is nothing transcendental or supernatural about it. Like Buddhism, Daoism, Jainism, Quakerism, and Satanism, it is generally considered a nontheistic religion. According to Klaeysen, Ethical Culture has around ten thousand members and classifies itself as a religion, but leaves it up to individual members to decide for themselves whether they experience it as such. It was founded by Felix Adler in New York City in the late 1800s. Adler was a renegade rabbi-in-training—seduced by the ideas of Immanuel Kant and Ralph

Waldo Emerson—whose ideas became too heterodox for Judaism. After being expelled from temple, he took up a professorship of Hebrew and Oriental literature at Cornell University, where he was accused of atheism and asked to leave. Perhaps frustrated by so much unwelcomeness, he developed his own "religion," which appeals to Klaeysen as a welcoming group that focuses on "deed not creed" (ethical behavior rather than race, ethnicity, sexual orientation, economic status, level of ability, or religious beliefs); social justice and activism; eliciting goodness in oneself and one another; ethical relationships with other people and the Earth; and spiritual recognition instead of religious salvation.

Notes

1 Søren Kierkegaard, *Philosophical Fragments, or, A Fragment of Philosophy by Johannes Climacus*, trans. David F. Swenson and Howard V. Hong (Princeton, NJ: Princeton University Press, 1962), 66.

2 Pew-Templeton Global Religious Futures, "The Changing Global Religious Landscape," Pew Research Center, (April 5, 2017), http://www.pewforum.org/2017/04/05/the-changing-global-religious-landscape/.

3 "The Changing Global Religious Landscape," Pew Research Center.

4 "The Changing Global Religious Landscape," Pew Research Center.

5 "The Changing Global Religious Landscape," Pew Research Center.

6 "The Changing Global Religious Landscape," Pew Research Center.

CHAPTER SEVEN

Hinduism

Deepak Sarma

There are so many types and varieties of Hinduism that it is difficult to offer a unified description, other than to reference a few specific concepts and practices. My account reflects the Hindu way of life that I experience that adheres to one particular *sampradāya* (tradition), namely the Mādhva tradition of Vedānta, founded by the theologian Madhvācārya in the thirteenth century in the Indian state of Karnataka.

Let me start by offering some generalizations about Hinduism and a Hindu philosophy of life, in spite of its diversity. First, what is meant by *karma* and its connection with causality?

Broadly speaking, all of the philosophical and religious schools extant in India, other than the Charvaka (materialist skeptic) and Abrahamic ones, shared a belief in the mechanism of *karma*, that one's actions in earlier lives affected both one's rebirth as well as the events that are to occur in one's future lives. The entity that was reborn is the *ātman* and is born again and again.

One accumulates some combination of *puṇya* (meritorious *karma*) or *pāpa* (demeritorious *karma*), popularly rendered in the West as "good" and "bad" *karma*. The accumulated *karma* manifests itself until it is depleted or until more is accrued. *Karma* is thus linked with a belief that one is reborn after one dies and that the type of body that one inhabits (and has inhabited in the past) is indexed to *puṇya* and *pāpa*. This cycle of birth and rebirth, in which everyone is bound, is called *saṃsāra* (worldly existence).

Karma is also intimately linked to *varṇa* (caste). One's *karma* determines which *varṇa* one is born into. There are, in this connection, four classes: *Brāhmins* (priestly class), *Kṣatriyas* (warrior or governing class), *Vaiśya* (merchant class), and *Śūdras* (laboring class). References to the creation of this system are found in the *Puruṣa Sukta* (Hymn to Primal Man)—a passage in the *Ṛg Veda* (Hymn 10:90), regarded by many Hindus as the earliest text in the Hindu canon. A Hindu way of life forces everyone to come to terms with this system, even if one lives outside of, or has never set foot in, India. One may believe that *varṇa* membership is an achievable, rather than hereditary, status, as do many converts and Hindu "reformers," arguing that the *Ṛg Veda*'s original egalitarian ethos was somehow distorted by unnamed actors. Another variant argues that class was not intended to be hierarchically arranged, but rather to be a classificatory system based on meritocracy. These "just so" stories are, of course, unverifiable.

One cannot simply abandon the doctrine of *varṇa* without calling into question the tenets of the *Ṛg Veda* and other core texts of Hinduism, such as the *Upaniṣads*, which reference caste.

The class system is undeniably problematic for many and offends anyone who embraces ideals of equality and social justice. Nevertheless, as a part of the Hindu worldview, Hindus have to either embrace, ignore, or reinterpret it. If one follows and propounds Hindu philosophy, one will eventually need to confront this social system, which is tied intimately with the very causal mechanisms of the universe.

I have sometimes embraced and sometimes rejected my *Brāhmin* heritage since first discovering it. Initially, and for some time after, I was surprisingly naïve about the discrimination inherent to the *varṇa* system. I recall embracing the identity it gave me as a status and uniqueness that buttressed my marginalized-minority American life.

Though the schools and traditions of Hinduism differ widely on the origins and precise function of these mechanisms of *karma* and *saṃsāra*, they all agree that they exist. They also all share an interest in ending this seemingly endless cycle and this desire is their raison d'être. The state that sentient beings enter after being liberated is called *mokṣa* among the Hindu traditions. In Buddhism this state is called *nirvana*. The status and characteristics of *mokṣa* differ vastly between schools of thought and traditions of Hinduism. Some, but not all, Hindu traditions offer systematic methods by which adherents can break the cycle and attain the desired end. Life as a Hindu means having *mokṣa* as the telos or endpoint, whether one thinks about it constantly or begins to think about it only when confronting what appears to be one's inevitable, if only temporary, death.

This belief in the causal mechanism of the universe that affects all sentient beings on the macrocosmic as well as the microcosmic scale is central to all Hindus. While not all Hindus may articulate it precisely, many continuously consider the causes and consequences of their actions, on the immediate present, on the future, and in an imagined or inferred past. Such reflections may pertain to everyday, mundane events. Not surprisingly, an extremely positive or extremely negative experience is chalked up to either *puṇya* or *pāpa karma*.

A few examples may be useful. Recently, when I was driving locally, I came within inches of having an accident. A careless driver failed to stop at a stop sign and in so doing entered my lane of traffic. I slammed on my brakes and steered away from his car, stopping only a few inches short of colliding with him. On the one hand, I felt anxiety about the *karma* I must have had to experience such a scary and unpleasant moment. On the other hand, I was grateful for my *puṇya* for not getting hit! Another example, which I like to use with college students in my classes, concerns their feeling of pleasure or pain in my class. If they are feeling the former and glad they have enrolled, then I suggest to them that it was because of their *puṇya karma* that they found themselves in my class. For the latter group, I ask them to consider that their current torture is a result of something they must have done in the past. It is easy to think about one's relationship in the world and with others in terms of *karma*.

When pressed on the issue of its origins or the location of *karma,* its ontological status, Hindus, even those professing the most systematic Hindu tradition, do not offer an explanation. Jains, in contrast, believe that *karma* is a physical particle that floats about and is attracted to sentient beings, depending on their actions and their intentions. Hindus are not concerned or bothered that the universe and *karma* were forever existent and will forever exist in the future. In this connection, unlike their Christian counterparts, Hindus are not disturbed with *anavasthā* (infinite regresses). The necessity to posit a "first cause" that had no previous cause, as the Christian philosopher Thomas Aquinas suggested, does not appear on the Hindu radar. So there are some metaphysical questions that are neither asked nor answered by Hindus. I am comfortable with this and feel no existential, philosophical, or logical need to look for, or require, a "first cause."

Bandha refers to the relationship of the *jīva* (enduring self) with the *deha* (the external body). Madhvācārya believes that *jīvas* are bound in a beginningless cycle of birth and rebirth. The *jīva* remains in *bandha* because of its *ajñāna* (ignorance) of *brahman* (the impersonal absolute) and of the universe. Its relationship with the *deha* ends only upon attaining *mokṣa*.

Madhvācārya never explicitly explains why Viṣṇu created the universe and all of its elements. It may be that Viṣṇu created it out of *līlā* (playful sport), though this explanation is functionally equivalent to the age-old assertion "God works in mysterious ways!" and just as satisfying. One may also venture that Viṣṇu periodically creates the universe for the sake of the *jīvas*. Within this universe, *jīvas* can manifest their stored *karma*, create new *karma,* and either maintain or break their existence in the cycle. The *jīvas* are bound by *puṇya* and *pāpa,* both of which, like *bandha*, are without beginning.[1] Viṣṇu is the actuator for the establishment of the universe, which is the location where *karma* can manifest, where suffering occurs and can end, and where *bandha* manifests and can cease. Beyond this Hindus neither ask, nor offer answers to, further metaphysical questions that arise from this belief. Or, if some response is proffered, such as attributing the unknowable to *līlā*, it is a kind of agnostic nonanswer. This, like the lack of origins of *karma*, seems acceptable to me.

Hindus resort to *karma* in order to explain both positive and negative events in their lives, and in what they observe in the lives of others. Suffering is thus inextricably linked to the consequences of actions, which are guided by and incur *karma*. In this way, *saṃsāra* is unavoidably pervaded by some degree of suffering. According to this mechanism of causality, agents (human and nonhuman) are directly responsible for their own suffering (physical, mental, spiritual, existential, and so on). While they may act in ways to mitigate this suffering, both in the immediate and in the long term (over future lives), there is a degree to which Hindus accept, and even embrace, its inevitability.

While this can be taken in a somewhat trivial way, as I suggested earlier concerning the suffering of my students, there are other, much more serious and profound scenarios. In a medical context, such an etiology can mean that some Hindus would welcome suffering rather than try to alleviate it. Palliative care, for example, may not be desirable if the Hindu believes that her suffering is the expression and manifestation of *pāpa* (demeritorious) *karma*. A Hindu may believe that relieving suffering may merely delay the manifestation of *pāpa karma*. The relief, then, would only be temporary and may even incur more *pāpa* and prolong or intensify the inescapable.

An example of this would be when suffering is tied to the requirement or desire to propitiate a god or goddess. Suffering can be understood as a test of faith or as a means for knowledge. Vaiṣṇavites (devotees of Viṣṇu), for example, may perceive suffering as a means by which one can increase *bhakti* (devotion) to the god Viṣṇu. Madhvācārya held that suffering made one aware of one's utter dependence upon Viṣṇu. This knowledge, gained through suffering, amplified one's *bhakti* and hastened one's attainment of *mokṣa*.

In some theistic models, devotees are concurrently rewarded or punished if they propitiate a god or goddess who can alleviate or penalize someone with suffering. Śītalā-devī, the smallpox goddess, is simultaneously benevolent and dangerous: she can protect or infect—bless or curse—devotees with smallpox and other diseases. Persons scarred by smallpox are believed to have been graced by her. Yet she is worshipped so that she does not inflict her *prasāda* (grace) upon her worshippers. In this case, suffering is directly a result of, and explicable by, the actions of the devotee.

Many Hindus find these explanations to be more satisfying than medical ones. They also lead some Hindus to accept medical diagnoses and to make medical choices that do not prolong life when prognoses are not favorable.

Just before beginning my research as a graduate student in India I sustained a significant and life-threatening traumatic brain injury. This left me with a variety of deficits and restrictions. When I told my teachers at the Mādhva *maṭha* (monastery) about it, they reasoned that there was some *karmic* mechanism at work, that it was a result of a previous action, and that my *karma* must have been good, ultimately, since I did, after all, survive.

If it is all *karma*, then what do gods and goddesses have to do with it? Some, but not all, Hindus believe in gods and goddesses who play a role in one's life and in the narrative of the universe. There are some Hindus, however, who believe that there are two levels of reality—conventional reality, which we inhabit and is illusory, and ultimate reality, toward which we should aspire (similar to the ones propounded by Kant and adherents of Mahayana Buddhism)—and therefore consider gods and goddesses to be a product of *māyā* (delusional thinking). For Madhvācārya, the universe is unquestionably real.[2] Viṣṇu, who is the pinnacle of the Mādhva system, governs all things.[3] Furthermore, correct knowledge of Viṣṇu and the nature and function of the universe are the prerequisites for *mokṣa*.[4]

Each Hindu believes that it is possible to be liberated from the cycle of birth and rebirth. They differ, though, on the process by which one attains *mokṣa* and on the experience of *mokṣa* itself. This does not mean that a Hindu philosophy of life embraces a relativism, where each and every path leads to *mokṣa* or that the experience of *mokṣa* is dependent on the beliefs of the individual. Rather, the history of Hinduism has involved debates and disagreements on how to attain *mokṣa* and what is precisely experienced thereafter. Some, for example, believe that *mokṣa* is obtainable by *jñāna* (knowledge) while for others it is made possible by *bhakti* (devotion) to a particular *deva* (god).

Hindus may or may not always be thinking about their *karma* and about how to attain *mokṣa*, the same way that many Christians don't always have sin and heaven on their minds. "Religious" and mindful Hindus, however, do reflect habitually on their current *karmic* status and their desire to break out of the cycle of birth and rebirth. That is, committed Hindus train, or in some cases retrain, themselves to have the right cognitive habits. They likely engage in rituals and meditative activities that confirm, solidify, and make beliefs, belief patterns, doctrines, and the like. For the Mādhva, for example, rituals and meditative practices performed three times daily solidify the right cognitive habits. As already mentioned, my meditations and rituals are oriented around the gradations and hierarchies.

For myself, my philosophy was informed by Madhvācārya's prescriptions. In fact, my work as a professor of Indian philosophy and Hindu religions is a way I can solidify the right cognitive habits, according to Mādhva Vedānta. In addition to my daily *sandhyavandhana* (morning meditation), my class preparations, my research, and my teaching permit me to study these texts, to reflect on them in the ways prescribed, to teach them to others, and to otherwise consider their content. My earlier work on the Mādhva school required me to learn the doctrine in depth, and therefore fulfill the injunction to do so. This repetition has the desired effect of making Mādhva doctrine a cognitive habit: when I hear the wind blowing outside my window as I write these words, I first think about the god Vāyu. Madhvācārya, of course, is an *avatāra* (incarnation) of Vāyu.[5] When I teach students about Vedānta in my Indian philosophy class, I am of course immersed in Mādhva doctrine. Correct knowledge of Viṣṇu and the nature and function of the universe is the prerequisite for *mokṣa,* and I am fortunate that I have the opportunity to teach and pursue research that can inform and further my experiences as a Hindu.

Suggested Readings

Flood, Gavin. *An Introduction to Hinduism.* Cambridge: Cambridge University Press, 1996. This is a basic introduction to the history of Hinduism, arranged thematically.

Sarma, Deepak. "When Is a Brahmin a *brahmabandhu,* an Unworthy or Wicked Brahmin? Or When Is the *adhikārin,* Eligible One, *anadhikārin,* Ineligible?" *Method & Theory in the Study of Religion* 13, no. 1 (2001): 82–90. An article about the insider-outsider problem as it is found, and exemplified, in Mādhva Vedānta.

———. *An Introduction to Mādhva Vedānta.* Farnham, UK: Ashgate Publishing, 2003. A short, philosophically oriented introduction to the Mādhva school of Vedānta.

———. *Classical Indian Philosophy: A Reader.* New York: Columbia University Press, 2011. This is an introduction to the exemplary themes and debates in Indian philosophy.

Notes

1 Madhvācārya, *Brahma Sūtra Bhāṣya,* 2:3:29.

2 Madhvācārya, *Viṣṇutattva(vi)nirṇaya,* 35.

3 Madhvācārya, *Tattvasaṃkhyāna,* 1.

4 Madhvācārya, *Mahābhāratatātparyanirṇaya,* 1:79, 1:85.

5 Madhvācārya, *Chāndogyopaniṣadbhāṣya*m, 3:15:1.

CHAPTER EIGHT

Judaism

Rabbi Barbara Block

Blessed are You, Eternal our God,
Ruler of the Universe,
Who has made me free.
> —One of the blessings
> practicing Jews recite every morning

I was born to two Jewish parents. According to traditional Jewish law, or *halachah*, I am Jewish by birth. *Halachah* recognizes me as a Jew even if I never engage in Jewish practice or subscribe to Jewish beliefs. In the United States today, unlike in the European communities of my ancestors, I could easily walk away from Judaism. There are Jews who leave both religious practice and the community behind. Recognizing this, we say that not only are those who convert to Judaism "Jews by choice"; *every* Jew who participates in Jewish life today is a Jew by choice.

Why, then, do I choose Judaism? Why do I choose to affiliate with the Jewish community, to practice Jewish rituals, and to live my life according to Jewish teachings? It is not merely because I was born to Jewish parents; nor is it simply because I attended Jewish religious school for eleven years and participated in Confirmation. Many from the same background have chosen to abandon Judaism. Nor is it because Judaism is all I know. I have done my share of exploration over the years, attending a Quaker meeting in my twenties and a Buddhist sangha in my forties. I have learned about Christianity from conversations with Christian friends over the course of a lifetime and from eighteen years working at two Catholic colleges. While I have found much to appreciate and admire in these traditions, I remain fully committed to Jewish life and practice.

I choose to practice Judaism because it offers a path to a rich and worthwhile life. Jewish study and practice bring meaning to my existence. But I am a Jew not only for the benefits that Judaism brings me as an individual. I practice Judaism because I believe it leads me to make choices that are better for the world. I teach Judaism because when I think of a world without people practicing Judaism—a world without Jewish spiritual practice and without observances such as Passover—I think of a world that is a less good place than it is.

Living a Jewish life means being in a relationship with a tradition. The path that is set before us by Judaism is not a rigid one. Tevye, the beloved hero of *Fiddler on the Roof*, says, "On the one hand . . . on the other hand." On the one hand, tradition teaches this. On the other hand, here is the situation. A Jewish philosophy of life is one that balances competing values and ideas. On the one hand, Judaism is rooted in tradition. On the other hand, we have persisted and even thrived for more than two thousand years by allowing that tradition room to breathe and change, to respond to new ideas and new realities. Even within the tradition, there are multiple voices; more than one truth is allowed and even encouraged.

The Talmud, compiled around the year 500 CE, records the discussion of competing ideas, even when one idea is ultimately chosen as correct. We find in the Talmud this story:

> R. Abba stated in the name of Samuel: For three years
> there was a dispute between the scholars of the House of
> Shammai and those of the House of Hillel, the former
> asserting, "The *halachah* [law] is in agreement with our
> views" and the latter contending, "The *halachah* is in
> agreement with our views." Then a *bat kol* [a voice from
> heaven] announced, "[The utterances of] both are the
> words of the living God, but the *halachah* is in agree-
> ment with the rulings of the House of Hillel." (Babylo-
> nian Talmud, Eruvin 13b)

Sometimes, we need to choose one road by which to arrive at a
destination. This story acknowledges that there might be several
roads that would work equally well. In this case, the words of
both sets of scholars "are the words of the living God."

This willingness to entertain more than one idea as worthy
and the respect shown for minority opinions are attitudes that
draw me to Jewish thought. Differences in opinion are appreciated and encouraged. Sometimes, they even provide a source of
amusement. In modern times, we like to quip, "Two Jews, three
opinions."

It should come as no surprise, then, that there is no single
authoritative Jewish philosophy of life. Our fundamental text, the
Hebrew Bible, is not a philosophical treatise. Jews have engaged
in philosophy since the Middle Ages, but there is no single work
of Jewish philosophy of any period that is considered authoritative. Rather than a liability, this diversity of voices is a strength,
providing a richness to Jewish thought.

What all Jewish philosophies of life have in common is a
grounding in Jewish texts. Jewish textual study is considered a
cornerstone of a good Jewish life. Study is an obligation, but also a
joy. As Tevye sings in *Fiddler on the Roof*, "If I were a rich man . . .

I'd discuss the learned books with the holy men seven hours every day. That would be the sweetest thing of all!"

Because textual study is fundamental to a good Jewish life, I want to highlight some of its key features. The primary texts of Judaism are all understood through the lens of commentary. At the heart of the Torah, in the middle of the book of Leviticus, we find the commandment, "You shall love your neighbor as yourself" (19:18). How is this to be understood? In a story related in the Talmud, a scoffer approaches Rabbi Hillel and says that he will convert to Judaism if Hillel can teach him the entire Torah while standing on one foot. Hillel responds with a negative formulation of Leviticus 19:18, saying, "What is hateful to you, do not do to any person. All the rest is commentary. Now go and study the commentary" (Talmud, Shabbat 31a). Love is an important emotion, but contrary to a favorite Beatles song, Judaism teaches that love is *not* all you need. We require guidance in how to show that love. We receive that guidance through the study of Jewish texts and the commentary on those texts. We say that the Torah is a tree of life. A tree lives and breathes and branches out, and so, too, does our understanding of our texts and our lives.

Jews of all the different denominations of Judaism study text and commentary. As a Reform Jew, I do not take the words of the Torah as literal or historical truth. Nevertheless, I do take these words seriously for the lessons they impart. I see the Hebrew Bible as a document that was written by many authors over a period of time. The text conveys timeless values, but some of the stories and commandments teaching those values have to be understood in the context of their times. For example, there are rules for taking a woman who is a captive of war as a wife. Today, we would reject this practice outright, as we do not condone the taking of captives. Furthermore, the woman is not allowed a voice in whether or not the man will be her husband. But in the context of its time, when captives of war were simply a given, the text is revolutionary in the consideration and protections given to the woman.

> When you take the field against your enemies, and . . .
> you take some of them captive, and you see among the
> captives a beautiful woman and you desire her and would
> take her to wife, you shall bring her into your house. . . .
> She shall spend a month's time lamenting her father
> and mother; after that . . . she shall be your wife. Then,
> should you no longer want her, you must release her
> outright. You must not sell her for money . . . you must
> not enslave her. (Deuteronomy 21:10–14)

The captive is given time to mourn and, once married, cannot be sold as a slave. While we would not condone taking a captive in this manner (although it still happens in many parts of the world; consider Boko Haram as one example), what we learn from the text for today is that even when we have power over another, we must be kind.

How Jews study the Torah is as important as the text itself. We are not supposed to study alone. "Get yourself a teacher and a companion," says Joshua ben Perachyah in *Pirkei Avot* (*Sayings of the Fathers*) 11:6. Study is traditionally done in pairs. The partners can keep each other on track, help avoid errors in interpretation, and enrich understanding. Most American education emphasizes individual accomplishment. Our papers are to be written by ourselves alone, and tests measure individual knowledge. This was true throughout my education: through twelve years of public school; in my private undergraduate experience; and in my career as a graduate student in philosophy. My seminary experience was markedly different. While we did have individual assessments, we were expected to have a study partner in text courses, and many of our class projects were done in groups. Not only was my learning deeper, but having study partners underscored the Jewish value of community, shifting the focus away somewhat from individual achievement.

Studying with different partners also reinforces another Jewish value. "Who is wise?" asks Ben Zoma. "The one who learns from every person" (*Pirkei Avot*, 44:1). As anyone who has studied or worked with a group knows, there are people whom we ordinarily would not choose as partners, and yet, they may well have something to teach us when we find it within ourselves to listen. I find this a useful lesson not only within the Jewish world, but in interfaith relations. To paraphrase Ben Zoma: "Who is wise? The one who learns from all traditions." I have learned valuable lessons from other traditions while maintaining my own identity and beliefs. This teaching also calls me to listen to those whose political opinions differ from mine. How wise our world would become if only we would all learn from each other!

Jewish texts are many and varied, and so, too, are the philosophies derived from them. There are, nonetheless, certain themes that permeate Jewish thought. One concept that is fundamental to a Jewish philosophy of life is the idea of *covenant*.

A covenant is an agreement between two parties, bringing them into relationship. In Genesis, God enters into a series of covenants with Abraham and his descendants, Isaac and Jacob, promising them land and progeny in return for following the rite of circumcision. This binds the family of Abraham to God.

The most important covenant for Jews is the one between God and the Israelite people that we entered into at Mount Sinai. It is this covenant that makes us Jews. God promises to treasure the people and to consider them "a kingdom of priests and a holy nation" in return for their obedience to God's commandments

(Exodus 19:5–6). God then reveals the Ten Commandments, followed by additional instructions for living. After God's revelation of the commandments, Moses repeats them to the people, and they respond, "All the things that the Eternal has commanded we will do!" (Exodus 24:3), thus agreeing to and entering into the covenant. In the retelling of this story, Deuteronomy asserts that all Jews, even those yet unborn, are present for the revelation of the covenant: "I make this covenant not with you alone, but both with those standing here with us this day before the Eternal our God and with those who are not with us here this day" (29:13–14).

The Israelites are able to enter into the covenant because they are a free people. This is no minor point. Fifty days before they arrive at Sinai, the Israelites are freed from slavery in Egypt. This freedom is celebrated in song during every worship service and is reenacted annually during the ritual of the Passover Seder, when we retell the story of the escape from Egypt. Like many Jews, I was little connected to Jewish communal life during my twenties, but come spring, I always found a Passover Seder to attend. During the Seder, we are commanded to see ourselves as though we ourselves were slaves in Egypt and were liberated. The fact of our slavery is repeated over and over in the Torah as a reminder to treat the stranger kindly: "You shall not oppress a stranger, for you know the feelings of the stranger, since you yourselves were strangers in the land of Egypt" (Exodus 23:9). The importance of freedom and of treating the most vulnerable among us well are core Jewish values that persuade many Jews to keep choosing Judaism, even when it is challenging.

The covenant into which we entered and which freedom made possible is a demanding one. One challenge of the covenant is being in relationship with God. I am the daughter of a Holocaust refugee who declared that he could not believe in a personal God after the murder of six million Jews. The challenge is particularly acute for me. I am not alone, however, in this struggle. The Israeli poet Uri Zvi Greenberg captures the tension of our relationship with God:

> *God, You taunt me, "Flee if you can!"*
> *But I can't flee.*
> *For when I turn away from You, angry and heartsick,*
> *With a vow on my lips, like burning coal:*
> *"I will not see You again"—*
> *I can't do it.*
> *And I turn back*
> *And knock on your door,*
> *Tortured with longing.*
> *As though you had sent me a love letter.*[1]

When thinking about God, it is important to consider: *What questions are worth asking?* Medieval Jews, like their Christian counterparts, tried to find proof for the existence of God, but I don't believe this is productive. Nor do I find it productive to try to pin down who God is or what qualities God has. Like Maimonides, a rabbi and philosopher of the twelfth century, I believe there is little or nothing positive we can say about God. Our finite minds cannot comprehend the infinite.

And yet, there are Jewish teachings about God that are instructive. One way of understanding the Torah is that it tells the story of humankind's developing understanding of God and of the way of life God would have us live. This idea is contained in a passage in the Torah itself, a passage that has been copied by the rabbis into the daily prayer service. When God appears to Moses at the burning bush, God says, "I am the God of your ancestors—the God of Abraham, the God of Isaac, and the God of Jacob" (Exodus 3:6). The rabbis ask the question, "Why does the text not read simply, 'God of Abraham, Isaac, and Jacob'? Is not God unchanging?" They answer that although God does not change, our understanding of God, and therefore our relationship with God, does change. Each generation conceives of God and experiences God in its own way.

The Torah is not the only Jewish text that teaches about God. Jewish prayer helps me to frame my relationship with God. Many Jewish prayers begin with a formula: "Blessed are You, Eternal One, Our God, Ruler of the Universe." While I do not believe that God is an omnipotent ruler, I find this formula worthwhile. Blessing God for things reminds me that not everything that happens is due to my own efforts. I sit here typing on my laptop. I take credit for learning how to type, for choosing my words, and for moving my fingers over the keyboard. But how did I come to have this body that allows me to see and to move and to learn? I cannot take credit for the design of my body or my mind, nor for their development. Remembering that I did not create myself and reminding myself that I cannot control all that happens serves to keep me appropriately humble. I cannot take complete credit for what I accomplish, nor am I entirely to blame for what is wrong in my life, for I do not have complete control over my world.

I also find the words that follow the opening formula to be helpful. One of my favorite sets of prayers is called "the miracles of every day." Every morning we recite the fifteen prayers in this set, each of which begins with the formula followed by something that we might take for granted. "Blessed are You . . . who gives the rooster the instinct to distinguish between day and night." Both the rooster and we are able to tell day from night, but how often do we stop to appreciate that fact? "Blessed are you . . . who stretches the earth upon the waters." When we experience floods, we recognize how wonderful is the ordinary order of things, which places land above water, but usually we are oblivious to this blessing. These prayers, which open our eyes to the everyday miracles around us, are a lovely practice of gratitude that anchors my day.

Some of the prayers in the set thank God for actions such as freeing the captive and clothing the naked. Judaism teaches that God does not accomplish these things alone. It is up to us to partner with God in repairing the world. The prayers function as a way of reminding us of our highest goals. They help us to focus our intentions. We praise God for freeing the captive; *we* need to free the captive. We praise God for clothing the naked; *we* need to clothe and feed and provide for the poor.

While there are some petitionary prayers, such as prayers asking God to make peace in the world, I do not see prayer as a method of manipulating God to give me what I want. One of my favorite modern readings, found in the Reform movement's prayer book, describes what I believe to be the true power of prayer:

> Prayer invites God's Presence to suffuse our spirits, God's will to prevail in our lives.
>
> Prayer may not bring water to parched fields, nor mend a broken bridge, nor rebuild a ruined city.
>
> But prayer can water an arid soul, mend a broken heart, [and] rebuild a weakened will.[2]

One prayer taken from Deuteronomy instructs me in my relationship with God and is a help in my life. The passage reads, "You shall love the Eternal your God, with all your heart, with all your soul, and with all your being" (6:5). This passage is recited every morning and every evening. When I recite it in the morning, I will often ask myself, *What is it for me to love God today?* and the answer will differ from day to day. One day, loving God might mean calling a family member; another day it might mean putting my desk in order or completing some task; or loving God might mean going to the gym or taking time for myself. The question about how I might love God functions better than any other I have found to help me focus on how I should live my life, even without a particular conception of God. In 2004, when I lost the job I had thought I would hold until retirement, I asked the question, *What is it for me to love God with all my heart, all my soul, all my being, in the next phase of my life?* The answer came back that to love God was to apply to rabbinical school. This would mean giving up the life I had built, giving up almost everything, at age fifty, to begin anew. I wondered, was there some other way to love God? But the answer that came back—the response that led me to become a rabbi—was true guidance that I have not regretted following.

I want to distinguish between asking how to love God and asking God to tell me what to do. I am leery of people on street corners and televangelists who proclaim that God has spoken to them and told them the Truth. There have been Jews throughout history who have professed to have heard directly from God, and there are Jews today who claim to be guided by God's voice. But the rabbis of the Talmud take a firm position that the days of the *bat kol*—the voice from heaven—are over. Prophecy as recorded in the Bible has ended. They make their point in this story about a dispute in which Rabbi Eliezer's answer to a ritual question differed from the answer of the rest of the group:

> It was taught: On that day Rabbi Eliezer answered all the answers on earth and they did not accept it from him.
> He said, "If the law is as I say, the carob tree will prove it"; the carob tree was uprooted from its place

one hundred cubits, some say four hundred cubits. They said: "We do not bring proof from a carob tree."

He came back and said, "If the law is as I say, the river will prove it"; the river flowed in reverse direction. They said: "We do not bring proof from a river."

He came back and said, "If the law is as I say, the walls of the House of Study will prove it"; the walls of the House of Study inclined to fall. Rabbi Joshua protested at them [the walls], saying to them, "If scholars defeat each other in the law, how does it benefit you?" They did not fall because of the honor of Rabbi Joshua but they did not straighten, because of the honor of Rabbi Eliezer, and still they incline and stand.

[Rabbi Eliezer] came back and said, "If the law is like me, from the Heavens they will prove it"; a *bat kol* [heavenly voice] came out and said, "What is with you toward Rabbi Eliezer, for the law is as he says in every instance?" Rabbi Joshua stood on his feet and said, "[The Torah] is not in heaven." (Deuteronomy 30:12)

What does "[The Torah] is not in heaven" mean? R. Jeremiah said: "Since the Torah was already given at Sinai, we do not pay attention to a heavenly voice, since You already wrote at Sinai in the Torah, 'After the majority to incline.'" (Exodus 23:2)[3]

The rabbis use this story to illustrate their point. We no longer look to a voice from heaven to decide matters. Nor do we believe that natural phenomena give us answers. We rely on the best judgment of the majority of scholars. The story continues with the rabbis imagining how God might respond to their assertion of authority.

> Rabbi Nathan met the prophet Elijah and said to him,
> "What did the Holy Bountiful One do in that hour?" He
> [Elijah] said to him: "God smiled and said, 'My children
> have triumphed over Me, My children have triumphed
> over Me.'"

Judaism offers many ways of conceptualizing God, our partner in the covenant. Through textual study, we learn about God, and through prayer, we develop a relationship with God. Over the generations, our ideas develop and our relationship with God changes. One thing that does not change, however, is the idea that through the covenant, God places demands on us.

Study of text and recitation of prayer lead us to knowledge of the covenant and bring us into relationship with God. But study and prayer are not enough. In *Pirkei Avot*, or *Sayings of the Fathers*, we read, "Simon the Just used to say: 'The world stands on three things: on Torah; on *avodah* [service]; and on *g'milut chasadim* [loving acts of kindness]'" (*Pirkei Avot*, 1:2). Textual study helps us to recognize what is kind and what is not, and prayer can help us set intention and inspire us, but these are incomplete without acts of kindness. Jewish tradition has developed many practices to help us move from knowledge and devotion to action.

One of these practices is called *teshuvah*, translated as "return" or "repentance." Jewish thinkers recognize that we make mistakes, and have developed a way to return to a better path. Return is not easy, however. In the twelfth century, Maimonides set out six steps for us to accomplish *teshuvah*; these steps are still studied and followed today, and it is a model that I find both compelling and useful.[4]

- The first step is regret. We cannot transform wrongdoing without first recognizing that we have done wrong. Ignorance is not bliss; we must examine our actions. We must truly feel remorse for what we have done.

- Second, we must renounce our error. This means that we stop making excuses for our actions.

- The third step is confessing our error out loud. If we have harmed another person, we must go to that person and admit what we did. If our transgression was against ourselves or against God, then we need to confess to God.

- Reconciliation, the fourth step, moves the focus from the one who has gone astray to the one who has been wronged. Reconciliation begins with a sincere apology, and continues with doing what is needed to heal the relationship. This may mean talking, listening, or giving the other space. This step can take considerable time and effort.

- The fifth step is to make amends. Perhaps this means making monetary restitution to the victim, or providing for their counseling or therapy. It is also appropriate to volunteer our time or make monetary donations to a cause related to our wrongdoing.

- Finally, we resolve not to repeat the offense. Maimonides wrote that we know we have completed our *teshuvah* when we find ourselves in the same situation in which we erred, but we do not commit the same offense again.

I will add to this practical wisdom a Hasidic story from the nineteenth century, which has often helped me regain my footing when I know I have done something wrong:

When you talk about and reflect upon an evil deed you
have done, you become the captive of your thoughts—
all your soul is utterly caught up in the evil, for you are
what you think. And then you are prevented from turning, for your spirit will coarsen, your heart grow infirm,
and, in addition, melancholy may disable you. After all,
if you stir the muck this way or that, it is still muck.
What is the use of weighing and measuring our sins?
In the time I am brooding on this, I could be stringing
pearls for the joy of heaven. That is why it is written:
"Depart from evil, and do good" (Psalms 34:15)—turn
wholly from evil, do not brood about it, and do good.
You have done wrong? Then balance it by doing right.[5]

There are many more practices that Judaism offers to help
us live a full and worthwhile life. I continue to choose Judaism
for the wisdom of its texts, the challenge of its covenant, and the
helpfulness of its practices.

Suggested Readings

Berkson, William. *Pirke Avot: Timeless Wisdom for Modern Life.*
Philadelphia: Jewish Publication Society, 2010. *Pirke* or
Pirkei Avot is a compilation of wise sayings of the rabbis of
the classical period. Several quotations from *Pirkei Avot* are
included in this chapter. *Pirkei Avot* is a tractate of the Mish-
nah, which was compiled in about 200 CE. Berkson's edition
includes helpful essays and comments about both historical
context and how we might apply this wisdom today.
Borowitz, Eugene B. *Choices in Modern Jewish Thought: A Partisan
Guide.* West Orange, NJ: Behrman House, 1983. Borowitz

explains the challenge of modernity to Judaism and provides a survey of responses from the outstanding thinkers of the modern era, including Martin Buber and Abraham Joshua Heschel. He presents four rationalist models and three non-rational models, followed by chapters on confronting the Holocaust, the theology of Modern Orthodoxy, and liberal Jewish thought.

Citrin, Paul, ed. *Lights in the Forest: Rabbis Respond to Twelve Essential Jewish Questions.* New York: CCAR Press, 2014. Forty Reform rabbis contribute essays to this easily readable work. The twelve questions addressed are grouped under three headings. Questions on God include "What is God's relationship to suffering and evil?" and "What is the connection between God and ethical values?" Section two addresses questions on our humanity, including "What does the concept of gender contribute to our understanding of being human?" and "What is your concept of soul and afterlife?" Section three, on the Jewish people, includes questions such as "As liberal Jews who value religious autonomy, how are the concepts of 'covenant' and 'commandment' relevant to us?" and "In what way is the Torah sacred text for us?"

Fackenheim, Emil L. *Encounters between Judaism and Modern Philosophy: A Preface to Future Jewish Thought.* New York: Schocken Books, 1987. One of the most important Jewish thinkers to address the Holocaust, Fackenheim will appeal to those who are familiar with Western philosophy. Chapters include "Elijah and the Empiricists: The Possibility of Divine Presence"; "Abraham and the Kantians: Moral Duties and Divine Commandments"; "Moses and the Hegelians: Jewish Existence in the Modern World"; "Idolatry as a Modern Philosophy"; and "Existentialist Finale—and Beginning."

Levy, Naomi. *To Begin Again: The Journey toward Comfort, Strength, and Faith in Difficult Times.* New York: Ballantine Books, 1998. Rabbi Levy's deeply personal book draws on her own experiences of suffering as well as the experiences of her congregants. Each chapter includes stories and wisdom gained from life's challenges and ends with a prayer.

Morinis, Alan. *Everyday Holiness: The Jewish Spiritual Path of Mussar.* Boston: Trumpeter, 2008. Mussar is an ethical tradition that is receiving renewed attention in many Jewish communities. Morinis's guide explains the historical roots of the tradition and how it can be practiced today. Mussar is a practice that addresses soul traits such as gratitude, humility, generosity, and more. One of the three sections of the book addresses each of eighteen different soul traits, with practical exercises to strengthen each trait.

Sonsino, Rifat. *Six Jewish Spiritual Paths: A Rationalist Looks at Spirituality.* Woodstock, VT: Jewish Lights Publishing, 2000. After considering what spirituality is and a historical survey of the Jewish spiritual quest from biblical times to the present, Sonsino presents six paths through which we might nourish our souls: acts of transcendence; study; prayer; meditation; ritual; and relationship and good deeds.

Notes

1 Uri Zvi Greenberg, "Like a Woman" adapted by Chaim Stern, in *Gates of Forgiveness* (New York: CCAR Press, 1993).

2 Elyse D. Frishman, *Mishkan T'filah: A Reform Siddur* (New York: CCAR Press, 2007), 165.

3 Babylonian Talmud, *Bava Metzia*, 59a–59b.

4 Adapted from Maimonides, *Mishneh Torah*, "Laws of Teshuva," 2:1.

5 *Gates of Repentance: The New Union Prayerbook for the Days of Awe*, ed. Chaim Stern (New York: CCAR Press, 1984), 240.

CHAPTER NINE

Christianity

Alister McGrath

Oh, I have slipped the surly bonds of earth,
And danced the skies on laughter-silvered wings;

. . .

put out my hand and touched the face of God.
—John Gillespie Magee Jr.
(1922–1941), "High Flight"

To speak of meaning in life, according to C. S. Lewis, is an act of rebellion against a "glib and shallow rationalism" that limits reality to the realm of empirical facts. It is to reach behind and beyond our experience of this world, to grasp and explore an intellectual framework that positions human beings within a greater scheme of things, and to allow us to see ourselves and our inhabitation of this world in a new way. It is to transcend the "surly bonds" of the observable, and discern a deeper realm of meaning and value, with clear implications for human existence. As the writer Jeanette Winterson remarked, "We cannot simply eat, sleep, hunt and reproduce—we are meaning-seeking creatures."[1] While empirical psychology (rightly) has little to say prescriptively about what the meaning of life might be, it certainly helps describe the kind of things we find meaningful to our well-being.

Meaning is about the way in which we make sense of the world, see significance in our lives, and locate ourselves within a greater scheme of things. While meaning can derive from many sources, particularly families of philosophical traditions such as Aristotelianism and Stoicism, it is widely recognized that religion (a deeply problematic category, by the way) has a particular capacity to provide people with a comprehensive and integrated framework of meaning, which both helps to make sense of their lives and worlds, and provides a way of transcending their own limited experience and situation by connecting them with something greater.

In a perceptive study, the novelist Salman Rushdie argues that religion has met three types of needs that have failed to be satisfied by secular, rationalist materialism.[2] First, it enables us to articulate our sense of awe and wonder, partly by helping us grasp the immensity of life and partly by affirming that we are special. Second, it provides "answers to the unanswerable," engaging the deep questions that so often trouble and perplex us. And finally, it offers us a moral framework, within which we can live out a good life. For Rushdie, religion or the "idea of God" provides us with a "repository of our awestruck wonderment at life, and an answer to the great questions of existence." Any attempt to describe or define people "in terms that exclude their spiritual needs" will only end in failure. Yet while religion in general is intimately linked to the (universal) human quest for meaning, it is important to respect the distinct identities of the various religious traditions. While there may be occasional parallels and synergies, each religious tradition has its own distinct concerns and emphases, which are resistant to assimilation or homogenization.

My own discovery of Christianity was somewhat belated, in that I came to it through an extended intellectual detour that took me through the fascinating territories of various kinds of atheism, both gracious and aggressive. As a teenager, I had no particular interest in the question of the meaning of life. I was then a metaphysically suspicious and intellectually minimalist natural scientist, who could see no grounds for believing either that there was any meaning in life, other than what I chose to impose upon an essentially amoral and chaotic world, or that the quest for such a meaning was in any way legitimate or productive. I was perfectly content to develop my own somewhat self-centered personal ethic, and took a certain perverse pleasure in knowing that, from my perspective, nobody had the intellectual resources to prove I was wrong.

Yet I arrived at Oxford University to study the natural sciences with growing doubts about the intellectual sustainability of this way of thinking. After much reflection, I stepped out of an atheist way of thinking and embraced Christianity. Here I found an approach to meaning that positioned me within a greater scheme of things—not one of my own choosing, but one that helped me identify who I really was and what really mattered. In this chapter, I shall make no attempt to defend or justify a Christian approach to meaning; my task here is simply to present and explore it. It is not my intention to commend Christianity, but to engage its associated frameworks of meaning.

I want to explain how Christianity offers such a system of meaning, and how this works out in practice. So what form of Christianity shall I be considering? Generalizing about the various forms of Christianity is notoriously difficult, and tends to be undertaken primarily by those with denominational scores to settle and axes to grind. What I therefore propose to do is to make use of C. S. Lewis's well-known concept of "mere Christianity"—a generous consensual Christian orthodoxy, which does not entail any specific denominational commitment.

In his influential *Mere Christianity* (1952), Lewis drew a pointed distinction between the common, shared assumptions of the Christian faith, and their more specific interpretation by individual denominations. He asked his readers to imagine a large hall, with doors leading to various rooms. The hall, for Lewis, represented the simple, consensual faith that underlies Christianity—what he himself termed "mere Christianity," picking up on a phrase used by the English writer Richard Baxter. The rooms represented particular ways of understanding and applying this basic Christianity—the various denominations that have developed over the centuries, each with their own distinctive approach to living out the faith.

Christianity has a highly developed understanding of the impact of religious belief and commitment on personal and social well-being, especially in relation to achieving authenticity and articulating responsibility. Although the basic intellectual framework that illuminates and informs the relation of spirituality and well-being is found in the New Testament, the foundational document of the Christian faith, the full development of these ideas, dates from later periods, particularly the "patristic age" (ca. 100–500 CE) and the Middle Ages (ca. 1150–1500 CE). For many, of course, the most convenient summaries of Christian beliefs are found in the early Christian creeds—such as those generally known as the Apostles' Creed and the Nicene Creed.

These creeds offer a truncated and convenient summary of the main elements of Christian belief for the purposes of teaching and public worship, but they fail to convey the conceptual and spiritual richness of Christianity, which is not their intention. Christianity is not primarily a set of ideas, but is rather an extended imaginative and rational reflection on the significance of its central figure, Jesus Christ. Above all, it represents an articulation of how human life is illuminated and subsequently transformed by Christ.

The creeds are merely sketches of understanding our world and ourselves that radiate outward from the historical person of Christ. Recognizing that no single mental map is good enough, the creeds use multiple maps—historical, geographical, legal, and theological—and invite us to superimpose one upon another to disclose Christ's significance for the human situation. In effect, Christianity offers a "big picture" of reality, which weaves together leading themes from both the Old and New Testaments, while focusing on the historical specificity of Jesus Christ as the embodiment of God in time and space.

The central Christian idea of the incarnation, in which God chose to enter into the place of human habitation, plays a very significant role in the Christian making of meaning. "The Word became flesh, and dwelled among us" (John 1:14). Since God chose to inhabit part of the creation, this act of divine incarnation is seen as affirming the importance of the created order; disclosing God's compassion and care for both the world and humanity; and making possible "salvation"—a transformation of the human situation that allowed those who embraced this new way of existence to live in hope.

For Christians, the term "faith" designates not a formal assent to a belief, but rather an act of trust and commitment to a way of envisioning our world, and exploring its implications for thought and action. In its first phase, Christianity did not see itself as a religion, as we would now use that problematic term, with a set of beliefs to which we give intellectual assent, but as a trustworthy and reliable way of thinking and living. Early Christian writers thought of their faith as a philosophy—an understanding of our world, our place within it, and what actions might be appropriate for us. Early Christian artwork occasionally depicted Christ as wearing a *pallium*—a philosopher's cloak—for this reason.

C. S. Lewis captures this well when he summarizes his own understanding of his faith: "I believe in Christianity as I believe that the Sun has risen, not only because I see it, but because by it I see everything else."[3] So how does Lewis's programmatic invitation to see everything through the illuminating lens of Christianity work out in terms of the human quest for meaning? In what follows, I will tease out how leading Christian writers have explored five core themes that would now be grouped together under the general framework of the "human quest for meaning."

1. An Alignment of Narratives

Christianity places a distinctive emphasis on the person of Jesus Christ, and rehearses the narrative of his life, death, and resurrection in its public worship. The New Testament frequently affirms that the Christian hope of eternal life in the future is linked with the experience of suffering in the present, and sees this link as expressed in the story of Christ's passion and crucifixion: "We share in [Christ's] sufferings in order that we may also share in his glory" (Romans 8:17). Early Christian spirituality, particularly during the extended period during which Christianity was marginalized and sporadically persecuted, stressed the alignment of individual believers' personal narratives with that of Christ, especially in relation to suffering and hardship. The wall paintings of Roman catacombs expressed this visually—for example, through depicting Christ as the good shepherd who carried his weary and fearful sheep through a dangerous world.

Although this theme of individual lives being transformed through relocation within this grander narrative has always been part of Christian reflections on the meaning of life, it has assumed a new importance since the Second World War. Retellings of the Christian narrative have become increasingly popular, allowing readers to locate their own quest for virtue, hope, and integrity. Some of those transpositions are immediately recognizable as such (C. S. Lewis's Chronicles of Narnia comes to mind); others, however, are more nuanced and subtle (such as J. R. R. Tolkien's *The Lord of the Rings*, and J. K. Rowling's Harry Potter series). For Tolkien, the Christian myth (Tolkien uses this term in its technical sense, as a "narrated imaginative worldview") has the capacity to connect with, illuminate, and transform individual personal narratives.

Others, however, have developed this idea in different directions. The theologian H. Richard Niebuhr's 1941 essay "The Story of Our Life" argued that Christians should focus on the "irreplaceable and untranslatable" narrative of faith that straddles the borderlands of history, parable, and myth.[4] Jesus's story was not an argument for the existence of God, but a simple recital of the events and an invitation to become part of that story. How participants understand being part of such a shared history is expressed in terms of a subjective, committed, and engaged attitude to existence, resting on a set of assumptions that need to be unpacked and given systematic formulation.

Niebuhr's essay saw a new interest emerge in the capacity of the Christian story to generate moral values and frameworks of meaning. Writers such as Stanley Hauerwas have explored how this narrative recognizes human brokenness and the need for forgiveness, and thus determines the context of corporate and individual formation, inviting Christians to align and connect the stories of their lives—both in terms of thoughts and actions— with the narrative of the Christian tradition. C. S. Lewis offered an accessible way of grasping this point in his Chronicles of

Narnia, showing how individual characters in the novel allow their personal narratives to become part of the greater story of Narnia itself—a story which they simultaneously inhabit and advance. While their individual identity and values remain, they realize, however, that they have become part of something grander.

2. *Finding Fulfillment*

The search for personal and communal authenticity and fulfillment is of central and critical importance to many people. From its outset Christianity both articulates and enables such fulfillment. Many early Christian writers presented Christianity as the fulfillment of the classic human quest for wisdom, and highlighted the way in which Christianity resonated with themes in the writings of philosophers such as Plato and Plotinus. Other early Christian writers located the significance of Christianity at a more existential level. For Augustine of Hippo, Christianity offered a vision of a God who was able to fulfill the deepest longings of the human heart. This is expressed in his famous prayer: "You have made us for yourself, and our heart is restless until it rests in you."[5]

For Augustine, this idea is partly descriptive and partly prescriptive. The fundamental theme here is that human beings have some inbuilt longing to relate to God (an idea often articulated in terms of bearing the "image of God"), so that finding and embracing God is thus about becoming what we are meant to be, and finding joy and peace in doing so. In this sense, it is perfectly reasonable to speak of a "Christian humanism"—as opposed to, for example, a secular humanism, which holds that religion is an improper and dysfunctional imposition upon humanity.

3. Inhabiting a Coherent World

The New Testament speaks of all things "holding together" or being "knit together" in Christ (Colossians 1:17), thus suggesting that a hidden coherence lies beneath the external semblances of our world. Christianity provides a framework that allows an affirmation of the *coherence of reality*. However fragmented our world of experience may appear, there is a half-glimpsed "bigger picture" that holds things together, its threads connecting in a web of meaning what might otherwise seem incoherent and pointless. This is a major theme in one of the finest Christian literary classics, Dante's *Divine Comedy*. As this great Renaissance poem draws to its close, Dante catches a glimpse of the unity of the cosmos, in which its aspects and levels are seen to converge into a single whole. This insight, of course, is tantalizingly denied to him from his perspective on earth; yet once grasped, this enables him to see his work in a new light. There is a hidden web of meaning and connectedness behind the ephemeral and seemingly incoherent world that we experience.

This way of seeing things engages what is perhaps the greatest threat to any perception of meaningfulness in life or in our world—its seeming disorder and incoherence. Yet the default position of contemporary Western culture tends to echo the view of the physicist Steven Weinberg, that the natural sciences disclose a meaningless universe. "The more the universe seems comprehensible, the more it seems pointless."[6] Nothing seems to fit together. There is no big picture. So do new scientific ideas destroy any belief in a meaningful reality? The English poet John Donne expressed similar anxieties in the early seventeenth century, as new scientific discoveries seemed to erode any sense of connectedness and continuity within the world.

Yet there is a deeper issue here. The philosopher John Dewey

(1859–1952) argued that the "deepest problem of modern life" was our collective and individual failure to integrate our "thoughts about the world" with our thoughts about "value and purpose."[7] If there is not an outright incoherence here, there is at least a *disconnection* between the realm of understanding the cognitive issue of how we and our world *function*, and the deeper existential question of what we and our world *mean*. Christianity offers a "big picture" of reality that values and respects the natural sciences, while insisting there is more that needs to be said about deeper questions of value and meaning. For philosopher of science Karl Popper (1902–1994), such "ultimate questions" lay beyond the scope of the scientific method, yet are clearly seen as important by many human beings.

Perhaps the greatest threat to any sense of coherence to reality is posed by the existence of pain and suffering. Christianity provides a series of mental maps that allow for illness and suffering to be seen as coherent, meaningful, and potentially positive in terms of fostering personal growth and development. Some of these maps—such as those offered by Augustine of Hippo, Ignatius of Loyola, and Edith Stein—portray illness as something that is not part of God's intentions for humanity, but which can nevertheless be used as a means of growth; other maps, such as that developed by Martin Luther, tend to see suffering as something God permits, with the objective of stripping away illusions of immortality and confronting human beings with the harsh reality of their frailty and transiency.

The philosopher and novelist Iris Murdoch is one of many writers to emphasize the "calming" and "healing" effect of ways of looking at the world that allow it to be seen as ultimately rational and meaningful. On the other hand, Christian theologians have, since the earliest times, argued that such seeming irrationalities as the presence of suffering in the world do not constitute a challenge to the meaning and purpose of Christian faith. Augustine of Hippo, for example, set out an approach to the presence of evil that affirmed the original integrity, goodness, and rationality of the world. Evil and suffering arose from a misuse of freedom, the effects of which are being remedied and transformed through redemption. Augustine argues that the believer is enabled to make sense of the enigmas of suffering and evil by recalling its original integrity and looking forward to its final renewal and restoration in heaven.

Such Christian frameworks of meaning encourage a positive expectation on the part of believers that something may be learned and gained through illness and suffering. They make available new ways of thinking about life, and catalyze the emergence of more mature judgments and attitudes. Although this consideration has clear implications for Christian attitudes to illness and their outcomes, it is also significant in coping with aging—an increasingly important phenomenon in many cultures.

4. A Sense of Self-Worth

In his "Late Fragment," the poet Raymond Carver spoke movingly of his longing "to call myself beloved, to feel myself / beloved on the earth."[8] It is a very human (and very natural) yearning, which helps us appreciate why so many regard personal relationships as being of such significance and find their sense of self-worth affirmed and validated through them. Yet it is a thought that is constantly subverted by reflecting on the apparent insignificance of humanity, when seen in its broader cosmic context.

Sigmund Freud famously argued that scientific advance has led to a radical reevaluation of the place and significance of humanity in the universe, deflating human pretensions to grandeur and uniqueness. Before Copernicus, we thought we stood at the center of all things. Before Darwin, we thought we were utterly distinct from every other living species. Before Freud, we thought that we were masters of our own limited realm; now we have to come to terms with being the prisoner of hidden unconscious forces, subtly influencing our thinking and behavior. And as our knowledge of our universe expands, we realize how many galaxies lie beyond our own. The human life span is insignificant in comparison with the immense age of the universe. We can easily be overwhelmed by a sense of our own insignificance, when we see ourselves against this vast cosmic backdrop.

So what answers might be given to this? Is our self-worth subverted, if not destroyed, by these reflections? Some would argue that we need to face up to our situation, whether in a bold act of intellectual defiance or in a gracious resignation to a bleak emptiness as we contemplate our limited role in the greater scheme of things.

Christian writers regularly engage these questions, often speaking of the radical reassessment of the value of human life that results from being "touched" by God—a theme that is found, for example, throughout the poetic writings of George Herbert. Herbert likens the graceful "touch" of God to the fabled philosopher's stone of medieval alchemy, which transmutes base metal into gold.

> *This is that famous stone*
> *That turneth all to gold;*
> *For that which God doth touch and own*
> *Cannot for less be told.*[9]

Through inhabiting the Christian narrative, we come to see ourselves, as the medieval writer Julian of Norwich famously put it, as being enfolded in the love of Christ, which brings us a new security, identity, and value. Our self-worth is grounded in being loved by God.

Earlier, I noted the importance of personal relationships in affirming a human sense of self-worth. Perhaps this helps us understand why the Christian idea of a personal God who loves individual human beings, and demonstrates that love through the life and death of Jesus Christ, is seen as so important by many spiritual writers. God is one who relates to us, and thence transforms our sense of value and significance precisely through this privilege of relationship. We matter to God.

Yet this notion of a personal relationship between a Christian and the living God is also integral to another aspect of the human quest for meaning—our longing to know who we really are. What is the ultimate basis of our identity? Some suggest that our identity is defined, determined, or informed by our genetic makeup, by our social location, and by countless other scientific parameters. We can be defined by our race, our nationality, our weight, and our gender. Yet all too often, identity is simply reduced to the categories we happen to occupy. So is there a better way of framing our identity? Part of the Christian answer to this question focuses on a relationship with God that affirms, whatever else we are, we are loved by God and individually known to God by name. We find identity, meaning, and value within the context of this relationship.

5. Coping with Trauma

Earlier, I noted the importance of the quest for coherence in life. One of the most significant challenges to any perception of coherence is trauma—the exposure to emotionally distressing events that not only seem to be senseless, but appear to challenge any notion of meaning in the world. There has been growing interest recently in the way in which certain specific features of the Christian faith relate to traumatic experience and establish a framework for posttraumatic growth. Psychological accounts of trauma generally place an emphasis upon the psychological and existential threats that trauma poses to human well-being. Not only does the experience of trauma pose a threat to human well-being and survival; it also calls into question core positive beliefs about the world or the individual through the shattering of personal assumptions that relate to the meaning of life and the value of self.

The central Christian narrative of the crucifixion and resurrection of Christ provides what is, in effect, an exemplary narrative of posttraumatic growth, with the potential to illuminate and transform the human situation. While Christianity shares a belief in a single God with Judaism and Islam, it offers a distinctive understanding of the nature of that God that sets it apart from the other Abrahamic religions. Knowledge of God is held to be linked to (and shaped by) the crucifixion of Christ. The gospel narratives depict this act of violence and brutality against Christ as leading to distress, incomprehension, and hopelessness on the part of the disciples, accompanied by radical questioning of existing ways of thinking that are now seen to be inadequate. Yet this gradually gave way to the identification of new and better ways of understanding these events, and an appreciation of how they acted as a resource for living in a world of violence and suffering.

The crucifixion of Christ called into question existing ways of thinking concerning the way in which God acts in history and in personal experience. This questioning of existing modes of understanding subsequently led to their reconstruction and renewal, enabling believers to make more sense of things, and better cope with the paradoxes of experience. The New Testament's accounts of the resurrection of Christ depicted this event as initially engendering fear, partly because of its unexpectedness, but partly also due to the challenge that this event poses to existing mental maps of reality. The distinctive Christian capacity to cope with suffering and trauma is ultimately grounded in the historical origins of the church in a traumatic paradigmatic context. In the aftermath of the shattering of certain unrealistic expectations, a new way of thinking encouraged and enabled Christians to face the paradoxes and uncertainties of suffering with a new confidence.

Conclusion

Christianity is a complex phenomenon, not easily reduced to simple description. Yet whatever else it may be, it is unquestionably concerned with the meaningful inhabitation of our world, and offers a developed and nuanced understanding of what that meaning might be and how it plays out in real life. Perhaps the capacity of Christianity to create a system of meaning is more easily appreciated through reading the autobiographies of reflective Christians than more academic works of Christian theology. C. S. Lewis's *Surprised by Joy*, Augustine's *Confessions*, and Paul Kalanithi's *When Breath Becomes Air* all explore how real individual lives are changed through the discovery of meaning. Each of these writers *embodies* a distinctively Christian understanding of meaning, allowing it to be seen as a way of living authentically, rather than as an impersonal set of principles or ideas.

Suggested Readings

Kalanithi, Paul. *When Breath Becomes Air*. New York: Random House, 2016. A very popular and influential account of the discovery of meaning in suffering, written by a neurosurgeon who was diagnosed with lung cancer. The narrative, published after the author's death, explores the failure of more technocratic approaches to meaning, and the specific ways in which he found the Christian narrative to generate and sustain meaning in the face of suffering.

Lewis, C. S. *Mere Christianity*. New York: HarperCollins, 2002. A classic rendering of the Christian view of life, with a particularly influential account of how the Christian narrative discloses the meaning of human experience.

McGrath, Joanna Collicutt. "Post-traumatic Growth and the Origins of Early Christianity." *Mental Health, Religion & Culture* 9, no. 3 (June 2006): 291–306. A thoroughly researched study of the importance of a narrative of suffering and death for the creation of meaning and significance for early Christians, bringing out both the importance of this general psychological question, and the specific role of the crucifixion of Jesus Christ as an interpretative tool for suffering.

Seachris, Joshua. "The Meaning of Life as Narrative: A New Proposal for Interpreting Philosophy's 'Primary' Question." *Philo* 12 (2009): 5–23. A stimulating exploration of the importance of narrative as a means of interpreting human existence, with reflection on the ways in which a narrative can render the universe and our lives within it intelligible.

Notes

1 Jeanette Winterson, *Why Be Happy When You Could Be Normal?* (New York: Grove Press, 2012), 68.
2 Salman Rushdie, "Is Nothing Sacred?", The Herbert Read Memorial Lecture, February 6, 1990, read by Harold Pinter, published in *Granta* 31 (spring 1990): 8–9.

3 C. S. Lewis, *Essay Collection: Faith, Christianity and the Church* (New York: HarperCollins, 2002), 21.

4 H. Richard Niebuhr, "The Story of Our Life," in *The Meaning of Revelation* (Louisville, KY: Westminster John Knox Press, 2006), 23–46.

5 St. Augustine, *Confessions*, trans. Henry Chadwick (New York: Oxford University Press, 2008), 3.

6 Steven Weinberg, *The First Three Minutes: A Modern View of the Origin of the Universe* (New York: Basic Books 1977), 154.

7 John Dewey, *The Quest for Certainty* (New York: Putnam, 1960), 255.

8 Raymond Carver, "Late Fragment," in *All of Us: The Collected Poems* (New York: Vintage, 2000), 294.

9 "The Elixir," in *The Works of George Herbert*, ed. F. E. Hutchinson (Oxford: Clarendon Press, 1941), 184.

CHAPTER TEN

Progressive Islam

Adis Duderija

In my early to mid-twenties and during my (short) career as a primary school teacher at a faith-based Islamic school in Australia, my initial curiosity in becoming better acquainted with my faith tradition forcefully grew into a fervent desire to become an Islamic studies academic. This sea change was primarily a result of my exposure to what here is termed "Progressive Islam" or "Progressive Muslim" thought.

As I increasingly fell in love with Progressive Muslim thought and the way of life informing it, it became apparent to me that I wanted to dedicate the rest of my life to realizing and attempting to be faithful to the ideals, objectives, and values of a Progressive Muslim worldview. This path, in practical terms, meant a life of prolonged financial insecurity for me and, eventually, my young family. I, perhaps selfishly, never looked back.

Some fifteen years down the road, the writing of this essay forced me to seriously ponder the question of what exactly drew me so strongly to a Progressive Muslim worldview. To answer it, however, I need to explain what I mean by it first.

One of the most powerful and influential books that made a lasting impression and acted as a major source of inspiration for me was a book titled *Progressive Muslims: On Justice, Gender, and Pluralism*, edited by Omid Safi and published in 2003. The book brought together fourteen leading Progressive Muslim scholars whose ideas about Islam not only captured my intellectual attention and imagination but also fully resonated with my personal ethico-moral compass and philosophical worldview. Written in the aftermath of the tragic events of 9/11, it presented an approach to Islam and its intellectual tradition that appealed to me on so many levels. As the subtitle of the book suggests—and as beautifully propounded by the contributors to the volume—Islam is discussed in terms of ethical beauty; rejection of religious fanaticism and extremism; prophetic solidarity with the oppressed; a Sufi-like philosophy based on a deep and abiding love of and longing for God; a strong commitment to social and gender justice—both theoretically and at a real-world level; opposition to the impoverishment of the human condition through his reduction to a *homo economicus*; and affirmation of religious pluralism. I thought to myself at the time that it was a breath of fresh air compared to mainstream discussions of Islam, especially in the hostile climate triggered by the launch of the so-called war on terror by the Bush administration.

The book set me on a kind of intellectual proselytizing mission. My PhD thesis on Progressive Islam was published in 2011, and I've since published a book on the imperatives of Progressive Islam, too. Just as important, a Progressive Muslim worldview also heavily informed (and still informs) my personal life choices and relationships—as a husband, father, son, colleague, neighbor, and citizen (of the world).

In what follows I will delineate features of Progressive Muslim thought and how they can translate to the life philosophy that I (try to) adhere to.

One feature of the Progressive Muslim worldview is what I term its epistemological openness and methodological fluidity. This, in essence, means that Progressive Muslim thought embraces a critically cosmopolitan outlook and welcomes and integrates ideas and values from outside its worldview. The proponents of Progressive Islam are engaged in ongoing dialogues with the progressive agendas of other cultures, religions, and civilizations. "Islamic liberation theology" openly "admits" its intellectual indebtedness to Catholic liberation theology as it emerged in South America in the twentieth century, and I do not see this as a reason why it should be considered any less Islamic for being so.

Furthermore, the Progressive Muslim worldview is characterized by its inclusive universalist impulse, contradicting claims that knowledge and values are exclusive products of certain cultures or civilizations. Progressive Muslim thought opposes binary thinking processes that ascribe concepts such as modernity and secularism to the West and fundamentalism and theocracies to Islamdom. When framed in terms of a philosophy of life, a practitioner of Progressive Islam is comfortable in accepting "foreign" values and ideas as long as they are consistent with a Progressive Muslim worldview and its overarching values and objectives. Put differently, a Progressive Muslim is not only open to the practical wisdom and cumulative experiences of humanity at any point in time, but can recognize and claim them as her own, justify them intellectually, and authentically integrate them into her worldview.

Epistemological openness and the cosmopolitan nature of Progressive Islam is further strengthened by its objectivist theology and ethics. Progressive Islam promotes the idea that all human beings are endowed with a God-given human dignity and the same degree of moral agency, regardless of differences in backgrounds, beliefs, or doctrines. All people are considered morally equal. The primary existential purpose of every individual is anchored in an ethics of responsibility and care for the entire well-being of all God's creation and for facilitating its flourishing. In the words of Omid Safi:

> At the heart of a progressive Muslim interpretation is a simple yet radical idea: every human life, female and male, Muslim and non-Muslim, rich or poor, "Northern" or "Southern," has exactly the same intrinsic worth. The essential value of human life is God-given, and is in no way connected to culture, geography, or privilege. A progressive Muslim is one who is committed to the strangely controversial idea that the worth of a human being is measured by a person's character, not the oil under their soil, and not their flag. A progressive Muslim agenda is concerned with the ramifications of the premise that all members of humanity have this same intrinsic worth because, as the Qur'an reminds us, each of us has the breath of God breathed into our being.[1]

Another element of a Progressive Muslim worldview is its subscription to a Sufi-like moral philosophy in which the Divine is most readily reflected in interhuman relationships that recognize the Divine spark in everyone. In Sufism, the Prophet Muhammad is the most faithful, practical embodiment of this Divine spark and is the model of the perfect moral being (*insan kamil*), to be emulated by believers in their everyday life practices and ethics. In many ways, a Progressive Muslim worldview represents a modern intellectualization of Sufism divorced from Islam's androcentric, highly rigid, and hierarchical structure.

Furthermore, Progressive Muslim theology is anthropocentric in nature, meaning that humanity, rather than God, takes center stage. This, in turn, translates into the idea of a God who is not fully graspable to us either through our intellect, mind, reason, or "the heart." The focus and foundation of Progressive Islam is the complex world of the human condition with its incredible diversity, including religious diversity. This makes it very difficult to think in binary terms, such as salvation and damnation. In addition, it is more open to, and accommodating of, the idea of religious pluralism. By suggesting that no religious tradition is capable of objectively and fully capturing the Divine, none can therefore claim a monopoly over God. And because God cannot be fully graspable, Progressive Muslim theology affirms the inevitability of pluralism, both in terms of religion and religious experience. This approach encourages people to be open to others, to resist dogmatism, and to be accepting of a wide range of interpretations about what "living a good life" means.

The sacred scriptures cannot offer us an unequivocal, clearly accessible, and once-and-for-all valid understanding of God through the simple process of reading and interpretation. Instead, the human interpreter—with her subjectivities and contingencies—is the most significant determinant of this continually evolving, dynamic process of interpretation mediated by reason. There is, in other words, an organic and dialectical relationship between revelation (i.e., texts) and reality (i.e., contexts). Furthermore, this theology gives precedence to reason-based ethics over religious law. Law must be in constant service of ethics and ought to change along with evolving ideas about ethics as developed by humanity (in contrast to divine command theory, which considers ethics to be laid down by God and which humans have to just blindly follow). Muslims believe that there are no more "revelations" in the form of Scriptures from God after

Muhammad. So, in the postrevelatory period, religious evolution is driven exclusively by reason and intellect (as opposed to scripture-based reasoning). Unlike traditional Islam and other nonprogressive religions, this theology not only embraces, but even thrives on pluralism, diversity—and what's fundamental to all of it—uncertainty in the face of an ungraspable God.

Gender justice, as part of a larger Progressive Muslim commitment to social justice, also strongly characterizes this philosophy of life. Safi describes this facet of the Progressive Muslim worldview beautifully:

> Gender justice is crucial, indispensable, and essential. In the long run, any progressive Muslim interpretation will be judged by the amount of change in gender equality it is able to produce in small and large communities. . . . Gender equality is a measuring stick of the broader concerns for social justice and pluralism.[2]

Progressive Muslims stand against the patriarchal and misogynistic elements of the inherited Islamic tradition, including resisting male guardianship over women—known as *qiwama* and *wilaya*—practiced in places such as Saudi Arabia and Iran; advocating for women's reproductive and health rights; as well as promoting women's religious leadership and authority through feminist approaches to knowledge building.

The activist element of what it means to be a Progressive Muslim is equally essential to the worldview behind Progressive Islam. Again, in the words of Safi:

> Progressive Muslims are concerned not simply with laying out a fantastic, beatific vision of social justice and peace, but also with transforming hearts and societies

alike. A progressive commitment implies by necessity the willingness to remain engaged with the issues of social justice as they unfold on the ground level, in the lived realities of Muslim and non-Muslim communities. Vision and activism are both necessary. Activism without vision is doomed from the start. Vision without activism quickly becomes irrelevant.[3]

The above discussion brings us to the poorly understood concept of *jihad*, especially in the West: the much-debated and frequently misunderstood concept of *jihad*, meaning "struggle." In Progressive Muslim thought, *jihad* is closely linked to the concept of *ijtihad*, meaning "creative interpretation." Indeed, an essential component of Progressive Muslim thought, according to Safi, is the *jihad* to exorcize our inner demons, and bring justice in the world at large, by engaging in a progressive and critical interpretation of Islam (*ijtihad*). Progressive Muslims wish to shift the current discourses on *jihad* from being primarily embedded in discussions pertaining to geopolitics, security, and terrorism to that of inner intellectual, ethical, and primarily nonviolent struggle, as well as resistance to forces that conflict with their overall Weltanschauung (worldview). In this respect, Progressive Muslims seek to follow in the footsteps of advocates of nonviolent resistance such as Martin Luther King Jr. and Mahatma Gandhi.

A Progressive Islamic worldview also strongly resists neoliberal market economics, which advance the interests of the global military-industrial complex, because they are responsible for creating great disparities between the Global North (with its lingering colonial and imperialist past) and the Global South. They also inform the forces that reduce a human being to primarily a consumer, a *homo economicus*. In this sense, the Progressive Muslim worldview has strong affinities with socialist and postcolonial critiques of neoliberalism and the global structures that sustain and enable it.

The above paints a broad picture of the main foundations of Progressive Muslim thought and the values, ideas, and objectives that characterize its worldview. Next, I briefly engage the question, why "progressive" in Progressive Muslim thought?

Reason one: The Qur'an and Sunna were fountainheads of Islamic teachings and were way ahead of their time in approaching contemporary ethical and legal issues. They were progressive in embracing a more ethical vision beyond what was considered status quo and customary. For example, not only was women's spiritual agency and equality with men recognized scripturally, but regressive practices such as female infanticide and the maltreatment and abuse of the most weak and vulnerable members of society—especially female orphans and the downtrodden—were strongly condemned, too. By extrapolating moral trajectories from these scriptural precedents, the proponents of Progressive Islam seek to construct new moral horizons that stay true to the original, scripture-based moral impetus but that also go beyond the letter of the texts.

Reason two: To emphasize the fact that ethical values like justice and fairness do not remain frozen in time. They, as collective human experience testifies, are subject to change, as God's creative powers have a direct bearing on our collective reason and our collective ethico-moral compass. These are manifested in living more ethical (and therefore more godly) lives and forming societies based on ethical beauty, justice, mercy, and compassion. Our aim is ever more faithfully to approximate the Divine as a source of absolute Beauty, Justice, and Mercy. This is only possible if our ethical systems do not remain frozen—as in the case of traditionalist and premodern approaches. Progressive Islamic theory does exactly that by being open and ever constructively responsive to the changing shifts in human consciousness and conceptualizations of justice and equality.

Reason three: To highlight the strong affinities in the kinds of theologies, interpretational approaches, and sociopolitical and ethical values that exist among progressive religious and spiritual movements worldwide, whose pillars affirm religious pluralism and a strong commitment to social and gender justice. A very good example of this would be the Network of Spiritual Progressives (NSP) and the philosophy that informs it. On its website, the NSP describes its philosophical vision:

> Our well-being depends on the well-being of everyone else on the planet and the well-being of the Earth. We seek a world in which all of life is shaped by peace, justice, environmental stewardship, love, care for one another, care for the earth, generosity, compassion, respect for diversity and differences, and celebration of the miraculous universe in which we live.

Then the NSP's vision of a "caring world" is described as a philosophy:

- Based on love, kindness, care, generosity, compassion, empathy, peace, nonviolence, environmental sustainability, and social, economic and environmental justice;
- Where we revere, honor and respect each other and the planet;
- Founded on a New Bottom Line—where institutions, corporations, social practices, government policies, our educational system, our legal system, and our medical system are judged efficient, rational and productive

to the extent that they maximize love, caring, kindness, generosity, justice, peace, ethical and ecologically sensitive behavior and enhance both our capacity to respond to others as embodiments of the sacred and our capacity to respond to the universe with awe, wonder, and radical amazement at the grandeur and mystery of all being.

Progressive Muslim thought and its worldview resonate with this philosophy. In practical terms this means living a kind of life that places a strong emphasis on promoting and embodying values such as personal integrity and responsibility; environmental sustainability; and a loving, generous, and compassion-oriented legal, political, social, and economic system. It does not support systems in which maximizing monetary profits is the overriding value and rationale.

Reason four: The concept of Progressive Islam exists for the same reason we have Sufi Islam, Sunni Islam, and Shi'i Islam. It's about affirming the fact that Progressive Islam has its own methodology of interpretation, its own theological orientation, and its own approach to conceptualizing the Islamic intellectual tradition.

Progressive Islam is sometimes labeled, especially by its critics, as secular or Western. However, as noted above, Progressive Muslim thought rejects binary conceptual categories such as secular or nonsecular and Western or Eastern. Progressive Muslims are critical of various secular ideas arising from the Age of Enlightenment that inform classical modernity, such as the existence of an objective reason/rationality and objective truth that operate outside history. Instead, they advocate that the quest for truth is sought in a dynamic relationship among revelation, reason, and the sociohistorical context in which all are embedded. According to this worldview, there is a harmonious relationship between rationality and belief, divine obligation and human rights, social and individual justice, religious morality and collective reason, and the human mind and divine revelation. So, the short answer to the question of whether Progressive Islam is secular or Western is not, for the reasons outlined previously.

Earlier I posed the question of why I find Progressive Muslim thought and its worldview so attractive. The answer is because of the kinds of ideas, concepts, values, and objectives that Progressive Islam embodies and promotes. More specifically, I love Progressive Islam's intellectual openness, its cosmopolitan character, its ethical vision, its strong focus on social and gender justice, its sensitivity to context, and its grassroots-activism-oriented theory and theology. Being a Progressive Muslim allows me to feel at home both as a global citizen who wants to contribute to the betterment of humanity and all creation, as well as someone who has strong roots in a specific intellectual and religio-cultural tradition.

Being a Progressive Muslim cannot be reduced to a specific approach to Islamic texts, politics, ethics, theology, and law, but it retains a sense of belonging to the cultural, ethical, and global Muslim religious community. In Arabic, this is called the *ummah*, and it manifests through partaking in the central spiritual and communal aspects of being a Muslim, such as prayer, fasting, and charity, even if less rigidly or in a different form. Although often critical of the mainstream approaches to many aspects of the inherited and dominant Islamic tradition, Progressive Islam deeply values this sense of belonging and, as such, traditional Islam profoundly informs the Progressive Islam worldview.

However, a specifically *Progressive* Muslim worldview provides me with more: an ethico-moral compass and grounding that I can use in my capacity as a world citizen, a Muslim, a husband, a father, and a human being enmeshed in a complex web of relationships, power structures, inequalities, and injustices, to which I can respond in an ethically sound, constructive, and meaningful manner.

Finally, a Progressive Muslim worldview provides me with intellectual and ethical tools that enable me to confidently and humanely engage with the big questions surrounding the meaning and purpose of life. In my view, Progressive Islam provides me with a philosophy of life that is meaningful, relevant, ethically beautiful, and intellectually satisfying. What more could I ask for?

Suggested Readings

Abou El Fadl, Khaled. *Reasoning with God: Reclaiming Shari'ah in the Modern Age*. Lanham, MD: Rowman & Littlefield, 2014. Provides a sustained set of arguments that underpin the aspect of Progressive Islam theory that views Shari'ah as an intellectually rigorous and ethically beautiful construct that is open to new systems of thought and sources of knowledge.

Akhtar, Shabbir. *Islam as Political Religion: The Future of an Imperial Faith*. New York: Routledge, 2011. One of the most important books on the idea of Islamic liberation theology and why Islam is a "political" religion.

al-Jabri, Mohammed Abed. *Democracy, Human Rights and Law in Islamic Thought*. London: I. B. Tauris, 2009. Offers a compelling case for reconciling, at a conceptual level, the contemporary ethical sensibilities informing the human rights discourse with that of Islamic ethics and law.

Duderija, Adis. *Constructing Religiously Ideal "Believer" and "Woman" in Islam: Neo-traditional Salafi and Progressive Mus-*

lims' Methods of Interpretation. Edited by Khaled Abou El Fadl. Palgrave Series in Islamic Theology, Law, and History. New York: Palgrave, 2011. Provides an in-depth discussion of how Progressive Muslims conceptualize and situate themselves and interpret the Islamic tradition (*turath*). It also deconstructs and delineates the assumptions informing Progressive Muslims' scriptural reasoning and compares them to that of the puritanical approaches.

———. "Progressive Islam and Progressive Muslim Thought." *Oxford Bibliographies*. Last modified October 27, 2016. DOI: 10.1093/OBO/9780195390155-0230. Identifies major works across many disciplines that fall under the category of Progressive Islam.

———. *The Imperatives of Progressive Islam*. New York: Routledge, 2017. An ultimate guide to the theory of Progressive Islam and its normative imperatives.

Hidayatullah, Aysha A. *Feminist Edges of the Qur'an*. New York: Oxford University Press, 2014. A comprehensive discussion of the attempts of Muslim feminist-minded scholars to interpret the Qur'an from a feminist perspective and some of the difficulties this poses at the level of scriptural reasoning.

Notes

1 Omid Safi, ed., introduction to *Progressive Muslims* (Oxford: Oneworld Publications, 2003), 3.

2 Safi, *Progressive Muslims*, 11.

3 Safi, *Progressive Muslims*, 6–7.

CHAPTER ELEVEN

Ethical Culture

Anne Klaeysen

Religion is very personal. Philosophy can be, too, of course, especially if one is passionate about ideas and lives one's life according
to philosophical precepts. But there's something about religion,
and the way it's practiced in the United States, that is emotional;
some say irrational and, potentially, dangerous. Tragic examples
abound. Some parents withhold lifesaving medical treatment
from their children for religious reasons. Too often, members of
the LGBTQ community are not only excluded from but also targeted by religious congregations—a transgender friend of mine
has been formally shunned by her Hasidic community. And it is
not unusual today to hear a politician proclaim loyalty to God and
church above the state, leaving his constituents to wonder how he
will represent them if they don't share his faith.

What I appreciate about Ethical Culture as a religion is how
reasonable it is and how it makes ethics come alive for me. No
creation myth or narrative about a God-made man and life after

death is involved; just a commonsense recognition that we are one with the natural world and what we do with our lives matters. Perhaps that is why our numbers remain so low: there's nothing especially mystical about ethics, although one could argue for its transcendence. I suspect that many people resonate with our message but are non-joiners, leading good lives without the need for intentional ethical community. I need community.

I am the product of a mixed marriage: my mother was Irish-Catholic, my father Dutch Reformed. In our rural village of Palmyra, New York (incidentally, the birthplace of Mormonism), where everyone was expected to belong to a church, this was no small matter. To keep his family together on Sunday mornings, my father converted to Catholicism, for which he was never forgiven by his parents. After all, it was a Catholic Spain that once conquered the Protestant Netherlands. Such is the power of historical memory and traditional religious affiliation.

My children are also products of a mixed marriage: I was raised Catholic and my husband Jewish. Neither of us converted. Instead, we found our way to the Brooklyn Society for Ethical Culture, where we were married and raised our two children. It was hardly a compromise, though, since we had both abandoned the religious faiths of our families. College and travel can do that sometimes: cognitive dissonance can lead to epiphany. That seems also to have been the experience of Felix Adler, who founded Ethical Culture in 1876 at the age of twenty-four. More about him later.

I was initially drawn to Ethical Culture, a nontheistic religion of ethics not unlike Buddhism, because, in the course of my research, I found nothing with which to disagree, as I had with other religions. It places deed above creed, and there is no catechism of beliefs to memorize. Emphasis is placed squarely on ethical experience. It starts with a deeply personal decision to attribute worth and dignity to every human being, distinguishing these from one's value to others, which is subjective and must be earned. We judge others and are, in turn, judged by our physical appearance, family and social connections, and the ways in which we do (or don't) make a living. Too often the question of "What can you do for me?" must be satisfactorily answered before any connection is made. What a different experience it can be to suspend judgment and simply behold the humanity in others, looking for and offering acceptance, even joining a community that seeks to make the world a kinder place for everyone.

Most important to me as a young mother was founder Felix Adler's admonition that "We should teach our children nothing which they shall ever need to unlearn; we should strive to transmit to them the best possessions, the truest thought, the noblest sentiments of the age in which we live."[1] There was much that I had to unlearn when I left home. I was a first-generation university student and traveled widely. Now that I was making a home for my children, I needed guidance. In their baby welcoming ceremonies at the Brooklyn Society, which their grandparents attended, Adler's words united us:

> The love of the parent is the warm nest for the fledgling
> spirit of the child. To be at home in this strange world
> the young being with no claim as yet on the score of
> usefulness to society or of merit of any kind, must find
> somewhere a place where it is welcomed without regard
> to usefulness or merit. And it is the love of the parents
> that makes the home, and it is his own home that makes
> the child at home in the world.[2]

It was really for my children's sakes that I joined Ethical Culture, something along the line of "It takes a village to raise a child," and I loved all the additional "grandparents" who supported our family. I attended Sunday morning platform services, taught in the Children's Sunday Assembly (aka Sunday School), and served on the board of trustees. I led parenting workshops and hosted potluck dinners. It would be years later before I chose this religion for myself and trained to become clergy.

Friend and colleague Randy Best grew up in the Ethical Society of St. Louis and told me that founder Felix Adler, who died in 1933, was treated there like an eccentric old uncle rattling around in the attic. Members scoffed at his arcane idealist philosophy with its "ethical manifold" and winced at a misogyny that relegated women to the Ladies' Auxiliary, worthy moral teachers of children but unworthy of becoming full members. Neither did he originally support women's suffrage. It wasn't until 1903 that the first woman, Anna Garlin Spencer, already a Unitarian minister, was hired as an associate leader at the New York Society for Ethical Culture. (She would later, together with another associate leader at the Chicago Ethical Society, Jane Addams, found the Women's International League for Peace and Freedom.) "Full" leaders, considered clergy, were all white men. Alas, it wasn't until 1960 that Barbara Raines was accepted into full leadership. Such is a founder's influence and the power of tradition. We women have since made up for lost time, outnumbering our male colleagues, as has happened in many professions today.

And yet there is something in Felix Adler's words that inspires me. A few years ago, I compiled some passages from his Sunday platform addresses for a guided meditation. In the introduction, I included this quotation from his *Reconstruction of the Spiritual Ideal* (1923): "The essential spiritual nature of man is not atomistic, but social. . . . In his inmost self, man is related to other selves in such fashion that he lives in them, and they in him." Adler valued what he called our "precious faculty of the imagination" to envision a society transformed by "creative energy unbound in every human breast; life that is mutual life enhancing other life."

Every meditation has a different theme—nature, water, light, and fire—based on images used by Adler. This practice, which also includes deep breathing and the relaxing of muscles, does not stay with one's individual experience; it connects every participant by imagining rays of light or streams of water carrying goodness around the circle. In other words, it's social, not atomistic. At the closing, the facilitator says,

> When you are ready, open your eyes. Slowly look around the circle. Remember the light that radiated from you reaching out to everyone else. Remember their rays coming back to you. Feel the gift that you are to yourself and to everyone in the circle. Feel the gift that they are to you. As Adler wrote, "The spiritual nature, the best in each person, does not need to be saved, it needs to be recognized."

Recognized, not saved. Other religions promise salvation and eternal life after death. See Jesus in your neighbor, Christianity tells us, and act accordingly. I choose to see my neighbor without any intermediary. Skip the middleman and get to work forging ethical relationships directly. That is what Felix Adler taught.

At monthly newcomer receptions for people exploring membership in the New York Society for Ethical Culture, I often tell a story about a young Felix who learns ethics from his parents and is sent back to Germany, where he was born in 1851, to pursue rabbinical studies so that he can eventually take the place of his father, Samuel, on the bimah of Temple Emanu-El, the first Reform Jewish congregation in New York City, founded in 1845. While abroad he witnesses chaotic political and social events, disapproves of his fellow students' licentious behavior, and writes home about his experiences like a dutiful son.

Most important for Ethical Culture was Adler's nascent study of philosophy, which he took up after being exposed to a literary criticism of Hebrew texts that contradicted the mythology of Moses receiving stone tablets from God. Like the New England transcendentalists of the nineteenth century, he was drawn to German philosopher Immanuel Kant's categorical imperative. Neo-Kantians who posited that God's existence could never be proven and that morality could be developed independent of theology caused him to reevaluate his own personal theology. This is the cognitive dissonance that I imagine he experienced, much as I did at his age when I studied world religions. We both became aware that our learned worldview was very narrow.

Adler returned home to give his first (and last) sermon, in 1873, at Temple Emanu-El, on "Judaism of the Future," a manifesto of Judaism as a secular religion for all of humanity. The trustees were impressed by his brilliance but did not offer him the position of rabbi. Instead, they endowed a nonresidency Professorship of Hebrew and Oriental Literature at Cornell University for him. His lectures there, tying ethics to contemporary issues, were popular and reported in the local press, resulting in his once again being called before a board of trustees. He was accused of atheism and relieved of his position.

And that brings us to the founding of Ethical Culture on May 15, 1876, in Standard Hall in New York City. Adler returned to the religious ideas he had introduced earlier and more fully developed them, creating a religion of ethics undivided by theology or ritual. He was fulfilling a hope that the transcendentalist essayist and poet Ralph Waldo Emerson, whom he admired and met in 1875, had expressed for "a church of ethics."

In the founding address, these words declare:

> Believe or disbelieve as ye list—we shall at all times respect every honest conviction. But be one with us where there is nothing to divide—in action. Diversity in the creed, unanimity in the deed! This is that practical religion from which none dissents. This is that platform broad enough and solid enough to receive the worshipper and the "infidel." This is that common ground where we may all grasp hands as brothers, united in mankind's common cause.

The principles of Ethical Cultural that Adler outlined that day were simple and revolutionary for his time, and are still pertinent today:

- The belief that morality is independent of theology;
- The affirmation that new moral problems have arisen in modern industrial society that have not been adequately dealt with by the world's religions;
- The duty to engage in philanthropy in the advancement of morality;
- The belief that self-reform should go hand in hand with social reform;
- The establishment of republican rather than monarchical governance of Ethical Societies; and
- The agreement that educating the young is the most important aim.

Again, as a parent, his closing words resonate with me:

We are aiding in laying the foundations of a mighty
edifice, whose completion shall not be seen in our day,
no, nor in centuries upon centuries after us. But happy
are we, indeed, if we can contribute even the least toward
so high a consummation. The time calls for action. Up,
then, and let us do our part faithfully and well. And oh,
friends, our children's children will hold our memories
dearer for the work which we begin this hour.

To have a religion of ethics means that behavior, not belief, is
most important. The theologian Paul Tillich once defined religion
as "one's ultimate concern," and so ethics is my religion. When I
was a child, I was taught that Catholicism was my religion, and
that it was the best one on earth. No one who wasn't a Catholic
would make it past the pearly gates of heaven, and that's what I
told a friend in the third grade. "You're a very nice person, Sherry,
and I like you, so I'm sorry that you won't go to heaven because
you're a Protestant." It was belief that was most important: Holy
Trinity, original sin, Immaculate Conception, etc. I could recite
the Apostles' Creed at mass every Sunday and still make a friend
cry because my religion emphasized belief. Rather than a confirmation into a belief, my children participated in a coming-of-age
program that included field trips to other faith meeting houses
and community service. I processed with my friends up to the
altar of St. Anne's Church in a white dress and veil to receive a
priest's blessing. My children stood at the lectern of the Brooklyn
Society for Ethical Culture to address its members on their ethical
growth and development.

Under Adler's leadership, the first generation of Ethical Culture members sprang into action with projects that included a
district nursing service and a hygienic tenement-house building
company. He was the founding chair of the National Child Labor

Committee, which hired, in 1904, his student Lewis Hine to document, in a series of photographs, the horrendous conditions under which children worked in fields, mines, factories, and on city streets. He also served on the Civil Liberties Bureau, which later became the American Civil Liberties Union (ACLU), and on the first executive board of the National Urban League. Other leaders and members were responsible for founding the National Association for the Advancement of Colored People (NAACP) and the Legal Aid Society, among other organizations.

Hudson Guild, a settlement house in Chelsea, was founded in 1897 by the Ethical Culture leader John Lovejoy Elliott. (His colleague, Jane Addams, had already founded Hull House in Chicago in 1889, the year that Elliott first heard Dr. Felix Adler speak, inspiring him to join Ethical Culture.) It brought together a number of clubs and programs for children, working women, and families that he had established since moving to Chelsea two years earlier and provided a platform for residents to organize to improve their neighborhood. The Guild opened the first free kindergarten in New York City in 1897, started the first Summer Play School in the city in 1917, and opened dental, prenatal, and well-baby clinics in 1919–1921. It also lobbied for the New York State Tenement House Act of 1901 and the approval of low-cost, city-funded housing in 1938.

The Guild remains active and has expanded its programs across the city. I love to visit, and every year attend the John Lovejoy Elliott Dinner honoring neighborhood activists young and old. In 2018, the board president read one of my favorite Elliott quotations:

> Just a word about neighbors. There is, of course, no such thing possible as a neighbor standing alone: it takes at least two to have any give and take. It really takes more

than two. Being a good neighbor is a great thing in our lives, something that is absolutely fundamental.

What then make up neighborliness? It is mutuality, reciprocal relations between people, and not only just from one to the other, but mutuality in all essential ways of living. That, I believe, is the deepest thing in all our lives.[3]

Perhaps most well known of Adler's projects in New York City was the Workingman's School that later became the Ethical Culture School and expanded to a campus in Riverdale called Fieldston. In 1910, a meeting house was erected on the corner of Central Park West and Sixty-Fourth Street adjacent and connected to the school. We finally had a home for our ethical community! Although the two institutions formally separated in 1995, our buildings share a heating and cooling system. When I take students on a tour of our women's homeless shelter, I tell them that we still share one beating heart.

The message of "deed above creed" that Adler heralded in 1876 is stenciled above a doorway in the lobby of our meeting house to remind us of our commitment to social justice. Also in our lobby hang a poster with the Universal Declaration of Human Rights and a photograph of Eleanor Roosevelt reading this document. One of our members, Rose Walker, a matriarch of the Brooklyn Society for Ethical Culture who lived to 104, often remarked that if Ethical Culture were to claim a sacred text, it would be this document. Time and time again we return to it for both inspiration and aspiration.

Mrs. Roosevelt was a longtime friend of the New York Society and supported the Encampment for Citizenship, founded in

1946 by the Ethical Culture leader Algernon Black to provide young adults from different religious, racial, and social backgrounds the opportunity to learn "the principles and techniques of citizenship . . . through lived experience." His notion was that if the victors of World War II claimed to have made the world safe for democracy, then a younger generation should know what true participatory democracy is. He was inspired by the Civilian Conservation Corps (CCC) and the American Friends Service Committee (AFSC) but wanted his program to reflect the real diversity of the United States and to teach young people critical-thinking skills, social activism, and leadership skills. Black and Mrs. Roosevelt were especially concerned about stereotypes, and hoped that, by living together for six weeks during the summer, "Encampers" would find the courage to break free of them.

Mrs. Roosevelt often hosted discussions, workshops, and "weenie roasts" at her Hyde Park estate. When the program was attacked by McCarthyite forces in the early 1950s, she defended it vigorously:

> The reason I think these Encampments are so important is that they are attended by citizens of different races and groups. They prepare people for thinking in terms of all people and not in terms of a selected few. Not only we in the U.S., but people all over the world, need young people trained to be good citizens with an ability to think with an open mind.[4]

The Encampment continued into the 1990s. Among its alumni are the civil rights activist and congresswoman Eleanor Holmes Norton; the cofounder of the Innocence Project, Peter Neufeld; the Manhattan borough president Gale Brewer; and the Fortune Society founder, David Rothenberg.

After a sixteen-year hiatus, the Encampment was relaunched in 2013 with a two-week pilot program in Richmond, Virginia, where the archives are housed at the James Branch Cabell Library Special Collections and Archives, Virginia Commonwealth University. Alumni can now access information and contribute their photos, letters, and journals. They financially supported a three-week program the following summer in Chicago that included the first Intergenerational Weekend, both a reunion for alumni and an opportunity for them to mentor new Encampers. No longer would participants return home without a support network; they could maintain contact with their peers and seek advice from alumni. Today we are able to provide a four-week summer experience to teens and several regional intergenerational programs across the country.

I sit on the board and co-chair meetings with the president, Ada Deer, an indigenous Encamper from 1954 who once led the Bureau of Indian Affairs. My friendship with her, and the memory of having learned about the Haudenosaunee (named Iroquois by the French for their oratory skill) growing up in the land of the Senecas in western New York State, led me to reach out to the American Indian Community House (AICH) in Lower Manhattan.

AICH, which serves 100,000 indigenous people living in New York City, is one of several partnerships the New York Society has made in recent years to fulfill our social justice mission. (Other partnerships include 350 NYC, Amnesty International, the Radical Age Movement, the League of Women Voters, and the Black Psychiatrists of Greater New York.) We host social gatherings, and their members have given presentations, including "Decolonizing NYC," at our Sunday platform services. At an American Ethical Union assembly in Albuquerque that focused on environmentalism, AICH arranged for us to engage with members of the local Laguna Pueblo and Navajo Nation, who taught us about their traditions. Our debt to those who lived on and loved this land long before our ancestors settled here is profound. We are aware of our government's genocide of their ancestors and work with them whenever and wherever we can.

Social justice kept me connected to my Catholic roots long after I abandoned its theology. I admired the Berrigan brothers, Philip and Daniel, who protested the Vietnam War; the Catholic Worker Movement founder Dorothy Day, who served the poor on the Lower East Side; and the "worker priests" of Latin America. Ethical Culture's call to action moves me to participate in coalitions, e.g., Interfaith Assembly on Homelessness and Affordable Housing, National Religious Campaign Against Torture, and New York Immigration Coalition, among others. Having marched in Washington, DC, in my youth against the war in Vietnam and for the Equal Rights Amendment, I continue to rally and march for every worthy cause, encouraging my family and members to join me. The best Mother's Day gift I ever received was a family trip to DC on May 14, 2000, for the Million Mom March, on the Mall, for commonsense gun laws.

This call to action is the logical consequence of putting deed above creed. Adler called Ethical Culture "a religion of duty." It is not enough to pay lip service to ethical ideals; one must work to realize them every day. A typical Sunday service should bring what he called "light and heat" to an ethical issue, not only illuminating what is wrong, but also passionately addressing its solution. Speakers are asked to tell us what we can do to help right the wrongs they bring to our attention, and we share half of the collection we take up each Sunday with other nonprofit organizations that share our values.

Felix Adler died on April 24, 1933, at the age of eighty-one. Legend has it that he entered a room where the Fraternity of Leaders was meeting and hesitated. Then he pulled out his pocket watch, looked at it, and said, "I think my time may be up." A few days later he died, and he was buried in a modest grave at Mount Pleasant Cemetery in Hawthorne, New York.

His book *An Ethical Philosophy of Life* (1918) outlines the development of his idealism from "The Hebrew Religion" to "The Teachings of Jesus" and his critiques of Kant and Emerson. In it he also develops his unique philosophy of worth and "The Ideal of the Whole." It is at the same time a dense philosophical treatise and an invitation to explore one's own philosophy. After all, the title has the indefinite article "An," not "The."

Ethics was Adler's religion but he expressed it in philosophical, not theological, terms. He offers what he calls "a system of thought and of points of view as to conduct, as these have jointly grown out of personal experience." The difficulty is in presenting ethics, which cannot be separated from the personal, as something objective. But he tries by positing the ideal of the whole with the concept of human worth at its core. "Why do men hold themselves and others cheap?" he asks. We are more than our usefulness; a man is "an end *per se*," possessing the quality of worth, which Adler claims belongs to "a supreme, a unique energy." Our knowledge of the world in which we live is extremely limited, but we can develop a plan by which to live. Within his ideal of the whole is an ethical manifold of unique individuals with myriad connections acting to elicit the distinctive characteristics of others. In some ways, he replaces the deity God with a transcendental ideal that holds humanity in an interconnected web and calls upon us to *recognize* one another *in* one another. That recognition and attribution of worth leads us to ethical behavior.

When I was a leader-in-training, I overheard one leader say

to another, "You have forsaken your father Felix Adler for your stepfather John Dewey." It was an indication of how Dewey's pragmatism had replaced Adler's idealism. Naturalistic humanism was in the ascendancy; in 1963, the National Leaders Council declared that Ethical Culture was rooted in humanism. This was little noticed by members who were busy arguing over whether Ethical Culture was a religion or not, the nuance of being a non-theistic religion of ethics continuing to pose a challenge. But it was an indication that a deity no longer needed to be replaced by an ideal. The study of science had fully revealed our humanity as part of, not separate from, nature. Not only had we evolved (and survived over other humanoid species) physically and intellectually; our morality also evolved, from early social interactions around the campfire, to clans and tribes and nations, to a sense of universal ethics. Having moved beyond theology, we needed to assess the ways in which philosophy could continue to inform our understanding of ethics in a world that was finally recognizing cultural differences around the globe.

While the philosophy evolved for the leaders of the movement, society members clung to Adler's "supreme ethical rule" and, I believe, rightly so. He expressed it in different ways, but the basic message is "Act so as to elicit the goodness (best, uniqueness, excellence, potential, etc.) in others, and thereby in oneself." It requires an empathy that the Golden Rule—"Do unto others as you would have them do unto you"—does not. It's dynamic and relational. I must engage with others to understand who they are and what they need. I must listen deeply, humbly, lovingly. The Golden Rule, by comparison, is egocentric and lacks imagination.

I recently held the hand of a member who knew she was dying and listened to her. She was worn out by the previous visits of family who kept asking her questions she couldn't answer, and she felt that they were harassing the hospital staff when, really, nothing more could be done for her. She understood that they all meant well and were probably anxious for her well-being, but no one listened to her. She felt disrespected and lonely. "I never thought dying would be like this," she said, "with pain and nightmares." "It's very hard," I said, and she replied, "Yes, it is." During a previous visit she had discussed her memorial with me. I took notes and reassured her that everything would be as she wished.

There have been times in my life, and I imagine in yours, as well, when a path seems to be revealed and a choice must be made. It can be subtle or strong. I've used the metaphor of the universe tossing pebbles against my window to get my attention. Sometimes it takes a boulder to come crashing through the pane. It's easy to ignore an invitation to try something new when old routines and doubts prevail. And yet there is something exciting about change, especially when it holds a promise of transformation: becoming more fully oneself.

Lay leadership training the summer of 1998, in a setting of wide natural vistas and among people whom I came to love, awakened in me a longing to grow. It was an expansive and inclusive feeling that gained clarity of thought and intention. It remained to discuss the future, as an Ethical Culture leader, with trusted family and friends.

September 11, 2001, was the first day of my internship at the New York Society. I learned what it meant to serve a community in turmoil. We grieved and raged together and tried to make sense of the world that had come crashing down around us. What responsibility did we have, and how could we make things better? "Overwhelming" doesn't begin to describe that year. First, there was the personal grief of individual lives lost: killed and literally lost in the debris, frantic calls to find loved ones in the chaos of those early days. I met with families for pastoral counseling and officiated at memorials. We held healing circles at the Society, safe places to share thoughts and feelings; open spaces to hold but not contain the grief and anger. Then there was the rampant patriotism and attacks upon Muslims that led to a war that most of our members protested.

I served other Ethical Societies as congregational leader and returned to the New York Society in 2008 to face new challenges of an aging membership. I am also Humanist Chaplain at New York University and Ethical Humanist Religious Life Adviser at Columbia University. The different demographics and needs of these communities provide much-needed balance in my professional life. While most baby boomers grew up in congregations, Millennial and Gen-Z cohorts did not and are, increasingly, as the Pew Forum on Religion and Public Life labeled them, "nones" and/or "spiritual but not religious (SBNR)." Many young people distrust faith institutions that they observe behaving hypocritically, especially in terms of social justice.

A phenomenon that I often experience on university campuses is the encounter between religious and secular students: "Oh, you're a Christian? I thought you were smart," and "Oh, you're an atheist? I thought you were a good person." These stereotypes are harmful and can be addressed with multifaith programming that includes secular and humanist groups. How well I recall the thrill of meeting students from different faiths, races, cultures when I was a student! Life in my hometown was homogenous and boring. If you didn't fit in, it was best to leave, so I did. I discovered people who were different in outward appearances but with whom I shared a curiosity and wonder about the world. There was more common ground than I had imagined, especially in terms of making that world a better place for everyone. Today on college campuses and in interfaith settings, we use a new and exciting vocabulary of identity, diversity, intersectionality, gender, and sexual orientation.

In addition to my congregational and campus responsibilities, I have the joy of officiating at life passage ceremonies. Earlier I mentioned my children's baby welcoming ceremonies at the Brooklyn Society. Welcoming a baby into the loving arms of parents and guiding parents, family, and friends is exquisite. Mentoring children for coming-of-age ceremonies always feels hopeful. And who doesn't love officiating at a wedding? Most of "my" couples have come from different faiths, cultures, and races. Some have been different genders, others the same. They all found acceptance and a warm embrace. My role is to facilitate their creative process and elicit their most authentic selves.

Strange as it may seem, I feel a special call to officiate at memorials. Survivors are vulnerable and openly share their stories. It is a time to both grieve a loss and celebrate a life. Forgiveness is important: some wounds are reopened; others are healed. I remind mourners that one service cannot hold the whole weight of their grieving; it is a communal step in a long process, and they can support one another throughout it.

Recently a member reminded me of something I had told him that inspired him to join our community. I said that I can take my whole self through the doors of our meeting house, leaving nothing behind, knowing that I will be seen for who I am and no one else. I hope that everyone feels that way. I hope that our ethical community can be a spiritual home, not in a supernatural sense, but in the meaningful connections we make with one another that both honor and transcend our individuality.

My faith is in the human potential for goodness. This faith is sorely tested, because I am by nature (and confirmed by the

Myers-Briggs Type Indicator) highly judgmental. Choosing to attribute worth and dignity to *every* individual is an ethical discipline that I practice in a community because I need others to honestly reflect back to me the effects of my behavior. I know my intent; they know the impact. Together we build a learning circle of trust that can encompass all of humanity. The challenges are great, but so are the rewards.

It may not be obvious to someone who joins us for a Sunday service or attends a workshop. We offer many programs that are not explicitly "ethical" in nature, but they are all opportunities to explore some aspect of our humanity, whether in a talk, concert, movie, play, or shared meal. And we are not limited to a particular belief or scripture. We find inspiration everywhere. At this year's intergenerational winter festival, I closed the program with a quotation from the Italian theoretical physicist Carlo Rovelli:

> Nature is our home, and in nature we are *at* home.
>
> This strange, multicolored, and astonishing world that we explore—where space is granular, time does not exist, and things are nowhere—is not something that estranges us from our true selves, for this is only what our natural curiosity reveals to us about the place of our dwelling. About the stuff of which we ourselves are made. We are made of the same stardust of which all things are made, and when we are immersed in suffering or when we are experiencing intense joy, we are being nothing other than what we can't help but be: a part of our world.[5]

And this realization, this understanding of what it means to be human, calls us to reach out to one another; not to make use of one another, but to recognize our worth and celebrate it. Idealistic? Definitely. It's also pragmatic and humanistic. And it takes time and patience. We can learn how to be better, not perfect, but it takes an intellectual and moral humility that is often not valued. We depend upon one another, not a supernatural deity in a transcendent realm, to make our world a better place for everyone.

Suggested Readings

Adler, Felix. *An Ethical Philosophy of Life: Presented in its Main Outlines*. New York: D. Appleton, 1918. This is a philosophical autobiography published over forty years after the author founded Ethical Culture. He traces his thoughts and influences. Although it is a rather dense tome, I read it as an invitation to develop my own personal philosophy. I found the chapter on "The Meaning of Forgiveness" helpful in my pastoral counseling training.

————. *The Reconstruction of the Spiritual Ideal: Hibbert Lectures*, delivered in Manchester College, Oxford, May 1923. New York: D. Appleton, 1924. This book starts with the sentence, "Out of the depths into which it has fallen humanity cries today for help." The author was devastated by the horrors of the First World War and felt that a spiritual ideal needed to be reconstructed in its aftermath. I resonate with the three "spiritual pains" that he identifies: a sense of human insignificance in the vast universe, an overwhelming and unquenchable need that many people experience, and "the need of relief from the intolerable strain of the divided conscience."

American Ethical Union (https://aeu.org/). This website is an excellent resource for members and newcomers alike, with links to existing Ethical Societies and information about starting new ones. In addition to current events information, it contains archives with history and social justice resolutions.

American Humanist Association (https://americanhumanist
.org/). For both secular and religious humanists, this website provides up-to-date information on local chapters, *The
Humanist* magazine and blog, training to become a humanist
officiant, and links to affiliates. Be sure to check out their
Center for Education (formerly the Humanist Institute),
which offers both online courses and in-person seminars
(http://cohe.humanistinstitute.org/).

Black, Algernon D. *Without Burnt Offerings: Ceremonies of Humanism.* New York: The Viking Press, 1974. Through anecdotes
and examples, the author relates his approach to conducting
ceremonies that emphasize human relationships. He invites
the reader to discard or reimagine ritual so that it serves the
needs of the individuals marking an important life passage.

Epstein, Greg M. *Good without God: What a Billion Nonreligious
People Do Believe.* New York: William Morrow, 2009. My
chaplain colleague (Harvard and MIT) has written a book
that brings humanism into the twenty-first century and provides resources to a new generation. Several New York Society
members found their way to us by reading this book.

Ericson, Edward L. *The Humanist Way: An Introduction to Ethical
Humanist Religion.* New York: The Continuum Publishing
Company, 1998. This book traces the roots of Ethical Culture in the broader humanist history, philosophy, and congregational movement. Of particular interest to me is his
clarification between "secular" and "religious" humanism, a
distinction that didn't exist until a footnote in a US Supreme
Court case.

Klaeysen, Anne. "A Different Kind of Immortality." *The Humanist
Prospect: A Neohumanist Perspective* 5, no. 1 (Autumn 2015):
2–26; and video of speech at Dying Without Deity: Perspectives on Death and Dying Symposium, The Institute for Sci-

ence and Human Values, April 10 and 11, 2015, at https://www.youtube.com/watch?v=TLxrkKTChGU. I participated in a symposium on death and dying by giving a speech and writing a journal article. These contain my approach to the subject and how I pastor family members.

———. "Humanism and the Expression of Love." In *Everyday Humanism*, edited by Dale McGowan and Anthony B. Pinn, 85–99. Bristol, CT: Equinox Publishing, 2014. This chapter gives attention to the manner in which humanism informs and influences the nature and meaning of human connection. In particular, it addresses life passage ceremonies.

New York Society for Ethical Culture (http://ethical.nyc/). This is the local website for my congregation. It contains an events calendar, videos, newsletters, and information on programs.

Radest, Howard B. *Toward Common Ground: The Story of the Ethical Societies in the United States*. Garden City, NY: Fieldston Press, Inc., 1987. This tome is for anyone interested in the early days of Ethical Culture and how it spread to other cities and countries. It includes historical details, concepts, and biographies.

Solomon, Robert C. *Spirituality for the Skeptic: The Thoughtful Love of Life*. New York: Oxford University Press, 2002. Since Ethical Culture employs philosophy rather than theology, I have found this book especially helpful in bridging the gap between theists and humanists, and assigned it in a course I taught on humanism at Union Theological Seminary.

Notes

1 Felix Adler, *Life and Destiny* (New York: American Ethical Union, 1944), 69.

218 · *Anne Klaeysen*

2 ———, *An Ethical Philosophy of Life* (New York:
D. Appleton, 1918), 252.

3 John L. Elliott, *Unconquerable Spirit* (New York: The Society
for Ethical Culture, 1942), 13.

4 "Who We Are," The Encampment for Citizenship, accessed
June 5, 2019, http://encampmentforcitizenship.org/who
-we-are/history.php.

5 Carlo Rovelli, *Seven Brief Lessons on Physics* (New York:
Riverhead Books, 2016), 79.

Modern Philosophies

Existentialism, Pragmatism, Effective Altruism, and Secular Humanism

The modern philosophies in this section—existentialism, pragmatism, effective altruism, and secular humanism—are just a few of the many that lend themselves to real-world application and concrete living.

In the late 1800s, Friedrich Nietzsche, a forefather of existentialism, famously declared that "God is dead." If God does not provide an answer as to why we are here or what we should do about it, we are left with a vacuum of values and meaning in the world. Nietzsche was not an advocate of nihilism. Rather, he warned about the effects of it, primarily decadence and hedonism in a moral void. While most of the existential thinkers acknowledged that the world is a nihilistic desert—which is why they thought existential dread was a perfectly understandable and natural state of being—they ultimately sought to overcome it. If there is no ready-made meaning, it is up to us to find our own and infuse our world with it.

As Skye C. Cleary notes, there are many different ideas about existentialism, and they all take different approaches to finding meaning in life. This makes it hard to pin down any specific rules or doctrines for existentialism; however, figuring it out for ourselves is an integral part of the existential project. Thus, existentialism tends to be more descriptive than prescriptive, and although Cleary is not officially an existentialist (few people would label themselves that way), she describes how some existential ideas have informed and influenced her life—particularly the search for authentically meaningful relationships.

John Kaag and Douglas Anderson do not consider themselves card-carrying pragmatists either, but they have both learned much from the American pragmatists—particularly from William James (1842–1910) and Charles Peirce (1839–1914)—especially about how to live despite the occasional desire not to. James and Peirce both went through suicidal struggles and existential crises upon reflecting on the futility and meaninglessness of existence. Kaag and Anderson write that Peirce was in despair about being "absolutely alone in the cosmos," and James worried that "individuals are always snuffed out before they can make a genuine or lasting mark."

The horrifying thought that science reduces us to biologically determined creatures with no control over our lives put James off the sciences and attracted him to philosophies of free will. Peirce's solution for the improvement of the world was to transcend our self-interest and greed toward love, care, and community—even if we do not end up making much of a difference. Constantly in a struggle between rugged individualism and community, these two pragmatists, knowing that their suicide would adversely affect others, thereby making its consequences ethically problematic, chose constantly to reaffirm the "live option," knowing that the alternative might be a valid one as well.

A relatively new social movement that places a special emphasis on the consequences of our actions is effective altruism, which encourages people to use whatever resources they have to do the most good they can. Effective altruism has deep roots in utilitarianism, such as the philosophy of Jeremy Bentham, who proposed an ethical system whereby a morally good action is one that produces the most good for the greatest number of people. In the twenty-first century, philosophers and writers such as Peter Singer, William MacAskill, and Kelsey Piper are popularizing effective altruism as a philosophy to be lived.

Many effective altruists donate money to charities, some spend their time working in realms where they can make the biggest impact, and others join communities and live in ways that minimize harm and cost. In her chapter on effective altruism, chapter 14, Piper explains how she does all three: she is a journalist who writes about poverty, emerging technologies, and factory farming; she lives with other effective altruists to save money; and she donates as much as she can to charities that she sees doing high-impact work. It sounds simple, but it quickly becomes complicated when we start to think about how you can do the most good: Which career? Which causes? And which charities? Piper points out that it is hard, but effective altruism provides a framework to reflect on these questions and to be more attuned to opportunities that can make the world a better place.

Secular humanism incorporates many elements of different philosophies of life that we have already encountered. Secular humanistic ideas—promoting the sciences, empirical validation of truth, observable knowledge, and human-centered ethics, while rejecting the supernatural and spiritual—are ancient. For example, around 600 BCE, members of the school of Indian materialism, or Lokāyata, were considered radical and heretical because of their skepticism about spiritualism, supernaturalism, and moralism, and their support for the sciences. The Iranian prophet Zoroaster (ca. 628–551 BCE), the Daoist Lao-Tzu (sixth or fourth century BCE), Epicurus (ca. 300 BCE), and Cicero (106–43 BCE) wrote about secular or humanistic themes, too. John Shook points out that secular humanism also incorporates some of the thinking of Socrates, Aristotle, and the Stoics, as well as elements of liberalism, utilitarianism, existentialism, naturalism, and pragmatism. Some of the more extreme secular humanists have even adopted nihilistic views. This is unusual, but it shows how accommodating secular humanism can be.

Given that secular humanism draws from so many sources, it might not be surprising that, as John Shook proposes, many people are probably secular humanists—or at least support the ideas of secular humanism—without knowing it. Key candidates for this category are people who are often referred to as "nones" because on surveys that ask "What religion are you?" they answer "None of the above." Around 16 percent of the world's population classify themselves as "unaffiliated."[1] That's more than 1.1 billion people. Not all of these will be secular humanists, but many of them will support similar values, such as equal rights, social and legal justice, political activism, separation of church and state, the right to be free from religion, and the value of rationality and science. Paul Kurtz (1925–2012), the founder of the Council for Secular Humanism, wrote that secular humanism includes "perhaps everyone who believes in the principles of free inquiry, ethics based upon reason, and a commitment to science, democracy, and freedom. Perhaps even you." Perhaps.

Note

1 Michael Lipka and David McClendon, "Why people with no religion are projected to decline as a share of the world's population," Fact Tank, Pew Research Center, April 7, 2017, http://www.pewresearch.org/fact-tank/2017/04/07/why-people-with-no-religion-are-projected-to-decline-as-a-share-of-the-worlds-population/.

CHAPTER TWELVE

Existentialism

Skye C. Cleary

In his famous lecture "Existentialism Is a Humanism," Jean-Paul Sartre (1905–1980) recounted the story of a woman who, when she swore, excused herself by saying, "I think I'm becoming an existentialist."[1] Existential philosophers do have a reputation for being scandalous and breaking social norms. Sartre and Simone de Beauvoir (1908–1986) were as famous for their philosophies as for their excesses of drinking, smoking, drug-taking, and affairs. If we take "the good life" to mean living fully, then the existentialists have plenty to say about that, and they speak from experience.

Some would argue that how philosophers live ought to be kept separate from their philosophy. Yet, the existential philosophers did not believe that. Friedrich Nietzsche (1844–1900), an intellectual grandfather of existentialism, proposed that all philosophy is autobiography. Indeed, existential philosophers such as de Beauvoir and Sartre explicitly set out to create a philosophy that could be lived and wrote copiously about their successes, failures, and challenges—not only in their scholarly works, but also in letters, autobiographies, plays, and novels.

Picture this: it's 1942 at the Parisian hotspot Bec de Gaz on rue Montparnasse when three friends—de Beauvoir, along with her short, ugly yet popular-with-the-ladies boyfriend Sartre, and the much-less-famous Raymond Aron—were chatting in between drags on their cigarettes about how their philosophical education had no practical value for everyday life. Like their fresh-out-of-college friends, they were bored with the Enlightenment's obsession with objectivity, detachment, abstract reasoning, logic, rationality, convention, restrictions, sensibility, and prudence, and the theories their teachers yammered on about while the real world was descending into World War II. As they drank apricot cocktails, they discussed how they longed for a philosophy that could really be lived—and thus the seed of existential philosophy was planted. Existentialism became popular because it provided a way of thinking that was conducive to dealing with great human suffering, the absurdity of existence, and the importance of individual freedom.

Georg Wilhelm Friedrich Hegel (1770–1831) was one philosopher that de Beauvoir and Sartre learned about at university. They thought that the problem with Hegel was that while he talks a lot about absolute ideals and what the underlying order to the universe might be, he doesn't say anything about how we should actually live, nor does he give us a reason to get out of bed in the morning. De Beauvoir and Sartre's generation was more interested in cocktails and coffee, jazz bars and walking in forests, emotions and black turtlenecks, freedom and creativity, and irrational things like passion.

Existentialism starts with the fact that we did not get a say in being born, but that is too bad, because once we are conscious, we must woman up. Every action is a choice, and there is no escaping that fact. Or, as Sartre put it, we're "condemned to be free."[2] This is a consequence of the maxim that "existence precedes essence,"[3] which means that we are thrown into the world first and then we are free to create ourselves through our actions. But there are some catches. One, our essence is forever elusive. It is never fixed in stone until we are physically fixed six feet under a stone. Death, Sartre says, is the moment in which we become complete. Two, with freedom comes the heavy burden of responsibility. Contra Dostoyevsky, if God is dead, anything does *not* go. We coexist with others, and so they must factor into our decisions. This realization of our freedom can also be terrifying because accountability for our choices lies squarely on our own shoulders. But not to worry, the existentialists also propose that anxiety is a fact of life, and the carrot at the end of the anxiety stick is authenticity. Authenticity is about creating ourselves by striving toward self-chosen goals. It is taking charge of our lives by actively choosing what we think is genuine and right. And three, there are plenty of facts of our existence that we can't change, such as our parents and the situations into which we are born. But what's important is how we strive creatively to surpass the given and how we free ourselves and one another from oppression, so that we can all be free to pursue authentically meaningful lives.

Existentialism tends to have a bad reputation—not only for swearing, but also for being an individualistic philosophy. Certainly, existential philosophers do look at the world through a predominantly subjective lens, but they also point out that it is only meaningful to talk about oneself in relationship with others. Sartre says that we would not know ourselves without other people: "Fundamentally, others are what is most important in us for our understanding of ourselves,"[4] and this makes existentialism very much a philosophy of relationships, which is what drew me to it in the first place.

228 • *Skye C. Cleary*

———

Corey Mohler, the author of the popular *Existential Comics*, tweeted the following guidelines for how to be an existentialist:[5]

1. Be super existential all the time.
2. Refuse to label yourself as an existentialist.
3. Lots of smoking.

It is funny because it is true that many existential philosophers smoked a lot—especially Sartre, de Beauvoir, and their frenemy Albert Camus. It is also funny because it is true that the existential philosophers did not want to call themselves "Existentialists." Gabriel Marcel, who is credited with coining the term in 1945, later rejected it. De Beauvoir and Sartre grudgingly accepted it, since everyone was calling them that anyway. Nevertheless, de Beauvoir and Sartre did spend a lot of time trying to "be super existential," or rather, live consistently with their existential ideas. "Being super existential" is not an actual achievable goal, because our existence is not static. Their emphasis was on becoming (authentic), which is a way of engaging in the world. Existentialism is something you *do*, not something you *are*.

The problem with calling oneself an Existentialist with a capital *E* is that it runs counter to everything that existentialism stands for. This is because, to paraphrase Monty Python's *Life of Brian*, we've got to work it out for ourselves. Signing up for a set of rules that someone else created is "bad faith," meaning that we are not being authentic. Sartre's famous example in *Being and Nothingness* is a waiter who fulfills his role to such perfection that he starts believing he is defined by his role as a waiter. But Sartre's point is that we are much more than we can describe in any fixed role. A waiter can never be a waiter. A waiter can play at it, but to believe that one is a role is bad faith because we are always becoming and growing, and so to view ourselves as some kind of fixed entity is to fool ourselves. It is to be a thing—like a rock—rather than a person with intentions and projects, with a past and a future.

I do not smoke, I do swear (probably slightly more than average), I do like cocktails, and although I would refer to myself as an existentialist thinker—or perhaps an existentially minded philosopher—Mohler is right: I would not label myself an existentialist. Even though you should view with suspicion anyone who labels themselves as an existentialist, we can still think about problems and challenges in life in an existential way.

Although I studied some philosophy in my undergraduate degree, it was a heavily analytical introduction. I did not hate it, but I did not love it either, and philosophy did not take hold of me then. I spent years being a well-behaved capitalist worker bee, moving from Sydney to New York City and working in equity arbitrage trading. When my work visa ran out, I returned home and completed an MBA.

Outside the classroom, it seemed that everywhere I turned I saw an urgency to find a husband and settle down. There are lots of phrases that a twenty-something unmarried woman hears frequently: *Your clock's ticking. You'd better be careful you don't get left on the shelf. Do you have a boyfriend? Is it serious? Why hasn't he proposed yet?* The assumption is always that if a significant other had proposed, you would have said yes, and that the man would have been the one to ask, and if he did and you said no, then there is obviously something wrong with you. I also found myself drifting toward what seemed to be all the wrong places for answers: pop culture, Hollywood films, and family and friends who had no more ideas than I did. People gave me books with titles such as *The Rules: Time-tested Secrets for Capturing the Heart of Mr. Right*. It is as vacuous as it sounds.

Without being fully conscious of it, I had internalized the pervasive assumption that love is about finding "the One" and living happily ever after. I was quite sure that I had no idea what that was all about and had mountains of questions: How do you know if you find the One? And is finding him or her and getting married how love goes? Is that the right thing to do? Aren't there other options? And what does marriage entail, anyway? With marriage "success" about as reliable as a flip of a coin, this narrative did not seem to be working out for most people. I knew there was something deeply amiss when a boyfriend complained that I spent too much time studying for my MBA when I should be hanging out with him, but I could not articulate what.

When matrimony and fertility—or rather the glaring scarcity thereof—come banging on your door and you happen to take an organizational behavior class in which the professor talks about freedom, responsibility, and anxiety in the workplace, it should not be surprising that existentialism captured my attention. I asked my professor what else she could recommend. At the next class, she handed me a piece of paper with the names of a few of Simone de Beauvoir's books. I started with the first— *The Mandarins*—and proceeded systematically to devour the list. It was as though I had just been flashed by the world outside of Plato's cave. Philosophy waltzed into my life, seduced me by dancing around, and gracefully shattering all the assumptions and expectations I had about life.

One of the things that attracted me to existentialism was de Beauvoir and Sartre's thinking about loving. They had multiple lovers, but considered themselves to be primary in each other's lives—meaning that, at least theoretically, they would always treat each other as most important. Undoubtedly, there were issues with their arrangement, including ethically problematic relationships with their students, jealousy, and time management (which, of course, are not exclusive to polyamorous couples). Freedom was their guiding principle, and relationship freedom was just one element of that.

Polyamory was not for me, but I did appreciate it as a valid option for others. I admired the fact that they threw everything that they were supposed to do out the window. They turned up their noses at societal expectations and created a relationship on their own terms. I also admired the respect they had for each other's independent projects. In de Beauvoir's *The Second Sex*, she talks about the tendency for women to give up their careers for their lovers. She quotes Nietzsche, who wrote:

> What woman means by love is clear enough: total devotion (and not mere surrender) with soul and body, without any consideration or reserve. . . . In this absence of conditions her love is a *faith*; woman has no other. Man, when he loves a woman, *wants* precisely this love from her . . . [6]

While this is an old-fashioned way of thinking about love, I saw much residual evidence around me that this was often, still, an implicit expectation—even if it is not politically correct to say so. Driving home one day in my car from a post-MBA event, I excitedly told my boyfriend, in the passenger seat, about a conversation I had with one of my professors about the possibility of my pursuing a PhD. There was silence. In my mind, I retraced the conversation, panicking slightly, about what I had just said. The problem, it seemed, was that if I were to do a PhD and have a career, I would have no time for him.

That relationship did not work out, and thanks to Nietzsche and de Beauvoir, I was beginning to understand why that attitude was not one I was interested in signing up for. A woman's love, de Beauvoir chides, "is a total abdication for the benefit of a master."[7] This was a critique, not a recommendation. I did love my boyfriend, but not if it required abdicating myself. Being for myself and being for him became mutually exclusive. De Beauvoir's description of authentic love was, for me, much more appealing:

> Authentic love must be founded on reciprocal recognition of two freedoms; each lover would then experience himself as himself and as the other: neither would abdicate his transcendence, they would not mutilate themselves; together they would both reveal values and ends in the world. For each of them, love would be the revelation of self through the gift of self and the enrichment of the universe.[8]

At the time, I didn't know if it was possible, but it was clear to me I wanted a partner who would respect my freedom as I respected his and who did not sulk about my ambitions.

According to Sartre, love, hate, sadism, masochism, and indifference are all part of the same cycle of human relationships. We need other people because although we can do a certain amount of introspection on our own, there are aspects of our being that we cannot know without others. The classic example is Sartre's voyeur. Looking through a keyhole to spy on others, you notice nothing wrong with your behavior. But if you hear footsteps behind you, only then do you think about how your actions might look to another person. Generally, the more we care about people, the more their opinions matter to us and the more desperately we want to know what they think of us—or control what they think of us—so that we can feel more complete, or at least have a more complete picture of ourselves. However, we can never fully do this and so, Sartre says, hell is other people.

Lovers can be great candidates for discovering new dimensions of our being because (often) they know us more intimately than anyone else. However, Sartre suggested that lovers can also be the worst people for this if they become complacent—in which case enemies play an important role in our lives. There is a film called *Burnt* starring Bradley Cooper and Sienna Miller about Michelin chefs. It is what I would call a film to watch on an airplane when you've seen everything you want to watch. Nevertheless, there is one noteworthy scene in which Cooper gets blind drunk and attempts suicide by putting his head in a sous-vide pouch (used for poaching food slowly and at low temperatures to seal in flavor and moisture). Cooper's arch culinary nemesis, played by Matthew Rhys, looks after him until he sobers up—and cooks him an omelet for breakfast. When Cooper asks Rhys why he helped him, Rhys explains that he needs him as a competitor, to push him to try things that he wouldn't have otherwise been inspired to do. They are not the sort of enemies that want to destroy each other. Rather, it is a constructive conflict, like elite sports teams who play against one another to become better.

Sartre makes a similar point in *Being and Nothingness*: "To realize tolerance with respect to the Other is to cause the Other to be thrown forcefully into a tolerant world. It is to remove from him on principle those free possibilities of courageous resistance, of perseverance, of self-assertion which he would have had the opportunity to develop in a world of intolerance."[9] I do not see this as license to go around making enemies and hating everyone in order to benefit from that—an inherent risk in such an attitude. Instead, we can look at this in a more positive way: enemies are sometimes inevitable. Sometimes people will (and do) hate us for things we do and say. The goal is not to try to be indifferent to it—that is next to impossible for many people anyway—but rather to appreciate that an enemy's perspective is valuable because it throws our being into question. We contemplate on the extent to which we screw up, whether we could or should have done otherwise, and if appropriate, consider what we might do better next time. Most people want to be liked, but thinking about those who hate us in this way can help us to reframe the situation and accept it as an opportunity to learn.

Not unlike Aristotle's ideal of great friends, Nietzsche's Zarathustra says, "Let your pity for your friend conceal itself under a hard shell; you should break a tooth biting upon it. Thus, it will have delicacy and sweetness."[10] While Zarathustra overstates it here—since there is a place for empathy and sympathy and we need them in the world now more than ever—the essence of what he is getting at is that a friendship that has space for agreement and disagreement, for enjoyment and challenges, is an ideal one.

It is hard to be a frenemy and to have them. The temptation is to block enemies on social media and ghost them—and sometimes people are so toxic that you must. When Lou Salomé (with whom Nietzsche was in love) ran away to live with one of his best friends, Nietzsche described her to friends as a "scrawny dirty smelly monkey with her fake breasts—a disaster!"[11] I agree with Nietzsche—not about bad-mouthing exes, but that the best sort of friends are those with whom you can push the boundaries of your existence. The ideal is to be and to have friends who are willing to be enemies when called for. I do not hate my ex-boyfriend, nor do I strive to be indifferent to him. I was certainly disappointed that our competing goals could not be reconciled, but my experience with him pushed me to reflect on my existence in ways that I would not have otherwise. For that, I am grateful.

Besides Martin Heidegger, most of the existential philosophers were not big on marriage. Søren Kierkegaard was engaged but broke it off. Camus married twice. Nietzsche was a (reluctant) bachelor his whole life. Sartre suggested he and de Beauvoir marry for practical, administrative purposes. If they were married, they could be posted to the same towns for teaching. De Beauvoir refused: since her teen years, she had been suspicious of marriage's societal baggage, such as gender roles and expectations, and she worried that Sartre would later regret it and resent her. They did not need an institution to validate their personal relationship because they created a commitment that was authentic to them.

Nevertheless, de Beauvoir's philosophy does not prohibit marriage either. She says, "There is no timeless formula which guarantees all couples achieving a perfect state of understanding; it is up to the interested parties themselves to decide what sort of agreement they want to reach. They have no *a priori* rights or duties."[12] De Beauvoir suggests that an authentic marriage is possible when neither partner is subject to conjugal servitude, both have economic responsibility, and both manifest their freedom in concrete ways, such as through independent careers. In simple terms: both partners are able to be self-sufficient.

So, when I fell in love with a person who thought my doing a PhD was cool, I wanted to marry him immediately. I didn't. (Well, not immediately.) As I worked my way through a dissertation on existentialism and love, we often discussed the structure of our relationship. Nietzsche was an unlikely source of inspiration on this topic. He had many conflicting ideas about marriage: on the one hand, he proposed that there's no such thing as happy marriages and if you see happy spouses, they are probably either lying to one another or lying to everyone else; and on the other hand, he acknowledged that while "the garden of marriage"[13] is not necessary for raising children, it can be a fruitful structure for doing so. In *Twilight of the Idols*, he celebrates procreation while defending Dionysian orgies by suggesting that having babies is a "will to life" and "the triumphant Yes to life beyond death and change; *true* life as collective continuation of life through procreation."[14] I did not exactly see having a child as part of the eternal return of my personal life, or think that marriage was needed to raise children. However, I did see these life choices—of both marriage and children—as potentially bold Yeses to life, and leaps into commitments. We were not as obsessed with freedom as were de Beauvoir and Sartre, and a joint mortgage and a party sounded like good ideas.

Ultimately, we said yes to both marriage and a child. When people ask us about our marriage and how my study of philosophy has influenced it, we joke "so far so good." Yet it is a serious statement, too: the existential influence is to recognize that relationships are contingent, no matter how much we try to secure them. One way to look at relationships is as a garden: we tend to it, nurture it, repair it when storms mess it up, and maybe even allow some wild patches to grow, just to see what flourishes there.

Existentialism is much more descriptive than prescriptive, meaning that it does not tell us specifically what to do in certain situations, nor is there a specific framework to guide our actions. However, existential philosophies can remind us to consider what is important to us (authenticity), that we always have choices (freedom) but we are not radically free to do whatever we please (responsibilities), and to consider the impact of our actions around us (consequences). It suggests that other people are vitally important because they challenge us and open up possibilities in ways that we do not always see on our own, and the best kinds of relationships are those that are constructively critical. Existentialism does not tell us how to live a "good" life, or even that we ought to aspire to it, but rather encourages inward reflection on how to live in authentically meaningful ways, and the side effect of that might be good. It is not a philosophy that people go around saying, "Hey, why don't you try being an existentialist?" but if you are the sort of person who lies awake at night thinking about the absurdity and horror of existence, staring into abysses, wondering why hell is other people, or simply feeling caught in webs of other people's expectations, then this might well be a philosophy worth reading more about.

Suggested Readings

Bakewell, Sarah. *At the Existentialist Café*. New York: Other Press, 2016. *At the Existentialist Café* is a lively group biography of the dazzlingly brilliant and revolutionary twentieth-century existential philosophers, including de Beauvoir and Sartre, as well as Albert Camus, Martin Heidegger, Edmund Husserl, Karl Jaspers, and Maurice Merleau-Ponty.

Cleary, Skye. *Existentialism and Romantic Love*. Basingstoke, UK: Palgrave Macmillan, 2015. In this book, I take an existential hammer to romance and emphasize the importance of freeing ourselves from misplaced expectations and flawed ideals about the nature of romantic loving, so that we can be free to reinvigorate our relationships in a way that allows for more authentically meaningful connections.

Cox, Gary. *How to Be an Existentialist, or, How to Get Real, Get a Grip and Stop Making Excuses*. New York: Continuum, 2009. *How to Be an Existentialist* is a good, fun introduction to existential themes, mostly based on the philosophy of Jean-Paul Sartre.

De Beauvoir, Simone. *She Came to Stay*. Translated by Yvonne Moyse and Roger Senhouse. New York: W. W. Norton and Co., 1954. *She Came to Stay* is de Beauvoir's first novel, and I think it's her most underrated work. It's about a ménage à trois and very loosely based on de Beauvoir's life and relationships.

————. *The Second Sex*. Translated by Constance Borde and Sheila Malovany-Chevallier. New York: Alfred A. Knopf, 2010. *The Second Sex* is de Beauvoir's most important work. She found herself pondering her existence in the world and began with the question: "What is a woman?" The answer, she found, was irritatingly complex. What started as an essay evolved into almost eight hundred pages of historical and philosophical analysis of women's situation.

Kirkpatrick, Kate. *Becoming Beauvoir: A Life*. London: Bloomsbury Academic, 2019. *Becoming Beauvoir* is an excellent, insightful, and philosophically rich biography that explores how Simone de Beauvoir attempted to live according to her philosophy and the challenges she faced in doing so.

Marino, Gordon. *The Existentialist's Survival Guide: How to Live Authentically in an Inauthentic Age*. New York: HarperOne, 2018. *The Existentialist's Survival Guide* is a thoughtful introduction to key existential themes, such as anxiety, death, authenticity, and love, drawing to a large extent on the philosophy of Søren Kierkegaard, but also others, including Camus, Nietzsche, and Sartre.

Nietzsche, Friedrich. *Thus Spoke Zarathustra*. Translated by R. J. Hollingdale. New York: Penguin Classics, 1969. In *Thus Spoke Zarathustra*, the Persian prophet Zarathustra takes a break from his hermitage in the mountains to spread the word that "God is dead" and to teach people about the Übermensch. It's one of Nietzsche's most important books, even though it is, as he wrote, "A Book for All and None."

Sartre, Jean-Paul. *Existentialism Is a Humanism.* Translated by Carol Macomber. New Haven, CT: Yale University Press, 2007. Sartre regretted publishing this lecture because he thought it oversimplified his ideas in *Being and Nothingness.* Nevertheless, I still recommend starting with this, and then tackling *Being and Nothingness.*

Notes

1 Jean-Paul Sartre, *Existentialism Is a Humanism*, trans. Carol Macomber (New Haven, CT: Yale University Press, 2007), 18.

2 Sartre, *Existentialism Is a Humanism*, 29.

3 Sartre, *Existentialism Is a Humanism*, 22.

4 Michel Contat, Michel Rybalka, and Jean-Paul Sartre, *The Writings of Jean-Paul Sartre*, trans. Richard C. McCleary, vol. 1 (Evanston, IL: Northwestern University Press, 1974), 99.

5 Existential Comics (@ExistentialComs), "How to be an existentialist: 1. Be super existential all the time. 2. Refuse to label yourself as an existentialist. 3. Lots of smoking." Twitter, September 26, 2017, https://twitter.com/ existentialcoms/status/912719586692276224.

6 Friedrich Nietzsche, *The Gay Science*, trans. Josefine Nauckhoff and Adrian Del Caro, ed. Bernard Williams (New York: Cambridge University Press, 2001), 227–28.

7 Simone de Beauvoir, *The Second Sex*, trans. Constance Borde and Sheila Malovany-Chevallier (New York: Alfred A. Knopf, 2010), 683.

8 De Beauvoir, *The Second Sex*, 706.

9 Jean-Paul Sartre, *Being and Nothingness*, trans. Hazel E. Barnes (New York: Washington Square Press, 1992), 530.

10 Friedrich Nietzsche, *Thus Spoke Zarathustra*, trans. R. J. Hollingdale (New York: Penguin Books, 1969), 83.

11 Rüdiger Safranski, *Nietzsche: A Philosophical Biography*, trans. Shelley Frisch (New York: W. W. Norton, 2002), 255.

12 Simone de Beauvoir, *The Prime of Life*, trans. Peter Green (Cleveland, OH: The World Publishing Company, 1962), 25.

13 Nietzsche, *Thus Spoke Zarathustra*, 95.

14 Friedrich Nietzsche, "Twilight of the Idols," in *Twilight of the Idols and The Anti-Christ* (New York: Penguin, 1990), 120.

CHAPTER THIRTEEN

Pragmatism

John Kaag and Douglas Anderson

William James and Charles Peirce, friends and the founders of American pragmatism, shared many things: ideas, writings, lectures. And an ongoing flirtation with suicide. Pragmatism, that most buoyant of American philosophies, actually, from the outset, wasn't buoyant at all. It was born of struggle, of crisis, personal and political, that shook men and women to the core. The clean and well-dressed arguments of contemporary philosophy often mask its less than ideal origins. But when one looks back at what philosophy originally meant in the United States, it is impossible, and indeed disadvantageous, to ignore them. The American transcendentalism of the 1830s wrestled with the true meaning and value of human independence, in an age that had proclaimed its freedom but didn't exactly know what to do with it. The pragmatism of James and Peirce inherited this philosophical project and understood its resolution—one that redefined the ideas of autonomy and togetherness—as essential to flourishing in both private and public life. Today, their crises make no small amount of sense, but so too do their respective solutions.

Our own relationship began as a teacher and his one-time student. We'd jog in the woods behind State College, Pennsylvania—the Happy Valley of Penn State—and discuss American pragmatism and why it might give a person a reason to keep running despite life's obstacles. Over many years, we became friends. Now we are both teachers—one in the belly of his career, one at the tail end. While it didn't come out in the early years of our relationship, it has become increasingly apparent that we always shared many things: a love of reading, a doubt concerning philosophy's practical worth, and deep insecurities about life's value. We were both drawn to thinkers who struggled with the question expressed by William James in 1895: "Is life worth living?" We aren't exclusively pragmatists, but we agree that James and Peirce still have a great deal to teach us, especially when it comes to this question. Each term we tell our students that philosophy isn't just an intellectual game. If it is a game at all, the stakes are unspeakably high. Pragmatists such as James and Peirce remind us that philosophy connotes the willingness to live or die—to live and die—for our thoughts. Thoughts matter: they can quicken our end, or help us survive, at least for the time being.

James suffered from depression from his teenage years on, his impulsion toward suicide a visceral reaction to the ancient idea, one pointedly expressed by Ecclesiastes, that "all is vanity": individuals are always snuffed out before they can make a genuine or lasting mark. For Peirce, a consummate scientist, considering one's self-destruction was cooler, calmer: a reflective activity brought on by a nagging sense that defined Peirce's later years that he was of little value to his wife and to society. As he wrote to James in 1905, it is "[my] duty not to allow myself to be a burden upon everybody, even if I have not already become so. It is my duty to get out, to make away with myself. I have considered the question maturely." More generally, Peirce's frequent breakdowns coincided with the mounting evidence that he was absolutely alone in the cosmos. Whereas James balked at the idea that single individuals could not effectively exercise their free will, Peirce carefully thought through the meaninglessness of a life lived in perfect isolation.

The existential crises of James and Peirce were grounded in two of the enduring concerns of classical American pragmatism and drove them to concentrate on seemingly disparate, but actually adjacent, concepts: the efficacy of individual freedom and the possibility of genuine communion. They also expressed two different facets of human experience; they embody, in turn, passion and reflectiveness in the face of uncertainty. Their world was not a stable, closed system created by a rational god but an evolving, contingent, precarious temporary home for human animals to make with their neighbors. It was shot through with the risk of real loss. But it was also the home of possibility, a site of making and doing. This was the universe of the pragmatists. The trick was to learn to walk on unstable ground, freely, with others.

It is easy to understand how James acquired his preoccupation with freedom and free will. He was the intellectual godson of Ralph Waldo Emerson, a close friend of his father, Henry James Sr. Emerson's "Self-Reliance," delivered in 1832, was regarded, in the words of Oliver Wendell Holmes, as "America's intellectual Declaration of Independence." The American Revolution may have secured political freedom, but intellectual and personal freedom was another matter entirely, and Emerson argued that it was high time for his fellow Americans to stand on their own philosophical feet. There was a buoyancy and hopefulness during this time in New England, inspired by belief that freedom could be achieved in more than name only. William James, however, was not born in the midst of this triumphant spirit, but reached intellectual maturity after the Civil War, a conflict that not only shook the nation's long-standing beliefs in absolutes and transcendent values—as Louis Menand argues in *The Metaphysical Club*—but also, and perhaps more important for James, cast serious doubt on Emerson's belief in the power of an individual's creative spirit.

The intellectual climate of America changed in the wake of the Civil War. Gone were the paeans to the sanctity of individual freedoms such as "Self-Reliance" and Thoreau's *Walden*, and in their place arose a pervasive faith in the progress of science. Science—measured, calculable, falsifiable science—came to be regarded as the best and safest way to understand the world. Although James's father was a Swedenborgian mystic, he encouraged his son's studies in biology and chemistry, and eventually proposed that William become a doctor. William, however, came to have other ideas. Chemistry was dead boring; biology was fascinating but deeply disturbing. Charles Darwin had published *On the Origin of Species* in 1859, and by the time James considered medical school, Darwin's friend Thomas Huxley had convinced many intellectuals that humans, like all other animals, were strictly controlled by the forces of nature and that their actions could be exhaustively described by way of physical laws.

The year 1870 was arguably James's worst. After returning to Cambridge from a biological expedition in the Amazon, he spiraled downward. At the center of his psychological crisis was his panic that human action was not free, and therefore that life itself was out of one's control. His biological studies did nothing to assuage his fears. "A fact," he wrote, "too often plays the part of a sop for the mind in studying these sciences. A man may take very short views, registering one fact after another, as one walks on stepping stones, and never lose the conceit of his 'scientific' function." The scientific conceit, James maintained, risked sacrificing the idea that humans could freely choose their own way in life, that the feelings and inclinations, which seem so vividly real, have some causal power. Life could not, should not, be boiled down to the workings of a biological mechanism.

James's desire for power—his hope that the world could be "up to us"—drew him away from his biological studies, toward a Frenchman who was in the process of constructing a philosophy of free will. Charles Renouvier was an unabashed loner, which might have been at least partially inspired by his argument that the individual will, even in total isolation, could be freely executed. In what became one of the most pivotal passages of classical American philosophy, James wrote in April 1870:

> I think that yesterday was a crisis in my life. I finished the first part of Renouvier's second *Essais*, and see no reason why his definition of free will—"the sustaining of one thought *because I choose* to when I might have other thoughts"—need to be the definition of an illusion. At any rate, I will assume for the present—until next year—that it is no illusion. My first act of free will shall be to believe that I have free will.[1]

This philosophical bootstrapping helped James through the "next year," and the year after that, for the next twenty-five years, until he wrote "The Will to Believe" in 1896. This essay, published when James was fifty-four, recasts the insight that James gleaned from Renouvier. The proof of free will might be wanting. Perhaps there is no definitive justification of its existence. But to believe and to act *as if* free will were viable is vitally important. It means believing that one's life is not determined in advance, that one has at least a modicum of choice over the matter of human existence. James's assertion of freedom was coupled with his focus on individuality; he was caught somewhere between the transcendentalism of Emerson and Thoreau that preceded him and the existentialism that followed. Unlike Peirce, James was intent to show the cultural changes that might be wrought by a single individual, and in that vein wrote his lecture "Great Men, Great Thoughts, and the Environment." And so James concludes in 1896 that "in truths dependent on our personal action, then, faith based on desire is certainly a lawful and possibly an indispensable thing." Championing free will and the importance of action, James often suggested pursuing the life of a rugged individualist, and some of his students and friends saw him as just that. James's student Dickinson Miller's brother visited one of James's classes and remarked that "He looks more like a sportsman than a professor."[2]

Peirce was intellectually alone, but he was never mistaken for a rugged individualist. He was a master of self-sabotage, and despite being one of the true philosophical savants of the nineteenth century, could never hold a stable academic position. He was largely despised by his contemporaries (save for James and Josiah Royce) and he lived out his later life in poverty in the hinterlands of northeastern Pennsylvania. Indeed, it was his near-total isolation that led him to the conclusion that James's Promethean individualism was somehow defective. For Peirce, beliefs were independent, living ideas that helped shape the world; they belonged to no one and to no time and place in particular. The history of the impact of an idea such as "justice" or "truth" was not the work of any one person or any one culture. The meaning and significance of these ideals were evolving and required the work of many people and many cultures. An intellectual, rugged individualism was bound to run aground on local dogma and fad-like creeds.

Whereas James's individualism necessitated a type of courageous self-mastery and assertion, Peirce's emphasis on community required yielding one's own interests to the human ideals of truth, goodness, and beauty. Egotism, conceit, arrogance, and self-interest had to be weeded out if the community were to be at all successful. Thus, love became the ground of Peirce's epistemology—a willingness to sacrifice one's personal interests for the ideal, to live with *agape* and *caritas*, love and care. "It is not by dealing out cold justice to the circle of my ideas that I can make them grow," he argued, "but by cherishing and tending them as I would the flowers in my garden." And so in the moral realm Peirce advocated a second community—an inclusive and growing "church of love." It is not surprising that in 1905, at the end of their friendship (James died in 1910), Peirce chided his superstar friend for not seeing the importance of community in a religious life.

Nevertheless, entering these communities did not relinquish us of our individual responsibilities to ideals; it simply gave these responsibilities context. Consistently, both existentially and conceptually, Peirce claimed that we each have some small, interconnected role to play in the growth of the universe. We each have talents that reveal our responsibilities and give us a place to operate in the overall improvement of things. This was Peirce's version of James's insistence that the world is "up to us." And our ability to play the roles we are offered hinges on our getting beyond our immediate desires and personal interests—"no man can be logical whose supreme desire is the well-being of himself or of any other existing person or collection of persons."[3] In Emersonian terms, we each have our modes of power, but these must be released within the fated contexts of the history of the cosmos. Interestingly, Peirce was in many ways more romantically minded than James and, by his own admission, was more philosophically attracted to the transcendentalism of Emerson and James's father. Peirce defended his great church of love and wondered out loud why James did not understand his own father's ideas. He was fascinated by our possibility of self-control in our beliefs and conduct, but he remained adamant that the road for creating change was narrow. James's inspiring gestures toward our making the world were always tempered by Peirce's stoic acceptance of life's burdens.

Both Peirce and James were meliorists—they had no hope for a "best" world but they believed that through pursuit of the ideals of beauty, truth, and goodness we could make any historical moment better. They knew that human fallibility and finitude meant that we could always backslide—we as a culture could always deny obvious facts (evolution or global climate change) and reject experienced goods (racial and gender justice). This is what James's student and, later, colleague George Santayana called a culture's "normal madness." And it was precisely this recognition of our ability to fail that led both of them to the importance of tolerance and inclusiveness. James learned this individually on a trip to North Carolina where he encountered a mountain life radically divorced from his own.

Now the blindness in human beings, of which this discourse will treat, is the blindness with which we all are afflicted in regard to the feelings of creatures and people different from ourselves.

We are practical beings, each of us with limited functions and duties to perform. Each is bound to feel intensely the importance of his own duties and the significance of the situations that call these forth. But this feeling is in each of us a vital secret, for sympathy with which we vainly look to others. The others are too much absorbed in their own vital secrets to take an interest in ours. Hence the stupidity and injustice of our opinions, so far as they deal with the significance of alien lives. Hence the falsity of our judgments, so far as they presume to decide in an absolute way on the value of other persons' conditions or ideals.[4]

Peirce arrived at the same conclusion after he became impoverished, but from the direction of community and its constraint on us as individuals. A church of love had to be universally inclusive to allow the flourishing of all amidst their differences, a community working together. He rejected the "gospel of greed" that sought wealth and comfort only for a few at the expense of others. These are American ideals that wax and wane within our culture, and they appear to be in serious jeopardy at present. Peirce and James remained friends to the very end. They understood each other, or rather understood the way that crisis or desperation could give birth to two different types of philosophical speculations. As they grew older, their friendship allowed their philosophies to cross-pollinate. Peirce, who in his youth was somewhat taken with the story of genetic determinism, later saw the world in a radically different way, embracing nonconformity and spurning the racist and classist arguments of modern eugenics. He learned that it was necessary to deviate from certain communities and abandon certain loyalties. James, meanwhile, became almost Peircean in the twilight of his life. The longtime champion of free will and an acolyte of decisiveness opens his final, posthumous book, *Some Problems of Philosophy*, with a Darwinian genetic story of the evolution of Western philosophy and concludes:

All our thinking to-day has evolved gradually out of primitive human thought, and the only really important

> changes that have come over its manner (as distinguished
> from the matters in which it believes) are a greater hesi-
> tancy in asserting its convictions, and the habit of seek-
> ing verification for them whenever it can.[5]

Between the poles of individualism and community, freedom
and constraint, pragmatism emerged as a genuinely American
philosophical outlook—and as a way of life.

Peirce's outlook on our place in the world, our need to know
our limitations, and the importance of caring for others in a community is instructive for looking at the end of life. Because of
his isolation, he reckoned his own end would not adversely affect
many people. Moreover, living with cancer, addiction, and a physical inability to sustain his household, he recognized that he had
become a burden to his wife. Peirce, ultimately, did not choose
suicide; he chose to continue to write. But in his situation, the
thought of choosing suicide seemed to him what James called a
"live option." Taking one's own life takes on different pragmatic
meanings in different situations. Peirce did not recommend suicide as a response to teenage angst. He was considering it from the
point of view of old age, a diseased body, depression, and a lack
of social worth. In this context, we are led to think of Hunter S.
Thompson. Like Peirce, he was living with pain, addiction, and
depression at the age of sixty-seven. He accepted his life without
regrets:

> My life has been the polar opposite of safe, but I am
> proud of it and so is my son, and that is good enough
> for me. I would do it all over again without changing
> the beat, although I have never recommended it to oth-
> ers. That would be cruel and irresponsible and wrong, I

think, and I am none of those things. Whoops, that's it, folks. We are out of time. Sorry. Mahalo.[6]

He was clearly becoming a burden on those around him and he had lost the freedoms of mobility that he so deeply cherished, unable even to get to his favorite bar unaided. In this context, his choice seems to us pragmatically reasonable—it seems in line with Peirce's pragmatic consideration of suicide. There is no "absolute" and acontextual judgment regarding suicide; its reasonableness or unreasonableness lives in the actual situation in which the thought arises. And, in the end, it is a choice—one of the small freedoms afforded us by the cosmos.

Hunter S. Thompson was a mind on fire. We do not pretend here to "understand" Thompson's life, writing, or angle of vision. What we think we understand is his choice of end. It's not a dark thought; on the contrary it's astoundingly pragmatic and liberating—a release to whatever modes of being linger on the other side. It's also not meant to hurt other folks—it's meant as an occasion for party and celebration. As we age there are energies still extant in our being, energies less steady and focused than when we're younger. These energies can come to lose context and the inner turbulence they create is just not worth the effort anymore. They offer us drugs—on this score, we'd rather go with Thompson and choose our own. The things one is offered to get out of depression simply take one away from the world. That "not being there" may be more devastating than a clean death. It's the moment when the music you hear is no longer heard by those around you. From the youth of exuberant community, when we shared the grooves through the electricity of the music, to the present, when we struggle to be with the groove and find those around us ahead or behind. It's the time when you have reached a pinnacle of life that you know you can't repeat. Where pragmatic reflection requires an ongoing engagement with one's slide into failure there is a freedom to be had in a simple choice. One doesn't angle for this situation, but we have no doubt it's a fairly common occurrence for those whose fires burn hot throughout a life.

In the exchange between James and Peirce, and their ultimate compromise, one feels the residual influence of an earlier thinker—the true originator of philosophy in America—one who is rarely regarded as a philosopher today but who inspired these two pragmatists in equal measure. Ralph Waldo Emerson's first series of essays, published in 1832, spurred his readers to empowerment but, at once, reeled them in by fate. As we read him, Emerson often intentionally paired his essays in thematic couplets. It was a way to remain self-aversive—cunningly undogmatic—even as one said what one believed, a way to maintain the Platonic balance that Emerson believed lived in the heart of a philosophical life:

> The balanced soul came. . . . He cannot forgive in himself a partiality, but is resolved that the two poles of thought shall appear in his statement. His argument and his sentence are self-poised and spherical. The two poles appear, yes, and become two hands to grasp and appropriate their own.[7]

Emerson carved out a place for the founding pragmatists and demanded that both be given equal hearing. It is likely that James and Peirce felt this undercurrent, and space for rapprochement, early in their lives. Emerson's "Self-Reliance" sets off in the direction of pure individual freedom, but "Compensation," its often overlooked sister essay, reminds us that all of our powers live and act in a largely determined world, the constraints over which we have no say. Later in his life, with slavery and impending war in view, the necessity of both of these positions came home to Emerson, at which point he wrote another book titled *The Conduct of Life* whose opening essays are similarly two-faced: "Power" and "Fate." The former echoes the individualistic call to arms of Emerson's early imperative: "Whoso would be a man must be a nonconformist." The latter, however, maintains that radical nonconformity is at best partial, and often counterproductive, since individuals are bound to their fated selves. He articulates an ideal in tension, elusive but beckoning, the only one suited to Americans like us: a freedom within brutal constraint.

Suggested Readings

Anzaldúa, Gloria. *Borderlands/La Frontera*, fourth edition. San Francisco: Aunt Lute Books, 2012. Yes, this is not written by a classical American pragmatist, but it accurately captures the pluralism that pragmatism was intent on preserving— and brings it up-to-date by applying it to the life of women and men on the border.

Bugbee, Henry. *The Inward Morning*. Athens, GA: University of Georgia Press, 1999. If you want to know what James meant by "the stream of consciousness," read this book.

McDermott, John J. *The Drama of Possibility*. Edited by Douglas R. Anderson. New York: Fordham University Press, 2007. If you ever want a guide to the existential side of American philosophy, this is the book for you. McDermott doesn't manufacture drama. He lives it.

Perry, Ralph Barton. *Present Philosophical Tendencies: A Critical Survey of Naturalism, Idealism, Pragmatism, and Realism, Together with a Synopsis of the Philosophy of William James*. New York:

Longmans, Green & Co, 1912. This gives a real sense of the
philosophical landscape in which pragmatism came of age.

Smith, John E. *The Spirit of American Philosophy*. Albany, NY:
SUNY Press, 1983. This is the best overview of the American
philosophical tradition, bar none.

Notes

1 Ralph Barton Perry, *The Thought and Character of William
   James*, vol. 1 (Boston: Little, Brown, 1935), 323.

2 Dickinson S. Miller, "A Student's Impressions of William
   James" in *Philosophical Analysis and Human Welfare: Selected
   Essays and Chapters from Six Decades*, ed. Loyd D. Easton
   (Boston: D. Reidel Publishing Company, 1975), 49.

3 Charles S. Peirce, "On the Doctrine of Chances, with Later
   Reflections," in *Philosophical Writings of Peirce*, ed. Justus
   Buchler (New York: Dover, 1955), 164.

4 William James, *On Some of Life's Ideals* (New York: Henry
   Holt and Company, 1912), 3–4.

5 James, *On Some of Life's Ideals*, 15–16.

6 Hunter S. Thompson, *Kingdom of Fear: Loathsome Secrets of a
   Star-Crossed Child in the Final Days of the American Century*
   (New York: Simon & Schuster, 2003), xxii.

7 Ralph Waldo Emerson, "Plato, or the Philosopher,"
   in *The Collected Works of Ralph Waldo Emerson*, vol. 4,
   "Representative Men" (Cambridge, MA: Belknap Press,
   1987), 31.

CHAPTER FOURTEEN

Effective Altruism

Kelsey Piper

On November 21, 2018—Giving Tuesday, the post-Thanksgiving day to give back to the world—I woke up at 4:45 a.m. I planned to donate $10,000 to two charities that I knew were doing extraordinary good, and if I made my donation right at 5:00 a.m., I could take advantage of Facebook's matching program. I'm not a morning person, and neither are most of my roommates—we usually sleep in until our two-year-old wakes us. But this morning I wasn't the only one up early.

I live with fellow effective altruists—like-minded people who've chosen to build our lives, in big as well as small ways, around doing as much good in the world as we can. I live with so many roommates because it lets us save money to donate. Effective altruism also guides our choice of careers. I left a job in technology to write about social issues such as global poverty, emerging technologies, and factory farming for the US news site *Vox*. Some of my fellow effective altruists are software engineers or stock traders, earning six-figure salaries, which enable them to donate to causes they care about. Others work in academia or at nonprofits on research questions. Effective altruism is a simple philosophy: we should dedicate at least some of our resources to making the world a better place, and we should ensure those resources get put to the best uses they can. It's a simple claim, but one that has transformed my life.

You can think about life philosophies in terms of two questions: What does this life philosophy answer for you? And what does it ask of you? I want to discuss effective altruism by answering these two essential questions.

Effective altruism appeals to me because it has the most compelling answers to the big questions: What should we do with our lives? Does anything matter in the long run? What should we strive for? How do we know if we're doing well enough? It also appeals to me because of what it asks of me. I think a lot of people want to aspire to something real, meaningful, complex, and challenging. The question at the heart of effective altruism is: Where are the problems in the world today where my effort can make the biggest difference?

I talk to a lot of people who worry that their life is kind of middling—adequate but a bit disappointing, a bit short of what they expected. They invariably feel that unless they were capable of pulling innocent people out of burning buildings (or the equivalent), they wouldn't feel as if they were making a worthwhile and meaningful difference in the world. If they saw a direct connection between their work or their funding of vital research, they would feel differently. What they frequently don't realize is that these are not silly or unrealistic things to aspire to—they're achievable for all of us. We all have the option of saving the lives of several children every year who will go on to live full, healthy, and promising lives. We may be able to achieve even more good.

Effective altruism asks that we set our sights at least that high. In return, it offers the opportunity to get impressive results with your time, your money, and your energy—to leave the world a much better place and to grow into a stronger, more capable, and better-informed person in the course of doing so.

So how do you do the most good in the world? That turns out to be a complex and demanding question. Effective altruism doesn't prescribe one answer or one way of getting to an answer, but there are certain principles that are core to the effective altruist approach. The first is that effective altruism is *outcome-oriented*. Effective altruism is interested in evaluating our choices by looking at their effects on the world. It's not enough to believe that a cause is important or a project is worthy—effective altruism is about identifying goals and evaluating the things you do by whether you're achieving results.

Most thinking about charity isn't outcome-oriented. We often think about whether a cause is worthy, or whether the recipients are deserving, or whether we will be ennobled or rewarded by offering assistance. Effective altruism asks a different question: What are the results? I find this satisfying—and important— because I firmly believe that ethics is about making the world not only a better place but the best that we can possibly make it. We need to judge ourselves on the basis of whether our contributions are making the world better.

The ethical philosophical tradition that effective altruism has the most in common with is utilitarianism. Utilitarianism, proposed in the eighteenth century by Jeremy Bentham, argued that "it is the greatest happiness of the greatest number that is the measure of right and wrong," so actions can be judged by how much happiness they create in the world. Bentham took this simple philosophy a long way. He concluded that slavery was a moral evil, when philosophers of his time defended it. He called for the abolition of the death penalty and opposed corporal punishment for children (an outlandish view at the time). He supported equal rights for women and even supported gay rights. By being outcome-oriented, Bentham got many things correct that his time period got wrong.

Not all effective altruists are utilitarians. Doing good in the world is an emphasis in many different ethical systems. But the philosophy that produces effective altruism is one that owes a great deal to Bentham and his intellectual heritage. Bentham laid the philosophical groundwork for not just utilitarianism but also other consequentialist moral systems—moral systems that hold that we should decide what's right and wrong by looking at what has the best effects in the real world, for varying definitions of "best." Effective altruism does not demand that you adopt a consequentialist moral philosophy in general. But it takes a *consequentialist approach* to altruism. When we're trying to do good, we should be judging ourselves by our results.

Effective altruism is also *cause-impartial*. Effective altruism asks us to generalize our impulse to do good. We may start out wanting to do good because we see a starving child, are grateful our own children are not hungry, and want to feed other children. Now, if someone saw a starving child and said, "I want to help, but only that one specific child," that would be a concerning failure to generalize the impulse. We should feel satisfied with a donation that feeds starving children, even if it is not the specific one in the photograph. We recognize that no child should starve.

When I see a starving child, I want to help. When I see a sick child, I want to help. When I see a crying child standing in the rubble of a war-torn city, I want to help. I should be open to the possibility that I can best help by providing food, or best help by providing vaccinations, or best help by pushing for better policy that prevents the next war. The important thing is that effective altruism asks us to pursue the question "How do I do as much good as possible?" wherever it leads us, which might mean we end up working on something quite different than the place where we started.

One nonprofit that attracts a lot of donations from effective altruists is the Against Malaria Foundation, which distributes insecticide-treated bed nets to affected communities. Malaria kills more than one million people every year, most of them children under the age of five. The Against Malaria Foundation is consistently rated by GiveWell (a nonprofit that recommends charities based on how much good they can accomplish with every dollar donated) as one of the most cost-effective charities in the realm of global health. A few years ago, I had the pleasure of talking with Rob Mather, the organization's CEO, about how he founded AMF. Amazingly, he started out by organizing swimming marathons to raise money for burn victims, after having seen a burn victim on the news and wanting to help. The swim fund-raisers were a success and left him wondering how many other people he could help. He eventually targeted one of the world's biggest killers of children and founded a highly cost-effective charity.

It can be intimidating to ask a question as big as "Where can I do the most good?" knowing you might have to make a major transition from helping local burn victims to providing bed nets on a global scale. But the world is big and complicated, and we shouldn't expect that the first causes we hear about, or the ones we have personal experience with, are also the places where we have the most leverage to do good. Cause-impartiality is critical for effectively getting results.

In addition, the effective altruist's approach to doing good is *universalist*. Effective altruists don't value some lives more than others because of skin tone or country of origin. If a charitable intervention in Bangladesh does more good than one in the

United States, we'll work in Bangladesh. Many people who start working to improve the world prefer to work on problems close to them. And there are some good, practical reasons to do that—it can be easier to verify the results, you might have specialized local knowledge, or you are less likely to unintentionally cause harm—which is often a problem with ill-conceived overseas charitable interventions.

But focusing exclusively on problems close to home can be myopic, too. People who live in the poorest parts of the world are typically much cheaper to help than people who live nearby. While it costs a lot of money to house a homeless person permanently in the developed world, cash transfers distributed by organizations like GiveDirectly in Kenya and Uganda can help whole families build a permanent home—with money left over for food, education, and livestock—for about a thousand dollars. When people are living on less than a dollar a day, money goes a lot further.

Effective altruism values all people equally, wherever they live. Effective altruism also encourages us to value future humans—making the world a better place for people who haven't yet been born. Those effective altruists who believe that animals experience pain and suffering will typically value the animals on factory farms as much as cats or dogs and believe that pain and suffering is an important moral priority, regardless of whether the being experiencing it is human.

A final core principle of effective altruism is that it is *maximizing*. This is best explained by comparing it to a perhaps oversimplified picture of "commonsense ethics," the moral principles we widely agree on as a society. Much of commonsense ethics are about clearing a bar for acceptable moral conduct. If you cheat, that's below the bar. If you donate to charity, that's above the bar.

If you're worse than the bar, you should feel guilty about being such a terrible person; if you're above the bar, you're doing fine.

Effective altruism approaches this with a different emphasis. One of the most popular books about effective altruism is *The Most Good You Can Do* by the Princeton bioethicist and philosopher Peter Singer. The title is telling. Effective altruism asks us to consider how to do *the most good that we possibly can.* When we have several options, we should consider which one is the best use of our resources, and we should do that. We might be uncertain. But "Is this good?" isn't the right question; we should try to ask "What is best?"

I've seen people struggle to grapple with this aspect of effective altruism in a few different ways. One is to be overwhelmed by guilt. If commonsense morality is about where we set the bar, effective altruism can come across as setting the bar impossibly high—as a claim that you're a bad person if you're doing any less than the best.

I tend to feel that the better approach is to dismantle the bar. There's no life you can live such that everyone in the world will acknowledge you are worthy as a person. And hopefully your friends and loved ones will encourage you in growing kinder, better, and more capable, even if you're already "good enough." "Where's the bar?" is a question that many people have a lot of anxiety around, but it's not a good guide to your ethical decision-making. As far as is possible, it's often healthier to replace that question entirely with a new one: "With whatever resources I've chosen to dedicate to improving the world, am I directing those resources as intelligently as I can?"

But that mind-set doesn't work for everybody. One thing I've found in the effective altruist movement is that, while we're united by a shared commitment to making the world a better place, we vary tremendously in how we relate to effective altruism—as a moral obligation, or as a compelling opportunity to do something real in a world where we often feel paralyzed and useless? For a lot of people, it's more actionable, constructive, and reassuring to know in advance what the expectations are for effective altruists.

In that spirit, Giving What We Can, an effective altruist organization, invites people to pledge 10 percent of their income—for the rest of their lives—to effective charities. I took the Giving What We Can pledge, and so have most of my friends. Donating 10 percent of your income isn't easy, particularly if you haven't planned a budget or if you run into unexpected expenses. I don't recommend it to young people in the first few years of their careers—building up your savings should be a higher priority. But I do think it's good for people to aspire to, and I think it's good to budget, save, and plan so that you can get to a place where you are able to donate 10 percent of your income. If you find the idea of a "maximizing" philosophy overwhelming, unappealing, or exhausting, the pledge can be a good way to make your effective altruist commitments concrete and bounded—and, hopefully, less paralyzing.

But while effective altruism can be construed very narrowly, limited to a philosophy you dust off once a year to make donation decisions, I've personally found that effective altruism affects my life in a much broader, pervasive, and daily way.

One of the most powerful things I've learned through involvement with effective altruism is the ability to research, evaluate, and weigh important and complex issues. Ten years ago, if I had wondered which policies did the most to reduce gun violence, or whether a new climate policy was a good idea, I'd have felt paralyzed—stuck reading opposing research with different viewpoints, with no way of evaluating which conclusions were true.

Effective altruism has nurtured my conviction that important questions like these do have a right answer and that we can and should be prepared to do research until we have a clearer picture of what's going on. It gets easier with practice to identify the most important pieces of a question—the one or two sub-questions that will be most decisive to the overall answer. I've become aware of how eager researchers are to see their work do good in the world and how willing they are to respond to questions and clarify complex issues.

I don't think it's a coincidence that I've grown more able to think about problems that are important to me. Effective altruism invites us to investigate large personal, epistemological, and moral questions about our self-worth and our place in the world that many of us were led to believe would be forever confusing, perhaps unanswerable. What are we supposed to be doing? Don't we have obligations to the poor? How do you make the world a better place? It teaches the skill of answering those questions by consistently applying the same core principles, leaning on research, and working with others who share the same concerns. All of this is essential if you want to answer the large moral questions effective altruism addresses. But it's also a valuable skill in other parts of life. Centering your life around an important question can make you better at answering any question in a systematic, principled way that gets you to the right answer even when it's surprising or counterintuitive. It can help you remember that even difficult questions can often be usefully approached and that even questions no one else seems to care about can matter immensely. That's a skill I am grateful for every day.

The habit of asking "Which of these is most impactful, and how do I focus my effort there?" pays dividends in one's personal life as well as in one's donations. I use this pattern of thinking to notice what I should spend my time on—I try to spend it in ways that produce concrete results in my happiness, my relationships, and my ambitions.

It is possible, of course, to take a habit like this too far or to be overwhelmed by trying to use these new tools and approaches in every aspect of everyday life. So do not start with such an all-in approach. Yet as a result of taking effective altruism seriously as a life philosophy, you are likely to find yourself applying the skills you've learned to tackle other things of importance to you.

I've laid out what makes the effective altruist approach to thinking about charity unique and distinctive, and the ways in which adopting these habits of thought can guide you in other important domains as well. But fundamentally, I believe that the way to seriously undertake effective altruism as a belief system is to first learn about some ways effective altruists have tried to answer our core question: What's the best way to do good in the world?

There is lots of research into different programs to address poverty, from training programs to vaccination programs to religious education. If you start reading, the evidence for any given program starts to look muddled. Some studies may find impressive results; others, however, might suggest that certain programs don't work at all. And then there is the even more basic question of whether charity is even the right way to try to make the world a better place. What about lobbying instead for better government policy, or working on the basic research that has enabled modern medicine? What about combating climate change?

It is not surprising that many people I talk to seem to despair of doing good with their money. They've heard stories about donations to well-meaning charitable programs that went to waste. They often feel ill-equipped to even start to answer a question as big as "What's the most valuable thing I can do?" I'm going to attempt to address those questions here, but I want to emphasize that I think the most important thing effective altruism offers, as a life philosophy, is not necessarily a simple and straightforward answer. Rather, effective altruism offers a healthier way to embrace the question. Effective altruism says that this question is important enough to build your life around—and of course any question important enough to build your life around is going to be *hard*.

But I want to avoid implying that, because the question is complex, no one can do any better than chance. We have a tendency to see that something is hard and conclude that ten minutes of effort won't make us much better at it—but ten minutes spent thinking about how to donate your money will allow you to make vastly better donation decisions than if you didn't think about it. Ten minutes and 10 percent of your income, if you're a person living in a rich country, will let you save several lives, every year.

If you're intrigued by effective altruism, there are four easily actionable things I'd like you to take away as a starting point. First, I highly recommend the book *Doing Good Better* by Oxford philosophy professor Will MacAskill. The book applies effective altruist principles to questions like fair trade, the ethical implications of high-earning careers, and how to ensure your donations do good. While this is a brief introduction to what effective altruism means and what it's like to live it, MacAskill's book will teach you a lot about how to do good with it.

Second, the charity evaluator GiveWell looks at interventions to tackle poverty and global health. When they launched ten years ago, their focus was quite broad—they looked at schools and health-care programs in the United States as well as programs in poor countries. What they found, consistently, was that the most promising programs to save lives, improve health outcomes, and increase income and consumption were all happening in poor countries. Today they recommend charities that work on cash transfers, deworming children with parasites, malaria prevention and treatment, and vitamin A supplementation. Sometimes the best way to understand a problem is to read about someone else's attempts to solve it, and GiveWell's work to identify the most cost-effective interventions in global health is exemplary.

I don't just recommend reading about GiveWell because it helps you do more good. As I discussed previously, one of the most valuable things I've received from effective altruism is a better understanding of how to answer hard questions. That's not just a skill set that helps you identify the best ways to do good—it also equips you to reason more carefully about everything else that you care about.

Third, I want to introduce a framework effective altruists use to identify promising causes. I think it's a framework applicable to far more questions than just the question "How do we do as much good as we can?" but it's easiest to explore there. It has three elements: neglectedness, tractability, and impact.

Impact is the most straightforward of these: How much good would we do by solving this problem? Heart disease kills vastly more people than malaria, so if you could invent a magic cure to one but not the other, you'd save more lives by curing heart disease. A nuclear war might cause the extinction of life on Earth, so preventing that would be tremendously impactful.

Tractability asks: How easy is it to make progress on this? For example, preventing nuclear wars might be the highest-impact thing around, but I don't know of any action I can take, day to day, that reduces its risk—so it doesn't score well on tractability. For a way of doing good to be promising, there needs to be a reasonable chance that spending your time and effort on it will make the world a better place. The war in Syria and accompanying humanitarian crisis is agonizing—but for most of us, there isn't a tractable avenue to resolving it.

Neglectedness is perhaps the most complicated of the considerations. Effective altruism is a small movement right now. Effective altruists are making decisions about only a small fraction of the resources spent on causes like global health (though in other areas, like animal welfare, effective altruists influence a much larger share of the resources available). Often, that means our effort is best spent on problems that get insufficient attention and discussion elsewhere. Climate change is a terrifying problem, but it's also one that thousands of scientists and millions of people are working on. So it's a good idea to check whether there's a neglected climate problem—one that's getting insufficient resources relative to its importance—before deciding to join the millions of others at work on a well-served problem. If a problem is underserved, it will often be more cost-effective to work on it.

Thinking about impact, tractability, and neglectedness will help you figure out where to prioritize your effort and energy and will help make sense of the projects other effective altruists are working on. Many effective altruists work on improving the welfare of farmed animals, because the impact is enormous— more than 50 billion animals raised for food every year[1]—and the problem is both tractable and neglected. Companies are typically willing to make animal welfare improvements when consumers demand it—but very few people have demanded it, as they mostly don't know much about the conditions on these farms.

Other effective altruists work on managing the development and deployment of advanced artificial intelligence. Experts in the field have estimated that the introduction of AI will be one of the most impactful events in our history—catastrophic if it goes wrong, and transformative if it goes well. There are a lot of understudied questions about AI, so additional time and money can improve our understanding of the problem—that's tractability. And, despite the significance of the issue, right now there are very few researchers working on AI safety and AI policy full time—which makes the issue neglected.

This framework, then, helps guide you in evaluating big questions and noticing when a cause might be one where there will be high-impact opportunities to do good.

Finally, I strongly recommend connecting with other people—not only other effective altruists but knowledge producers and researchers in relevant academic fields, from development economics to welfare biology to philosophy. Anyone can make the world a better place in a strategic, smart, and thoughtful way. However, you'll benefit greatly from being connected with the researchers who are working full time on these questions. As a reporter, it is part of my job to talk with development economists about the interventions they find most promising and the ongoing efforts to take promising results from a pilot program and produce a cost-effective, large-scale program that is robust enough to be scaled. At its best, effective altruism is deeply integrated with the research communities trying to answer the questions we care about. Doing good in the world is complicated, and we need answers to be backed by evidence, clear reasoning, expertise, and a careful commitment to results.

As I said earlier, I think a philosophy of life can be evaluated by asking what it offers to you and what it demands of you. For effective altruism, these are very closely intertwined. You're asked to sacrifice to do good, but in return you get real and important results, as well as a life filled with meaning and purpose. You're asked to spend a lot of time thinking about complicated, intimidating questions, but you will learn how to approach hard questions and come away with a clearer picture of the world. I've found learning about effective altruism to be humbling. It leaves me with an awareness of how complicated the world is and how much diligence we need to exercise to get the results we want from our actions. It also leaves me with a deep appreciation for all of the knowledge that has already been generated. Medical researchers have developed vaccinations and eradicated diseases. Geneticists have engineered better crops and vastly improved agricultural yields. Billions of people have been lifted out of poverty by economic growth.

These gains are fragile. Dangerous mistakes or unintended consequences in the next few decades might undo them. But humanity is capable of achieving a great deal—and I want to ensure that my piece of that does as much good as it can. So I get up early, once a year, to donate 10 percent of my income wherever I believe it will do the most good. Next year I'd be honored to have you join me.

Suggested Readings

Bentham, Jeremy. *The Works of Jeremy Bentham*. Published under the Superintendence of his Executor, John Bowring. Eleven volumes. Edinburgh: William Tait, 1838–1843. Bentham is an inspiring writer because he got so much right—from slavery to gay rights to women's rights to sexual liberation—in a time when almost no one was considering these issues. He's best read with an eye to these questions: What would it take to be right about the issues of tomorrow, today? What approaches to reasoning and moral logic was Bentham putting into practice? There's a lot here even for people who don't end up agreeing with utilitarianism in either Bentham's or subsequent formulations.

MacAskill, William. *Doing Good Better*. New York: Avery, 2015. Will MacAskill is a researcher at the Global Priorities Institute at Oxford and one of the philosophers who founded effective altruism. His book explores how we can do good in the world and what we learn from a serious look at the question. He covers effective altruist topics from global health to civilizational risks. It's a great place to start for understanding the ideas effective altruists talk about.

Singer, Peter. *The Life You Can Save*. New York: Random House, 2009. Peter Singer laid the foundations of effective altruism with one challenging thought experiment: Are you obliged to ruin your nice suit to rescue a drowning child? From there, he builds up to questions of moral responsibility to distant people, the case for giving much more to charity than most people do, and practical advice on how to end global poverty.

Note

1 Alex Thornton, "This is how many animals we eat each year," World Economic Forum, February 8, 2019, https://www.weforum.org/agenda/2019/02/chart-of-the-day-this-is-how-many-animals-we-eat-each-year/.

CHAPTER FIFTEEN

Secular Humanism

John R. Shook

Many people are already in agreement with secular humanism, though they may not realize it. Being a secular humanist does not depend on joining the right club, paying dues, and attending meetings. Living a secular life, and relying on humanist values, is enough. Being nonreligious does not mean that one must live without greater purpose in one's life, or living without moral standards. It has never been true that only religions can explain why life has meaning for us and how ethical principles guide us. Perhaps you have thought that science understands far more about nature than ancient scripture. Perhaps you do not expect churches to have the best answers to tough problems that people encounter nowadays. If so, then you may be thinking about alternative ways to contemplate life, in ways that secular humanism has already explored. If you celebrate during the holidays or meditate for some stress relief, those practices can look a little religious, but you've made up your own mind about what those things mean to you. That's fine—secular humanism accommodates lifestyle diversity, and defends the freedom to think for yourself.

Religions too often view humanism and secularism as dead-end roads for people who are losing moral direction, forgetting tradition, abandoning higher purpose, and gratifying selfish desire. Religious people are led to imagine that "humanism" must mean "humans make themselves all-important." And religions typically view "secularism" only as "power politics without morality or civility." Neither of these narrow perspectives are justified. Humanism does affirm that humanity is ready to take responsibility for what our societies are doing and where our planet is headed. Secularism holds that government makes the life plans of all citizens better when no religion can make the government's laws serve God's plan. That separation of church from state ensures that responsibility for the future is not left to divine providence, but instead to democratic participation. This combination of secularism with humanism to form secular humanism allows everyone to choose their life goals without fear of losing their individual liberties.

Locally, secular humanism can take many forms. There are welcoming communities of like-minded people for regular gatherings and celebrations of life events. There are also organizations devoted to advocating atheism and/or science. Many secular people put their humanist energy into all sorts of charitable organizations. They may also be engaged in political activism for civil rights and liberties, public policy reforms, educational standards, environmental projects, and many more social causes. Secular humanism, while grounded in philosophical values and virtues, is not merely a private lifestyle choice that ignores social problems and political issues. Democracy itself is at stake.

Secular humanists are proud to support full and equal rights for all, and they take the side of those struggling for social and legal justice. They have supported pro-choice on abortion, reproductive freedom, equal pay for equal work, anti-discrimination policies, free speech and freedom of expression, the separation of church and state, the teaching of evolution in schools, the availability of stem cell therapies, the right to dying with dignity, and the application of science to real-world problems. Hundreds of secular and humanist organizations large and small, found in most countries around the world, take part. The umbrella organization for humanism, the International Humanist and Ethical Union, lists nearly 150 affiliates. Humanists UK in Britain and the Center for Inquiry and the American Humanist Association in the United States are national-level organizations that publicize their resolutions on political and social issues and participate in legal actions against religious intrusions into civil rights and liberties.

Secular humanism resists violations of people's rights caused by religious doctrines, but it should not be viewed as an enemy of religion. Neither humanism nor secularism claim that religion is entirely bad for humanity or that religions should disappear. Disgruntled voices among atheists will be heard saying such things, but there is nothing about humanism or secularism as philosophies of life that tell nonreligious people to hate religion or religious people. Secular humanism does urge everyone to love this life, trust their natural abilities, and take care of each other. This is not a new message of wisdom for humanity.

Humanistic philosophical traditions are as old or older than the religions around today. Humanistic ideas arose in Greece and Rome, and early Indian and Chinese thought. In the West, the Renaissance revived humanist ideals. Then the Enlightenment advanced human reason and democracy over dogmatic tradition and monarchy. No longer should citizens be treated like children. As the modern world emerged, what citizens decide for themselves would be the law, not what priests interpret from their scriptures. Since the late nineteenth century to the present day, secular humanism has been the philosophy most devoted to this confidence in humanity's maturation.

Secular humanism is a philosophical worldview, not a narrow ideology. It incorporates wisdom from ancient sources, such as Socrates, Aristotle, and Stoicism, blended with modern liberalism and utilitarianism, and infused with an existentialist sensibility, a naturalistic perspective, and a pragmatic optimism. Socrates represents the courage to question and debate. Aristotle correctly understood human beings as reasoning animals. Stoicism's view that everything in the world is usefully interdependent is a positive alternative to the religious notion that nature is corrupted or degrading. The quest for more freedoms and opportunities for everyone is a liberal principle inherited by secular humanism, and it pairs well with the utilitarian tenet that social institutions should advance the greater good for everyone. What is good and meaningful about life is right here within human experience, as existentialism emphasizes. And the good things in life are enhanced, not diminished, by applying knowledge of the natural environment around us. Finally, and perhaps most importantly, secular humanism confidently offers itself as a practical method for improving the human condition, undaunted by more challenges that are surely coming.

Despite its impressive heritage and its large influence on modernity, most people do not know much about secular humanism. If someone has heard of it, that is usually due to complaints they have heard about it, from religious conservatives who criticize secular humanism as an evil and dangerous way of thinking. Perhaps what these conservatives fear most is secularism, more than humanism. Secularism insists that government should treat religion neutrally, so that religion cannot control the lives of nonreligious people. Too often, religions think that unless religious people are allowed special powers and privileges to advance religion and affect the lives of many people outside of church, they are not getting legal equality. Religious conservatives are particularly offended when government is unable to help religion enforce its dogmatic religious ethics, such as making abortion illegal, or preventing women from controlling their reproductive health. For these conservatives, government is never neutral—if their denomination isn't receiving special powers and privileges from the government, they can only perceive discrimination and injustice. That "for us or against us" viewpoint leads toward the undemocratic destination called theocracy, where religious leaders can wield influential political powers. Secularism must resist that political direction. All people should enjoy personal religious liberty. Yet that liberty must include the freedom to be nonreligious, too. Secular humanism understands why people walking away from churches is a horrifying sight for those theocrats. However, freedom from religion, personally and politically, must be a primary individual right alongside others.

Secular humanism is not merely a political agenda or a stand against fundamentalism, and it is not just for self-proclaimed atheists. It has no sacred texts or creeds, but it does have reasonable ideas about how the world works and making the most of this earthly life. Humanism finds worth and dignity in every human life, and celebrates excellence in humanity's achievements. Adding "secular" to humanism emphasizes how our rights and duties are not assigned by God, but instead asserted by people taking responsibility for their future. Strong democracies condemn intolerance and guarantee inclusion for everyone under one equal rule of law. In order for reason to guide our future instead of faith, science is the better method for understanding nature and repairing our planet. This opportunity can become a bridge between religionists and secularists, since as many religious people around the world are now comfortable with science and endorse democracy (after centuries of battles, both intellectual and military). Hopefully that degree of collaboration can continue to expand.

Secular humanism has communicated its worldview in a variety of manifestos, which typically repeat tenets found in the *Affirmations of Humanism: A Statement of Principles*, composed by Paul Kurtz. Kurtz, the philosopher at SUNY Buffalo who popularized the usage of the term "secular humanism," was the founder of the Council for Secular Humanism in 1980, and the *Affirmations* have appeared regularly in issues of CSH's magazine *Free Inquiry* since the early 1980s. Here are a select number of affirmations capturing the core of secular humanism: [1]

- We are committed to the application of reason and science to the understanding of the universe and to the solving of human problems.
- We deplore efforts to denigrate human intelligence, to seek to explain the world in supernatural terms, and to look outside nature for salvation.
- We believe in an open and pluralistic society and that democracy is the best guarantee of protecting human rights from authoritarian elites and repressive majorities.
- We are committed to the principle of the separation of church and state.
- We are concerned with securing justice and fairness in society and with eliminating discrimination and intolerance.
- We want to protect and enhance the earth, to preserve it for future generations, and to avoid inflicting needless suffering on other species.

- We respect the right to privacy. Mature adults should be allowed to fulfill their aspirations, to express their sexual preferences, to exercise reproductive freedom, to have access to comprehensive and informed health-care, and to die with dignity.
- We believe in the common moral decencies: altruism, integrity, honesty, truthfulness, responsibility. Humanist ethics is amenable to critical, rational guidance.
- We believe in optimism rather than pessimism, hope rather than despair, learning in the place of dogma, truth instead of ignorance, joy rather than guilt or sin, tolerance in the place of fear, love instead of hatred, compassion over selfishness, beauty instead of ugliness, and reason rather than blind faith or irrationality.
- We believe in the fullest realization of the best and noblest that we are capable of as human beings.

People who are not religious and agree with these beliefs are rightly classified as secular humanists. However, secular humanists are not limited to these beliefs, and usually have additional perspectives and convictions. Secular humanism can overlap with other compatible philosophies, and it need not be an exclusive view of life. No one is just a secular humanist. It is not meant to completely define you as a person. The most important thing is to feel confident about your own judgment, and knowing who you really are.

You could never give a thought to humanist or secular manifestos and simply live your nonreligious life. However, secular humanism offers an enriching wisdom tradition and helpful guidance about life's toughest questions. These include the kinds of issues that religions assume can only have religious answers. And you do not have to feel alone in your journey. You can meet secular humanists through local organizations about atheism, skepticism, philosophy, humanism, and free thought. Thanks to the Internet, anyone can find events offering enjoyable alternatives to church.

Again, you do not have to tell everyone there's no God. Just say "I'm a secular humanist" if anyone needs to know. Or, mentioning "humanism" as you describe yourself and your values can also work. Be careful about saying that you are "spiritual but not religious," unless you really mean it. Doing yoga or meditation, or communing with quiet forests and vibrant sunsets, are enriching experiences available to secular humanists. But if you think that cosmic energies or spirits exert unnatural influences, or you suspect that mystical experiences reveal something beyond this life, that is not secular enough for secular humanism. There are humanists who need some spirituality and churchly ceremony; "religious humanist" is an appropriate label for them.

Speaking of labels, it can seem like a lingering vestige of religion to even need one. Why should there be labels for nonbelievers, while religions have denominations as labels? We need to look at where secular humanism fits into the bigger picture. Plenty of people, perhaps as much as 15 percent of the world, do not think of themselves in terms of a religious label, or regard themselves as part of a religion. Research into religion has shown this to be accurate. On the topic of religion, do you feel like you are "None of the Above"? Demographers have a category for those who can't be easily categorized: the nonaffiliated or the "nones." No matter how long a list of religions are given, the nones do not pick one as theirs. The nones have reached around 20 percent in America and 30 percent across Europe, with rising numbers also observed in developed and developing countries from Mexico and Brazil to India and Japan. A large portion of nones still believe in a god of their own preference, but they aren't very religious by other measures, because they rarely attend religious services and infrequently rely on religion to guide their lives.

Research into these nones has asked people whether religion plays a large, small, or no role in guiding their lives, or in making moral decisions, as well as how often they attend religious worship or whether they got married in a church or temple. The personal importance of religion has been steadily dropping in America and most European countries for decades. But the eye-grabbing headline from these polls is always about God. The standard "God question" used by polling goes like this: "Do you believe in God or a universal spirit?" The percentage of adults saying no has reached between 5 and 10 percent in many Western countries including the United States, and an even higher percentage in some European and Asian countries. People unable to say yes to this question are nonbelievers, and if religion plays no significant role in their lives, either, then they are quite secular, even if the label of "atheist" is unappealing to them. The meaning of "secular" is not "anti-religion" (as some religious people suppose), but just "worldly." If you have no need for a god to guide the cosmos or an immortal soul to enjoy an afterlife, then you are wholeheartedly focused on this earthly life, where the wisdom of secular humanism is grounded.

An earthly focus allows secular humanism to develop a world-view unlike religion and its unearthly promises. The repudiation of everything about religion is the preoccupation of the secularist, not the typical secular humanist. Staunch secularists let antipathy against religious ideas dictate their views, as if the very opposite of religion must be the truth. Secular humanism's overriding aim is to build a coherent worldview, not just to contradict whatever religions have preached. Positive philosophical engagement is required. Other nonreligious philosophies, if they similarly prioritize equality and freedom and respect science, will tend to converge with secular humanism. Secular Buddhism, for example, agrees with the essentials of humanism, and secular humanism can incorporate psychological and ethical insights from Buddhism.

Secular humanism works more like an accommodating framework than a rigid set of doctrines. However, that framework also filters out incompatible ideas, including some views cherished by strict secularists. Even if you haven't read the outpouring of secularist writings, only a little familiarity with this genre is needed to see what I mean.

Secularists who don't know or don't care about humanism are common enough, so we can start there. Condemning religion for its irrationality, or for its complicity with immorality and injustice, keeps many secularists busy. Depicting atheism as having all reason and morality on its side is also a frequent secularist tactic.

For secularists who think in terms of this "religion or reason" dichotomy, morality does not come from religion, so it must be based in reason. Separating morality from religion also leads secularists to deny that there are moral rules for all humanity, since religion gets obsessed with such rules, such as commandments from God. After all, there is no otherworldly origin for morality, so morality only comes from humanity. Some secularists observe how morality displays differences from culture to culture, so they accept cultural relativism. Others think that morality is not about where you happen to be born, but about what you personally value. This view is moral subjectivism, and it can seem preferable to the way that religions require unwavering, unthinking obedience. These examples show how a compulsion to contradict religion drives secularists toward neat conceptual divisions and simplistic views about morality.

The secularist declaration of independence from religion often amounts to just contrariness on the question of life's meaning as well. Religions preach that the divine world assigns purpose to the human world. They accuse atheism of leaving humanity without any greater purpose and there are plenty of secularists willing to agree. There's no higher purpose to life's existence at all, many will say, because life was not put here in the universe to serve some ultimate end.

The boldest among secularists have adopted the pose of cold nihilists announcing the complete meaninglessness and absurdity of life. That type of nihilism is hard to live out in practice—typical secular people do not talk or act like nihilists. Secularists do worry that what can actually deprive life of all meaning is a supreme being that controls life's meaning. Perhaps a life without religion could also open a way to an authentic life of meaning. The overall purposelessness to life in the universe is no reason to suppose that your life or my life cannot be meaningful. Social activities, intellectual pursuits, and noble ideals keep people inspired and engaged as a means to imbue life with purpose. Secular humanism expects that the opportunity for creating what is meaningful in life is a responsibility that rests upon each person.

Secular humanism does not expect something supernatural beyond us to tell us who we really are, nor does it find that anything unnatural within us, such as an immortal soul, will accomplish that goal, either. Skeptics in the empiricist tradition after David Hume detect no center of a "self" and no laws dictating the stream of ideas though the mind. This empiricism allies with indeterminism: events are not entirely caused by prior events, so the future could go in any number of directions. Indeterminism appeals to secularists hostile to the religious mantra that everything must happen precisely according to God's plan. Perhaps there is no greater freedom than freedom from mental compulsion. Some religions, such as Christianity, say that only their religion's view of the immortal soul can guarantee that people have free will. Should secularists deny that free will is real? Psychological determinism, which says that we cannot change or control where our thoughts will go, does not sound very liberating. Are we just machines, really controlled by blind forces causing us to want what we want and decide what we decide? There are many influences that contribute to who we are. From our genetic inheritance and our months in the womb, through every moment of our lives down to the present, we absorb and digest what impacts us. Everything going on inside us must ultimately have some origin outside us, in the present or the past. Only magical thinking expects that today's choices are unaffected by yesterday's events. All the same, what does secular humanism say about human freedom?

Perhaps the feeling that, when we make a choice, we are choosing between two options that are both possible is just the feeling of an illusion. According to determinism, there can only be one future in which every event necessarily happens, thanks to the past. But a person cannot be held responsible for a deed that was necessarily going to happen. Psychological determinism, by saying that we cannot possibly act otherwise, seems to remove our responsibility for our behavior and assigns it elsewhere. Could all the fault for our actions be really in our genes, or our upbringing, or somewhere in society, and so on? Or perhaps physics has eliminated the possibility of free will and moral responsibility. With natural laws firmly dictating everything that happens at the macro-level of nature (setting aside quibbles over quantum-level chanciness), this physicalist determinism makes it impossible for anything about us or anything affecting us to be otherwise than precisely what it is.

On morality, meaning, and freedom, secularists have been talking about a wide variety of options. The cacophony of secularist complaints against religion illustrates why there is no single secularist position. Each secularist can make their particular opposition to something about religion as clear as they are able to, but checking for broader consistency among alternatives is not so easy. Inconsistencies can pop up all over the place, and inconsistencies would weaken the case for secular humanism. For example, if reason sets what is moral, then moral relativism is wrong; if psychological indeterminism is valid, then rational morality is impotent; if social purposes give us meaning, then psychological determinism's denial of purpose must be misguided; if cultural relativism prevails, then there are no universal human rights; if physical determinism is accurate, then "choosing" personal values is a sham; if values are so personal, then egoism steers morality; if there is no personal responsibility, then morality is a fiction; and any combination of nihilism, cultural relativism, and determinism leaves little room for the individual pursuit of meaning. How should secular humanism avoid these dilemmas? Even if an astute secularist only takes stands against religion that are compatible with each other, such as aligning personal values with indeterminism or pairing nihilism and determinism, there are multiple positions that remain possible. Must a secular humanist subscribe to rationalist ethics or moral subjectivism? Personal choice or psychological determinism? Human rights or cultural relativism?

Secular humanism rightly looks to reason and science, but lingering there is not enough. Religions hasten to tie secularism down to materialism, and link materialism with egoism, nihilism, and anarchy. Compared to that portrayal, spirituality or even supernaturalism might look sane and safe.

Philosophical defenders of humanism and secularism over the past two hundred years have included a few nihilistic materialists and anarchists. However, most of them articulate a moderate position on morality, responsibility, freedom, and rights. Secular humanism finds that human life is meaningful and worthy, for no better reason than we judge life to be meaningful and worthy.

Needing to be told by a higher authority how life is meaningful only deprives our lives of their intrinsic worth. Dignity and autonomy cannot depend on someone else, not even a god, who decides that you are worthy—one must affirm one's own right to live for oneself.

Secular humanism did not invent the ideas of human dignity and moral worth, but it staunchly upholds them, even if religions forget their importance from time to time. Universal human rights must not be diminished just because a sacred text echoes a prejudice against homosexuality or a church tradition places men above women. Respecting other people's rights displays a mature level of moral responsibility, displayed by nonreligious people no less than religious people. The notion that the nonreligious are more immoral and criminal is yet another oft-heard religious prejudice with no basis in fact. What about nihilism, though, and its amorality? Nonreligious people can live a meaningful and responsible life according to secular humanism, so it must reject nihilism.

As for what science says about free will, people are evidently controlling their conduct and making moral choices, using their inherited and acquired abilities, without waiting for science to finally decide that nature is completely deterministic or it is somewhat indeterministic. Human freedom does not depend on some indeterministic aspect of nature (quantum events, for example) since responsibility could not be grounded on just chance according to humanism. Therefore, freedom and responsibility exist in and through natural forces and energies, not in spite of them. There is no unnatural free will from an immortal soul, but natural freedom is amply exercised by intelligent organisms like humans. We adjust our course of actions in pursuit of goals, we can do this more or less considerately, and we are rightly held responsible for those choices and goals. This view of natural freedom is called compatibilism: freedom of choice and action exists even in a completely deterministic universe. A naturalistic view of intelligent freedom, such as the view preferred by humanism, could just as well hold that the degree of determinism in the universe is irrelevant, so long as there are enough stable laws of nature to make choices effective. Secular humanism's affirmations of freedom and responsibility are not hostage to scientific theories, such as quantum mechanics, or to philosophical arguments over determinism.

Nor are freedom and responsibility necessarily diminished by local conditions and social influences. Environmental effects on us can be enabling and empowering, too. Freedom improves as others instruct and advise us from birth. Freedom evolves as humans discover more opportunities yielded by nature for fresh pursuits. Growing intelligence correlates with enlarging freedom. Science's knowledge has proven to be the most empowering resource yet devised by human intelligence. Denying science, as religion often does, disrespects the mind and disempowers humanity.

Our capacity for morality is basically biological, but our childhood socialization instructs us in specific moral codes. Moral expectations will vary somewhat across cultures, with ample overlap on basic virtues and moral rules. There is no need to reduce moral values to personal desires or attitudes, so moral subjectivism is mistaken. Secular humanism respects cultural pluralism, but it does not endorse cultural relativism. Morality may vary, yet there are universal ethical standards regardless of whether everyone is ready to respect them or not. The equal humanity and moral worth of all, the importance of basic rights, the protection of inquiry and learning, and the condemnation of injustice and oppression are not waiting for final approval by nations still subjugated by political or religious tyranny.

Secular humanism holds all peoples to these fundamental

ethical obligations, and morally condemns any violations. It remains unimpressed by rhetoric about "Who's to say what is really right and wrong?" The answer can only be: "We all do!" What grounds those objective ethical norms about equality and rights? Nothing less than the objective reality of human persons who deserve them. Each person already intuits their self-worth. If anyone doubts their own unconditional equality, that is because an ancient prejudice or pernicious myth has made them feel unworthy or afraid.

The status of moral worth and equality comes with ethical obligations. One's virtuous character cannot be left to chance, any more than human rights can be left to happenstance. We can turn again to secular humanist Paul Kurtz, who listed what he called "Ethical Excellences" that every person should acquire and cultivate:

- First is the excellence of autonomy, or what Ralph Waldo Emerson called self-reliance. This means a person's ability to take control of his or her own destiny. . . . Such a person is self-directed and self-governed.
- Second, intelligence and reason rate high on the scale of values. To achieve the good life we need to develop our cognitive skills [and] good judgment about how to make wise choices and how to live.
- Third is the need for some self-discipline within the domain of passions and feelings. . . . Recognizing the harmful consequences that imprudent choices may have upon ourselves and others.
- Fourth, some self-respect is vital to psychological balance. . . . A person needs to develop some appreciation for who he or she is and a realistic sense of one's own

identity. . . . Some confidence that one can succeed is essential for the good life.

- Fifth, and esteemed highly on the scale of values, is creativity, the fountainhead of innovation and invention, the boundless spirit of novelty and discovery. . . . We can add to the sum of bountiful joys implicit in the fullness of life, but only if we dare to do so.
- Sixth, we need to develop high motivation, be ever ready to seize the opportunities in life, to undertake new departures in thought, experience, and action. The motivated person finds life intrinsically interesting and exciting.
- Seventh is an affirmative and positive attitude toward life. . . . We can and do express our potentialities, and we can and do capture opportunities that arise or that we can create.
- Eighth, an affirmative person is capable of *joie de vivre*, the intensity and passion of joyful experiences. This expresses the full range of human pleasures and satisfactions, . . . tasting life to the fullest.
- Ninth, if we are to live well, we should be concerned about good health as a precondition of everything else. . . . We need to love others and be loved by them, to share our everyday lives with friends and companions; to belong to significant communities of interaction and inquiry, work, and play; and we need times for solitude and quiet reflection.
- Tenth, all these excellences clearly point to the goodness of life. . . . The end, purpose, and goal of life is to live fully and creatively, making each moment of beauty and brilliance count. . . . Every moment of life

is precious, intrinsically good in itself and for its own sake.[2]

These ideas about living a worthy and good life could look like yet another lifestyle choice, but they must be more than that. They are good advice for anyone, no matter where your life's journey is going. Secular humanism is not just an alternative to religion. No matter who you are, its ethics will help to enhance your life and the lives of everyone around you. And no matter where you live, the principles upheld by secular humanism improve your society and the stability of the world we share. We owe that much to each other, because we are worth it.

Suggested Readings

Barker, Dan. *The Good Atheist: Living a Purpose-Filled Life without God*. Berkeley, CA: Ulysses Press, 2011. Barker, a former evangelical preacher, tells inspirational stories of people choosing their purposes and creating meaningful lives. With faith in one another, caring communities can ignore religious threats of damnation.

Batchelor, Stephen. *Secular Buddhism: Imagining the Dharma in an Uncertain World*. New Haven, CT: Yale University Press, 2017. Valuable Buddhist practices are transcending their Asian cultural origins. A preeminent secular Buddhist himself, Batchelor conveys the essence of meditative traditions freed from supernatural views of *karma* and reincarnation.

Berlinerblau, Jacques. *How to Be Secular: A Call to Arms for Religious Freedom*. Boston: Houghton Mifflin Harcourt, 2012. The protection of religious liberty for all is not about permitting a religion to force everyone to obey its commandments. Only a wide separation between church and state fulfills the Constitution.

Dennett, Daniel C. *Freedom Evolves*. New York: Viking, 2003. There is no place for free will in a natural world, but the freedom to control our actions and meet responsibilities is not threatened by science. In fact, biology can explain how these abilities evolved, and how human beings use them to live well.

Epstein, Greg M. *Good without God: What a Billion Nonreligious People Do Believe*. New York: HarperCollins, 2009. A large portion of humanity is enjoying nonreligious lives with dignity and wisdom. Epstein identifies their shared ethical values, and he explains why those values would improve the whole planet.

Grayling, A. C. *The God Argument: The Case against Religion and for Humanism*. New York: Bloomsbury, 2013. Arguments for God are no longer convincing, and commandments handed down by religion are no longer needed. The future should be guided by humanist values, such as tolerance, freedom of expression, reason, and democracy.

Hecht, Jennifer Michael. *Doubt: A History: The Great Doubters and Their Legacy of Innovation from Socrates and Jesus to Thomas Jefferson and Emily Dickinson*. New York: HarperCollins, 2004. There have always been skeptics toward religion in every age. Hecht's fascinating narrative recounts their courage and honesty, so that their devotion to truth and independent thinking can inspire us today.

Kurtz, Paul. *Affirmations: Joyful and Creative Exuberance*. Amherst, NY: Prometheus Books, 2004. Religions portray the nonreligious as sad and selfish people, but Kurtz sees the enthusiasm for life and the love for beauty and goodness in every person. Living affirmatively with joy is the birthright of all humanity, not just those serving a deity.

————. *What Is Secular Humanism?* Amherst, NY: Prometheus Books, 2007. In a concise and clear way, the guiding values and core principles of secular humanism are outlined and defended.

McGowan, Dale. *Parenting beyond Belief: On Raising Ethical, Caring Kids without Religion*, second edition. New York: Amacom, 2016. McGowan recruits the best advice from parents, teachers, doctors, psychologists, and philosophers about raising moral and freethinking children. There is guidance about common issues, such as religious family members, holidays, coping with grief, and finding nonreligious communities.

The Oxford Handbook of Secularism. Edited by Phil Zuckerman and John R. Shook. New York: Oxford University Press, 2017. Many chapters discuss the foundations of humanism and secularism, and explore the issues and tensions between religions and nonreligious philosophies.

Shook, John R. *The God Debates*. Malden, MA: Wiley-Blackwell, 2010. This compendium of arguments against God supplies commonsense refutations of a variety of religious beliefs. In addition, this book explains detailed counterarguments against theological positions.

Notes

1 The full statement is found in Paul Kurtz, *Affirmations* (Amherst, NY: Prometheus Books, 2004), 13–17. Also available at http://www.secularhumanism.org/index.php/12.

2 Kurtz, *Affirmations*, 52–60.

Conclusion

It is a common theme among social and cultural critics that the spiritual crisis in which modern humanity finds itself is partly a product of our having lost the psychological security and certitude allegedly enjoyed by our premodern ancestors. For them, a philosophy of life was rarely expressed or even explicitly entertained, but was woven into the fabric of the given world and forms of life in which a person lived. The overt quest for meaning and significance and consolation was one pursued by small numbers of highly educated philosophers and theologians, devoted to the life of the spirit and mind. The widespread interest today in these questions is at least in part a legacy of modernity: of multiple scientific revolutions and the challenge they posed to traditional religion and the picture of the world it once painted; of industrialization and the migration of whole populations from rural to urban areas; of the condensing of the once-extended family down to the minimal, isolated nuclear one; of mass literacy;

of democracy and modern capitalism and the endless and often bewildering choices with which they confront us; of a general loss of faith in institutions; and of the ever-present possibility of our utter destruction, by way of advanced technology and warfare.

Despite the challenges posed by modernity, religion maintained its hold on the public psyche, in combination with an early Cold War–inspired patriotism and some degree of cultural feel-good-ism, well into the 1950s, and the search for significance, meaning, and consolation remained a relatively specialized affair. Especially in the West, it was the societal loss of faith in institutions, as a result of numerous wars and political scandals, and the social dislocation and experimentation of the 1960s that broke this artificial calm and gave rise to the various movements—then characterized under the umbrella of "human potential"—that would lead us to the place in which we find ourselves now, where the explicit desire to find a deeper conception of oneself and one's life is widespread, across almost every stratum of our society. The rapid advancement of modern communications and the global distribution of American and Western media ensured that this interest in consciously adopting a meaningful path in life would take on a truly international scope. And just as the human potential movements of the sixties and seventies provided a window into the anxieties, yearnings, and questionings of people in those difficult, tumultuous decades, so the religions and philosophies of life that we see people pursuing today—of which this book contains what we hope is a somewhat representative sample—give us a view into the spirit of our own age. That there are practitioners of ancient philosophies and updated versions of traditional religions represented in our collection brings this view into even sharper relief.

The modern philosophies of life—and those ancient religions and philosophies adapted to modern purposes—reflect a relatively tight, overlapping set of concerns that aim at addressing the characteristics and problems of the modern worldview. By far the greatest concern is an emphasis on the moral sphere of life, with self-mastery and self-control and fortitude in the face of chaos coming closely behind. This should hardly surprise anyone even casually attuned to the tenor of life in modern, technological societies.

The logic of capitalism, especially in its contemporary, neo-liberal form, is ultimately mercenary and amoral, and for many of us, social isolation and atomization have left our charitable instincts satisfiable chiefly by way of impersonal and distant charities. Our increasing inclination to engage with one another through social media, rather than in person, has rendered our interactions ruder and coarser. Media saturation in general has left us overstimulated, numbed to experience, and alienated from our own feelings. (Something Susan Sontag observed in her 1964 essay "Against Interpretation," in which she wrote that "Ours is a culture based on excess, on overproduction; the result is a steady loss of sharpness in our sensory experience.") The sheer amount of information and choices with which we are confronted every moment of every day has left us spiritually and emotionally vertiginous. The self-discipline and moral commitment at the heart of modern Aristotelianism, Stoicism, Buddhism, Daoism, effective altruism, and Ethical Culture; the human connectedness central to modern Hinduism, Confucianism, pragmatism, Christianity, Judaism, and Progressive Islam; the quest for healthy, pleasurable experience that defines contemporary Epicureanism; the desire to learn to live with and embrace radical freedom characteristic of existentialism and secular humanism—they all speak, and constructively react, to the distinctive societal and cultural failures of our particular moment in the modern age.

In this regard, the entries dealing with religion in our volume provide a sharp contrast and, in doing so, a great deal of clarity. Those chapters discuss supernatural beings and events; transcendent metaphysics and cosmologies. They are infused with a yearning for a picture of the world and of our place in it, different from the one given by the modern sciences and modern philosophy; one in which human concerns have a cosmic, rather than merely a terrestrial or personal significance. Few to none of the modern philosophies of life—or the modernized ancient ones—are directed toward satisfying these kinds of needs, on the ground that they do not fit with the scientific view of the world. For some, the sense of the sublime is satisfied by nature and need not extend beyond it, and the "unanswerable" is understood as that which science has not answered yet or as something that cannot be answered in principle. The extent to which such ideas continue to inspire so many living in the modern world—billions of people nowadays do strive to live according to the orthodoxies of premodern religions—indicates the extent to which science has neither answered nor eliminated many of the old human concerns and yearnings. Indeed, despite the sometimes sharp differences among the religions and philosophies of life examined in this volume, there seem to be universal principles that were as valid two millennia ago as they are today: the need for meaning and a sense of agency, compassion for others, and the notion that cooperation and pro-sociality are the best ways to ensure human flourishing, regardless of one's metaphysical views.

Will the updated religions and ancient philosophies as well as the new philosophical approaches meet the challenges of the immediate and distant future? One can never be sure. The technological age has barely begun, and the potential to transform not just human life but human nature itself appears nearly limitless. Sickness and disease may cease to play a meaningful role in human life. Robotics and automation may render work, as traditionally conceived, no longer necessary. Life spans may dramatically increase, with people living well into their hundreds. Futurists and transhumanists go so far as to imagine that our future will be essentially *posthuman*. The challenges such developments will pose, the new concerns they will raise, and the pressures on the human (or posthuman) experience they will impose are impossible to predict. But one thing we can be sure of is this: the people of these future eras will seek out their own philosophies and religions, and they will provide as fascinating a window into their souls as our current philosophies and religions do ours. That is why we have offered fifteen possibilities to learn from, ponder, and perhaps adopt as your own compass to navigate life.

Contributors

Douglas Anderson is the former chair of the department of philosophy and religion at the University of North Texas. Now retired, his work has focused on American philosophy, the history of philosophy, and the relation of philosophy to cultural practices. He is the author of several books and numerous articles including *Philosophy Americana: Making Philosophy at Home in American Culture*, *Conversations on Peirce: Reals and Ideals*, *Strands of System: The Philosophy of Charles Peirce*, and *Creativity and the Philosophy of C. S. Peirce*.

Barbara Block is the rabbi of Temple Israel of Springfield, Missouri. She was ordained at Hebrew Union College–Jewish Institute of Religion in 2010. She holds an MA in Hebrew Letters from HUC-JIR; an MA in philosophy from the University of Minnesota; and a BA in ancient Greek from Carleton College. Before coming to Springfield she served Congregation Beth Aaron in Billings, Montana. Prior to entering rabbinical school, Barbara spent twenty years working in higher education as an academic adviser, administrator, and instructor in the Twin Cities. Her interest in the rabbinate was kindled when she became a founding member of Shir Tikvah Congregation in Minneapolis in 1988 and met the first female rabbi in Minnesota.

Hiram Crespo is the author of *Tending the Epicurean Garden* (Humanist Press, 2014) and the translator of several other books, a bilingual blogger at *The Autarkist* and *El Nuevo Día*, and the founder of societyofepicurus.com. He lives in Chicago, has contributed content to many outlets in both Spanish and English, and has a BA in Interdisciplinary Studies from Northeastern Illinois University.

Adis Duderija is a lecturer in Islam and society at Griffith University in Queensland, Australia. He received his PhD in 2010 from the University of Western Australia. He taught at the University of Melbourne and the University of Malaya in Malaysia prior to joining Griffith University in 2017. His research interests include Islamic hermeneutics, with specific reference to gender and interfaith relations, Progressive Islam, and neotraditional Salafism. He has been publishing extensively on all these subjects for more than a decade. His sole-authored books include *Constructing a Religiously Ideal "Believer" and "Woman": Neo-traditional Salafi and Progressive Muslims' Methods of Interpretation* (Palgrave, 2011) and *The Imperatives of Progressive Islam* (Routledge, 2017). Duderija is an activist-minded scholar and is a world-leading expert on the theory of Progressive Islam.

Owen Flanagan is James B. Duke Professor of Philosophy at Duke University. He also works with the Center for Sustainable Development at Columbia University on initiatives that connect ethics with happiness and sustainability.

John Kaag is a professor of philosophy at the University of Massachusetts, Lowell. He is the author of *Hiking with Nietzsche: On Becoming Who You Are* (Farrar, Straus and Giroux, 2018), an NPR Best Book of 2018, and *American Philosophy: A Love Story* (Farrar, Straus and Giroux, 2016), an NPR Best Book of 2016 and a *New York Times* Editors' Choice. His writing has appeared in *The New York Times*, *Harper's Magazine*, *The Christian Science Monitor*, and many other publications.

Anne Klaeysen is a clergy leader at the New York Society for Ethical Culture, a Humanist Chaplain at New York University, and a Humanist Religious Life Adviser at Columbia University. She holds a DMin from Hebrew Union College in pastoral care and counseling, serves on the faculty of the Center for Education of the American Humanist Association, and has taught classes on humanism at Union Theological Seminary.

Alister McGrath is Andreas Idreos Professor of Science and Religion at the University of Oxford and director of the Ian Ramsey Centre for Science and Religion. McGrath is a public intellectual who has played a leading role in the debate about the "new atheism" and is author of the international bestseller *The Dawkins Delusion?* (Veritas, 2010), as well as many academic monographs. His most recent book is *The Territories of Human Reason: Science and Theology in an Age of Multiple Rationalities* (Oxford University Press, 2019).

Kelsey Piper earned her BS in symbolic systems from Stanford University, where she was the founder and first president of Stanford Effective Altruism. She then joined the founding team of Vox's Future Perfect, a partnership with the Rockefeller Foundation to support journalism focused on the most important stories facing the world today, from global poverty through climate change and risks to human civilization.

Deepak Sarma is a professor of Indian religions and philosophy in the Department of Religious Studies at Case Western Reserve University. He also has a secondary appointment in the Department of Bioethics in the CWRU Medical School. Sarma is the author of *Classical Indian Philosophy: A Reader* (Columbia University Press, 2011); *Hinduism: A Reader* (Blackwell, 2008); *Epistemologies and the Limitations of Philosophical Inquiry: Doctrine in Mādhva Vedānta* (Routledge, 2005); and *An Introduction to Mādhva Vedānta* (Ashgate, 2003). After earning a BA in religion from Reed College, Sarma attended the University of Chicago Divinity School, where he received a PhD in the philosophy of religions. His current reflections concern cultural theory, racism, bioethics, and postcolonialism.

John R. Shook is a research associate in philosophy and a faculty member of the Science and the Public EdM online program of the University at Buffalo, New York. He also is a lecturer in philosophy at Bowie State University in Maryland. He coedited with Phil Zuckerman *The Oxford Handbook of Secularism* (Oxford University Press, 2017), and his most recent book is *Systematic Atheology: Atheism's Reasoning with Theology* (Routledge, 2018). For many years Shook has worked with secular and humanist organizations. He has been the director of education and a senior research fellow for the Center for Inquiry; the education coordinator for the American Humanist Association; a mentor with the Humanist Institute; and president of the Society of Humanist Philosophers. Shook is currently the editor of the journal *Essays in the Philosophy of Humanism*.

Bryan W. Van Norden is Chair Professor in Philosophy in the School of Philosophy at Wuhan University (China), Kwan Im Thong Hood Cho Temple Professor at Yale-NUS College (Singapore), and James Monroe Taylor Chair in Philosophy at Vassar College. A recipient of Fulbright, National Endowment

for the Humanities, and Mellon fellowships, Van Norden has been honored as one of the professors profiled in *The Best 300 Professors* in the United States by *The Princeton Review*. Van Norden is author, editor, or translator of nine books on Chinese and comparative philosophy, including *Introduction to Classical Chinese Philosophy* (Hackett, 2011), *Readings in Later Chinese Philosophy: Han to the 20th Century* (Hackett, 2014, with Justin Tiwald), *Readings in Classical Chinese Philosophy* (2nd ed., Hackett, 2005, with Philip J. Ivanhoe), and most recently *Taking Back Philosophy: A Multicultural Manifesto* (Columbia University Press, 2017).

Robin R. Wang is Robert Taylor Chair Professor in Philosophy at Loyola Marymount University, Los Angeles and a Berggruen Fellow (2016–2017) at the Center for Advanced Study in the Behavioral Sciences (CASBS), Stanford University. Her teaching and research center on Chinese and comparative philosophy, particularly on Daoist philosophy. She is the author of *Yinyang: The Way of Heaven and Earth in Chinese Thought and Culture* (Cambridge University Press, 2012) and editor of a few books. She was a credited cultural consultant for the movie *The Karate Kid* (2010).

About the Editors

Skye C. Cleary, PhD MBA, is a philosopher and the author of *Existentialism and Romantic Love* (Palgrave, 2015). She teaches at Columbia University, Barnard College, the City College of New York, and Think Olio, and previously taught at the New York Public Library. Skye is the managing editor of the American Philosophical Association's blog, and her work has been published in *Aeon*, *The Paris Review*, *The Times Literary Supplement (London)*, TED-Ed, *Los Angeles Review of Books*, and others.

Daniel A. Kaufman is a professor of philosophy at Missouri State University. He hosts the *Sophia* program on MeaningofLife.tv and edits and publishes *The Electric Agora*, an online magazine devoted to the intersection of philosophy, the humanities and sciences, and popular culture. He lives in Springfield, Missouri, with his wife, Nancy, a high school teacher, and their daughter, Victoria.

Massimo Pigliucci is the K. D. Irani Professor of Philosophy at the City College of New York. His books include *How to Be a Stoic: Using Ancient Philosophy to Live a Modern Life* (Basic Books, 2017); *Nonsense on Stilts: How to Tell Science from Bunk* (University of Chicago Press, 2010); and *A Handbook for New Stoics* (with Gregory Lopez, The Experiment, 2019). He blogs at patreon .com/FigsInWinter.

Copyright Acknowledgments